Viella Historical Research
21

Political Objects in the Age of Revolution

Material Culture, National Identities, Political Practices

edited by

Enrico Francia, Carlotta Sorba

viella

First edition: October 2021
ISBN 978-88-3313-847-3

The publication of this book has been funded by the University of Padua, Dipartimento di Scienze Storiche, Geografiche e dell'Antichità (DISSGeA).

Cover illustration: Joseph-Louis-Hippolyte Bellangé, *Le marchand de plâtres ambulant, colporteur de figurines napoléoniennes* (1833). Paris, Musée du Louvre

POLITICAL
objects in the age of revolution : material culture, national identities, political practices / edited by Enrico Francia, Carlotta Sorba. - Roma : Viella, 2021. - 229 p. : ill. ; 23 cm. (Viella historical research ; 21)
Indice dei nomi: p. [217]-226
ISBN 978-88-3313-847-3
1. Cultura materiale - Europa - Sec. 18.-19. 2. Oggetti - Aspetti politici - Europa - Sec. 18.-19. 3. Oggetti - Aspetti socio-culturali - Europa - Sec. 18.-19. I. Francia, Enrico II. Sorba, Carlotta
306.46094 (DDC 23.ed) Scheda bibliografica: Biblioteca Fondazione Bruno Kessler

viella
libreria editrice
via delle Alpi, 32
I-00198 ROMA
tel. 06 84 17 758
fax 06 85 35 39 60
www.viella.it

Contents

Enrico Francia, Carlotta Sorba

Introduction: The Political Life of Objects*

Why some things matter. This was the subtitle of a seminal volume edited by Daniel Miller, which in 1998 took stock of the new research area of "material studies", the common ground of a range of different disciplines and investigative perspectives, including anthropology, sociology, literature, archeology of the past and present and, of course, history.[1] Since then, studies on the materiality of the past have proliferated, evidence of the exciting potential of taking a material approach to delve into different historical themes and topics. Fabrics, household goods and bodily accessories, previously studied above all by specialists in fashion and decorative art history, have become important sources in analyses of highly relevant historical phenomena, from religious practices in the early modern era to the consumer revolution that took place in the 17th and 18th centuries, to name but two of the best-known research areas in the new history of material culture.

The importance of things, the vitality and mobility of objects, their ability to offer different viewpoints on the life of the past are all elements that have emerged with strength and clarity in many recent studies, and these themes have also been analysed in a number of methodological contributions, further defining new investigative approaches and directions.[2] Material culture frames all of our actions and experiences, and it also helps create them. It has thus become increasingly obvious, even in the historiography, that materiality is an integral and unavoidable part of every culture, and that the social world cannot be fully understood without it. Despite this, the point Miller raised (which can be expressed more generally as *why things matter*) still seems a somewhat open question, and it is difficult to escape the impression that new perspectives and approaches on the complex and hitherto insufficiently investigated relationship between us and things can and should be

* The introduction was jointly conceived by the two editors, but sections 1, 4 and 6 were written by Carlotta Sorba and sections 2, 3 and 5 by Enrico Francia.

1. *Material Cultures: Why Some Things Matter*, ed. by Daniel Miller, London, UCL Press, 1998.

2. See, in particular, *Writing Material Culture History*, ed. by Anne Gerritsen and Giorgio Riello, London, Bloomsbury, 2015; *History through Material Culture*, ed. by Leonie Hannan and Sarah Longair, Manchester, Manchester University Press, 2017; "Storia e cultura materiale: recenti traiettorie di ricerca. Interventi di Fabio Dei, Giorgio Riello, Beverly Lemire, Manuel Charpy, Leora Auslander", ed. by Alessio Petrizzo and Carlotta Sorba, *Contemporanea*, 3 (2017). See also the recent *Oxford Handbook of History and Material Culture*, ed. by Ivan Gaskell and Sarah Anne Carter, Oxford, Oxford University Press, 2020.

developed further. To focus clearly on a past that fully includes material aspects, however, we must partially change our perspective and open analytical pathways in which materiality has a role in shaping the research questions themselves. We believe this to be the case for the topics covered in this volume, in that they open potentially fruitful new research trajectories with a focus on the political sphere and objects that assume political meanings, values and uses, in very different ways. Let us attempt first of all to provide a definition of the area that we will investigate here. What do we mean when we speak of political objects? As will become clear in the chapters that follow, this definition can include a very wide range of objects: artefacts of various kinds and substances, but also natural elements or bodily remains turned into relics. They are produced and/or disseminated with a political purpose (and therefore explicitly or allusively with a politically oriented message); or they acquire political meaning in different ways: as the remains of an event, as images of a figure or a politically connoted behaviour, or even as bearers of a political narrative, again either explicit or allusive.

In the chronological framework we propose, they became part of a public political sphere which, in its modern forms, was still under construction. In fact, we have chosen to focus on a phase that in our opinion was very significant in the political use of materiality, namely that moment of transition that is remembered in Western societies as the Age of Revolutions, roughly from the 18th-century revolutions to 1848, and its legacies. At that time, as we seek to show, objects acquired an increasingly important role in the processes of politicisation and mobilisation that accompanied, preceded or followed the revolutionary episodes.

Before arriving at the heart of our argument, we should recall that the initial idea for this work dates back to an event organised in Padua in September 2016: a workshop to compare new research on the material history of 19th-century politics that brought together many of the scholars who have subsequently contributed to this volume.[3] At the centre of our investigation, then and now, was the political life of objects and the many forms that it could take in the past. Thus, we examined not only the social life of things, which was already well outlined in Fernand Braudel's and Daniel Roche's seminal works and in the volume edited by Arjun Appadurai,[4] but also the political dimension, whose outlines we felt deserved a substantial study, above all for the many opportunities that materiality seemed to offer in this context, by opening different avenues of investigation: from the emotional, nostalgic and memorial dimensions of objects to aspects of their production, consumption and material gain, right up to the essentially political elements that they embody (belonging, ideological orientations or control over them).

3. We would also like to credit those who have been unable to contribute to this book but who have nevertheless made an important contribution to our collective discussions: Gianenrico Bernasconi, Gian Luca Fruci, Maria Alexandra Lousada and Anna Novikov.

4. For an overview of the impact of Arjun Appadurai's book (*The Social Life of Things: Commodities in Cultural Perspective*, Cambridge, Cambridge University Press, 1986), see Fabio Dei, "La vita sociale delle cose trent'anni dopo: quale svolta negli studi di cultura materiale?", in *Storia e cultura materiale: recenti traiettorie di ricerca*, pp. 441-444.

There is a further element that prompted the original event and which, a few years later, still motivates this book: objects are still little used in the historical analysis of contemporary society, probably also as a result of the greater wealth of written sources as compared to those from the medieval and early modern eras and the more consolidated primacy of written sources. In actual fact, the material available is much more plentiful and more eloquent than might be imagined, as the contributions that follow show, and it certainly does not deserve to be relegated to the antiquarian sphere, as has often happened in the past.

1. *Materiality and the history of politics*

Many recent studies have argued that bringing materiality into the investigation of the past has important implications for the very practice of making history. "Like words in the postmodern 1980s", Frank Trentmann wrote, "things today are shaking our fundamental understandings of subjectivity, agency, emotions and the relations between humans and non-humans".[5] It is an interesting, if perhaps daring, analogy. Putting the material world of things at the centre of research does not mean simply adding one more item to our research agenda. It means modifying it: promoting, on the one hand, a significant expansion of the historical archive towards areas that still appear to have a lot to offer (museums, collections, historical sites); on the other hand, raising new questions even around the usual contexts. This was certainly the case for the *Risorgimento*, the process of building Italian national unity and independence, the studies of which have undergone a significant and important change of direction in recent years and around which some of the contributions in this volume are appropriately focused.[6] Not only has the morphological reinterpretation of the national-patriotic discourse certainly contributed to this important review, but so has a decisive new sensitivity towards its communicative, media and emotional aspects, as well as towards the embodied practices of politics, and therefore the bodies and things of patriotic mobilisation.

What are the implications of allowing objects within the framework of the cultural history of politics? It goes without saying that we are talking about an area of research that, perhaps for longer and more stubbornly than others, has remained tied to an approach based exclusively on written sources. It is therefore important to begin to understand what pathways and specificities can be identified in the association between the material world and politics. The material history of politics is, first and foremost, a way of cross-referencing different analytical

5. Frank Trentmann, "Materiality in the Future of History: Things, Practices and Politics", *Journal of British Studies*, 48 (2009), pp. 283-307.

6. On the re-reading of the period of the *Risorgimento* in recent historiography, see *Risorgimento Revisited: Nationalism and Culture in Nineteenth Century Italy*, ed. by Silvana Patriarca and Lucy Riall, London, Palgrave Macmillan, 2012; Maurizio Isabella, "Rethinking Italy's Nation-Building 150 Years Afterwards: The New Risorgimento Historiography", *Past and Present*, 217 (2012), pp. 247-268.

perspectives that rarely interact: in particular political history (ideas, their circulation, appropriation and socialisation) with the consumption practices that objects represent so well. Furthermore, such a perspective can lead us to focus more fully on its various implications. Politics is not made up only of words and writings but also of non-verbal expressions, rituals, gestures, colours and objects. Extending our investigation to them, as we propose to do here, means acquiring greater complexity, rather than simplifying matters, since the impression that objects take us back to the past with tangible immediacy is little more than an illusion. In actual fact, material evidence is often more ambiguous and virtually polysemic than a verbal text and, above all, it must be re-framed in its original context, which is sometimes far from simple.

Therefore, if working with objects is not particularly easy, they nevertheless allow us to take significant steps forward in the investigation of tangible individual and collective experiences. On the one hand, this brings us towards a deeper knowledge of the nature and functioning of the symbolic and communicative aspects of political action, and on the other towards a better understanding of the performative dimensions. On the political front, it is particularly clear, in fact, that objects are not only a key element in symbolic communication (and sometimes crucial to affirming one's identity and belonging), but they "embody" messages of various kinds and, in their materiality, perform important tasks and roles. Many of the objects we see talk and tell in their own ways; they show varying degrees of "loquaciousness", as Lorraine Daston would say,[7] and, in some cases, they contribute to the action or to a plan of action.

In embracing a pathway of this kind, we are certainly indebted to the field of anthropology, but more generally to a "practical turn" that cultural history has definitely embarked on in recent years, identifying in experience, even in its material and performative aspects, the most significant and crucial intersection between the discursive order and individual action, between social conditioning and the agency of individuals.[8] On the first front, the strictly anthropological one, the ideas of "social drama" and "ritual communities", proposed by Victor Turner, can first and foremost be brought to bear in understanding certain moments of political protest and in defining the outlines of a dramatisation that used clothing and accessories, corporeal and otherwise, as one of its main tools.[9]

Similar perspectives can be identified in many cases of political mobilisation, in situations in which the theatrical nature of protest combined – often more than

7. *Things that Talk: Object Lessons from Art and Sciences*, ed. by Lorraine Daston, New York, Zone Books, 2004, p. 11.

8. For an overview of the centrality of practices as long-term consequence of the cultural turn, see Gabrielle Spiegel, *Practicing History: New Directions in Historical Writings after the Linguistic Turn*, New York, Routledge, 2005. See also Carlotta Sorba, Federico Mazzini, *La svolta culturale. Come è cambiata la pratica storiografica*, Rome, Laterza, 2021.

9. An interesting application of the investigation on the performativity of actions and behaviours can be found in Simon Gunn, "Analysing Behaviour as Performance", in *Research Methods for History*, Edinburg, Edinburgh University Press, 2012. On Turner's suggestions, see in particular *From Ritual to Theatre: The Human Seriousness of Play*, New York, PAJ Publications, 1982; and Victor Turner, *The Anthropology of Performance*, New York, PAJ Publications, 1986.

it juxtaposed – performance and the surveillance of revolutionary disorder.[10] More generally, it might be said that an analysis of objects and clothing opens up to a kind of "political ethnology" focused on single specific situations. Enquiring into the forms of political action through material objects gives us a deeper insight into specific aspects of the actions and behaviours of men and women of the past and can also tell us something about the mindsets by which they lived, expressed themselves and shared their political allegiances in a given historical context.

There is also another aspect to consider, and that is, to quote Daston once again, the fact that things not only "repeat the human voice" but express their own presence in the processes analysed. Much has been said in recent years about the "agency of objects", as conceptualised above all by Bruno Latour in his Actor-Network Theory.[11] Thanks to its materiality and the gestures it prescribes, an object is considered, in Latour's definition, an "actant", fully participating in the action configuration. The positions expressed by historians on this point differ, but the debate is open and of considerable interest, once again showing the fruitfulness of the dialogue between historiography and cultural theory. According to Ivan Gaskell, author of a number of methodological essays and studies on various "tangible things", attributing agency to things can only be a form of catachresis, that is, an attempt to use a metaphor to define a phenomenon that does not yet have its own specific definition.[12] So, in his opinion, it is human action, the uses that are made of things, that remain at the centre of every historical investigation, while our interest in materiality consists above all "of its capacity to mediate human relationships among individuals and social groups across space and time". Others, however, have pointed out that the apparently alienating reference to the "ability of things to act" entails something more, in particular the recognition that objects can prescribe new bodily practices and plans of actions, and play an active role in many human experiences. An object or artefact, as a technical mediation of the imperative it incorporates and translates, sparks reactions and influences the social world. An interesting example, which would certainly need further investigation, might be that of the ballot box, which symbolises the prominence acquired by the ideal of political rationality that we define as democratic.[13]

10. See ch. 7 of Carlotta Sorba, *Politics and Sentiments in Risorgimento Italy: Melodrama and the Nation*, Cham (Switzerland), Palgrave Macmillan, 2021.

11. See Bruno Latour, *Reassembling the Social: An Introduction to Action-Network-Theory*, Oxford-New York, Oxford University Press, 2005. For a brief overview of the arguments around the presumed agency of objects, with philosophical and sociological reflections, see also *History through Material Culture*, pp. 19-20.

12. This is discussed in Ivan Gaskell, "History of Things", in *Debating New Approaches to History*, ed. by Marek Tamm and Peter Burke, London, Bloomsbury, 2019, pp. 217-232, 239-246 and also emerges in the edited volume *Tangible Things: Making History through Objects*, ed. by Laurel Thatcher Ulrich, Ivan Gaskell, Sarah Schehner and Sarah Anne Carter, Oxford-New York, Oxford University Press, 2015.

13. This topic was discussed by Gianenrico Bernasconi during the workshop which prompted this book. See also Yves Déloye, Olivier Ihl, *L'acte de vote*, Paris, Presses de la Fondation nationale des sciences politiques, 2008.

Latour's is a theoretical source used today across countless spheres in an attempt to reread the dynamics of social interaction in more sophisticated and topical forms and to take non-human factors into account. What we can say about our area of research is that politics is undoubtedly an embodied activity, and one which Latour would say is situated in a "framework" made up of practices, places and a universe of objects that, like the patriotic snuffboxes in constitutional Spain (Álvaro París and Jordi Roca Vernet) or the commemorative ceramics of Peterloo (Simon Morgan), represent all that remains of a series of actions whose highly specific density is now not so easy to grasp. It is thus not a question of forgetting about human intentionality in the use of objects or putting it to one side; rather, it is a question of taking a few steps forward towards a more general rethinking of the very concept of "materiality", in the direction of what has recently been defined as the "material engagement approach".[14] And it is therefore to consider the material world – in the present as in the past – not as something separate and distinct from human existence, but linked to it in a close and organic relationship that has a strong impact on our mental and cognitive experiences.

To sum up, then, we can say that the political objects we shall discuss (pocket-sized, decorative, clothing or other) represent both a form of language – which communicates, sometimes more evocatively than directly, a political message and a narrative – and a practical device incorporating actions and programmes of action. And it is precisely in the practical sphere that these objects would seem to be especially capable of shedding light on aspects that evade other types of analysis. As condensed forms of different dimensions (materiality, the symbolic and communicative dimensions, their agency and performance effectiveness), we might say that the objects speak to and act in the political sphere, helping to structure narratives of various levels of coherence, shape subversive or legitimising actions, creating links and allegiances and building what we call the political sphere.

2. *Material culture in the Age of Revolutions*

Between the mid-18th century and the first decades of the 19th century, what contemporaries themselves called the "Age of Revolutions" unfolded. As John Adams wrote in 1815, in his assessment of the American, French and South American revolutions, "the last twenty-five years of the last century, and the first fifteen years of this, may be called the age of revolutions and constitutions".[15]

14. See Chris Gosden, *Rethinking Materiality: The Engagement of Mind with the Material World*, Cambridge, McDonald Institute for Archaeological Research, 2004, and Lambros Malafouris, *How Things Shape the Mind: A Theory of Material Engagement*, Cambridge (MA), MIT Press, 2013.

15. Cited in David Armitage, Sanjay Subrahmanyam, "Introduction: The Age of Revolutions, c. 1760-1840 – Global Causation, Connection, and Comparison", in *The Age of Revolutions in Global Context, c. 1760-1840*, ed. by David Armitage and Sanjay Subrahmanyam, New York, Palgrave Macmillan, 2010, p. xiii.

It is a definition that is now widely used and that, over time, has gone through different historiographical readings in terms of its chronology, causes, spaces and contexts.[16] Despite the variety of approaches and interpretations, historians agree in identifying some elements that characterised the nature of these revolutions and that would profoundly distinguish the societies involved: the attack on monarchical and class institutions; the emergence of the idea of popular sovereignty; the insistent emphasis on freedom, expressed in political, civil and emancipatory terms;[17] the appearance of new social actors on the public stage; the emergence of national claims that questioned the very existence of empires. One of the main factors that guaranteed the success – albeit, in many cases, temporary – of the revolution and profoundly modified the nature of politics, was the powerful arrival of new communication tools, made available by what has been called the contemporary media revolution: the improvement of printing techniques favoured the appearance of newspapers, pamphlets and low-cost books; new reproduction techniques made the wide dissemination of illustrated prints and periodicals possible.[18] The extraordinary editorial and visual production that characterised these decades meant not only that the words, symbols and faces of the new politics became the heritage of a public opinion with ever-broader boundaries, but it also brought about a change in the nature of the political message. No longer confined to debates among the educated elite, political discourse was articulated through new genres and narrative forms (e.g. melodramatic devices), bursting through private and intimate spaces and prompting, more than a rational conviction, an emotional participation.

Political objects belong with these forms of the visualisation and communication of revolutionary ideals and were a specific and significant element of them. They were often objects used on a daily basis, re-semanticised in a political-revolutionary key through the reproduction of the symbols, colours, effigies and faces of the new political protagonists; or they were newly-designed clothing accessories – such as Phrygian caps and rosettes – designed to identify an individual's belonging or contribution to revolutionary dramatisation. The messages conveyed were sometimes easy to interpret, but, where revolutionary or subversive ideas needed to move underground, they appeared as allusion, disguise or metaphor, which could only be deciphered by the initiated. This

16. The books that have contributed to defining this category are, above all, Robert Roswell Palmer, *The Age of the Democratic Revolution: A Political History of Europe and America, 1760-1800*, 2 vols, Princeton (NJ), Princeton University Press, 1959-1964, and Eric J. Hobsbawm, *The Age of Revolution, 1789-1848*, London, Weidenfeld & Nicolson, 1962. More recently, the topic has been analysed from a global perspective by Christopher A. Bayly, *The Birth of the Modern World, 1780-1914: Global Connections and Comparisons*, Oxford, Blackwell, 2004, ch. 3; *The Age of Revolutions in Global Context, c. 1760-1840*; Wim Klooster, *Revolutions in the Atlantic World: A Comparative History*, New York, New York University Press, 2017.

17. See Janet Polasky, *Revolution without Borders: The Call to Liberty in the Atlantic World*, New Haven-London, Yale University Press, 2015.

18. See Gian Luca Fruci, Alessio Petrizzo, "Visualità e grande trasformazione mediatica nel lungo Ottocento", in *Il lungo Ottocento e le sue immagini. Politica, media, spettacolo*, ed. by Vinzia Fiorino, Gian Luca Fruci and Alessio Petrizzo, Pisa, ETS, 2013.

is what happened, for example, in the first half of the 18th century with the Jacobites, when objects marked with symbols and texts of political propaganda kept alive the claims of the last followers of the Stuarts in a context marked by repression and control.[19] A century later, the *Carbonari* used objects with symbols and allusive words as an effective form of non-verbal communication, so as to identify affiliates and escape police checks.

The spread of political objects in this phase was linked to another contemporary revolution, namely that of consumption, which first affected England and then moved to continental Europe and beyond. It was precisely the English scholars of the 18th century who were among the first to highlight the importance of the material dimension of politics, closely related both to the expansion of the market in goods destined for pleasure and personal and domestic beautification, and to the expansion in the number of consumers of these objects: no longer just aristocrats and rich bourgeois, but also artisans, shopkeepers and manual workers.[20]

The political revolutions of the late 18th century – the American and the French – were therefore marked by the presence of an extraordinary number of political objects. In France, where the revolution took on the characteristics of an "epochal medial event",[21] the images that represented the ideals, colours and symbols of the Revolution were reproduced not only on paper products (calendars, almanacs, caricatures, playing cards, prints, drawings, flyers), but on a large number of artefacts in daily use (clothes, furniture, crockery, wallpaper). Alongside this, we observe the creation and dissemination of specific clothing accessories, and at times actual outfits, which more or less clearly marked the identity of the wearer or, in any case, his membership in a group.

Beginning with Lynn Hunt's pioneering research,[22] the historians of the Revolution, especially those who have attempted to decipher the various forms of political communication, have turned the material culture of revolutionary politics into a lively field of research, following several major analytical and interpretative lines. For Richard Taws the objects of everyday life – re-semanticised in political terms – precisely because of their "ephemeral" nature made it possible to modulate and modify a message that was in itself constantly evolving. Therefore the "images and objects made during the French Revolution were [...] a primary site for the formation of both individual subjectivities and wider national or political

19. Murray Pittock, "Treacherous Objects: Towards a Theory of Jacobite Material Culture", *Journal of Eighteenth-Century Studies*, 34/1 (2011), pp. 39-63; Neil Guthrie, *The Material Culture of the Jacobites*, Cambridge, Cambridge University Press, 2013.

20. See, for example, John Brewer, "Commercialisation and Politics", in Neil McKendrick, John Brewer, John Harold Plumb, *The Birth of a Consumer Society: The Commercialisation of Eighteenth-Century England*, London, Europa Publications, 1982, pp. 197-262; Katrina Navickas, "'That sash will hang you': Political Clothing and Adornment in England, 1780-1840", *Journal of British Studies*, 49 (2010), pp. 540-565.

21. Rolf Reichardt, "The French Revolution as a European Media Event", *European History Online*, accessed at http://ieg-ego.eu/en/threads/european-media/european-media-events/rolf-reichardt-the-french-revolution-as-a-european-media-event, published 27 August 2012.

22. Lynn Hunt, *Politics, Culture, and Class in the French Revolution*, Berkeley, University of California Press, 1984.

community identities".[23] Leora Auslander has highlighted how the governments and intellectuals of the Revolution were interested above all in those materials that had a public dimension (clothes, clothing accessories, architecture), while they did not worry too much about designing objects to decorate domestic spaces.[24]

Whereas historians of the revolutions of the late 18th century have paid specific attention to the role of political objects,[25] the studies devoted to the material culture of politics in the first half of the 19th century are fewer and far between. This limited interest was prompted in the first place by what we mentioned at the beginning of this introduction and what has been reiterated by the authors of one of the few articles devoted to this topic in the context of Victorian England: "It could be argued that historians of Victorian politics have little need to incorporate material culture into their research as they enjoy an embarrassment of text-based riches – the papers of individuals and organisations, the extensive Victorian press, printed memoirs and pamphlets, to name but a few of the most mined sources".[26] However, the wealth and, in some cases, overabundance of written documents did not prevent a specific space from being reserved for the materiality of politics in at least three areas of research. The first has been devoted to the forms of political radicalism that developed in Europe in the first half of the 19th century, often closely related to revolutionary events. Thus, for example, in the case of England, scholars such as James Epstein and Paul Pickering have identified in the forms of non-verbal and symbolic communication of radical and reformist movements – Chartism in particular – the preferred tool in the construction of their political identity and dissemination of their message.[27] Moreover, the use of these alternative forms of political communication was motivated by these movements' limited access to the traditional media of the time and the negative image conveyed by the latter. Across the Channel, Emmanuel Fureix has

23. Richard Taws, *The Politics of the Provisional: Art and Ephemera in Revolutionary France*, University Park (PA), Pennsylvania State University Press, 2013, p. 21.

24. Auslander compares, in particular, clothes and architectural projects, on the one hand, and house furniture on the other: Leora Auslander, "Regeneration through the Everyday? Clothing, Architecture, and Furniture in Revolutionary Paris", *Art History*, 28/2 (2005), pp. 227-247. On revolutionary clothing, see Nicole Pellegrin, *Les vêtements de la liberté: Abécédaire des pratiques vestimentaires en France de 1780 à 1800*, Paris, Alinea, 1989; Lynn Hunt, "Freedom of Dress in Revolutionary France", in *From the Royal to the Republican Body*, ed. by Sara E. Melzer and Kathryn Norberg, Berkeley, University of California Press, 1998, pp. 224-250; Richard Wrigley, *The Politics of Appearances: Representations of Dress in Revolutionary France*, Oxford, Berg, 2002.

25. On the American Revolution, see Michael Zakim, *Ready-Made Democracy: A History of Men's Dress in the American Republic, 1760-1869*, Chicago, University of Chicago Press, 2003; Leora Auslander, *Cultural Revolutions: Everyday Life and Politics in Britain, North America, and France*, Oxford, Berg, 2009.

26. Mark Nixon, Gordon Pentland, Matthew Roberts, "The Material Culture of Scottish Reform Politics, c. 1820 - c. 1884", *Journal of Scottish Historical Studies*, 32/1 (2012), p. 28.

27. James A. Epstein. *Radical Expression: Political Language, Ritual, and Symbol in England, 1790-1850*, New York, Oxford University Press, 1994; Paul A. Pickering, "Class without Words: Symbolic Communication in the Chartist Movement", *Past and Present*, 112 (1986), pp. 144-162.

considered the material dimension of politics in the light of political iconoclasm in the first half of the 19th century in France, analysing how regime changes and revolutionary moments were deeply marked by attacks on the symbols and effigies of political opponents.[28]

The second area of investigation of the material culture of politics in the 19th century is that linked to studies of the 1848 revolution. For a long time used by the historiography only in illustrative and/or decorative terms, the numerous political objects present in the great European revolution have been analysed as an expression of an ongoing "politicisation", as capable of generating a system of symbols and visual emblems with the function of identifying the nature and distinctive elements of the people who wore them, distinguishing them from others and allowing viewers to recognise and identify them.[29] In particular, as was also the case for the French Revolution, the attention of historians has often been directed towards the way revolutionaries-patriots dressed, analysing them in the light of the construction of a national "fashion" and its relationship with specific cultural traditions.[30]

Finally, objects marked with politically relevant images and symbols have been considered within the research devoted to reconstructing the popularity and success of 19th-century political leaders. In recent years, this area of investigation has seen new developments, mostly aimed at showing how between the 18th and 19th centuries in the Atlantic area extraordinary attention was paid to the new protagonists of public life. Within this culture of celebrity, politicians were talked about and presented using the tools made available by the ongoing media revolution, which included political objects.

The protagonists of this construction of political celebrity were first and foremost the military leaders and "builders of nations", from George Washington to Napoleon Bonaparte, from Simón Bolívar to Giuseppe Garibaldi. In England

28. Emmanuel Fureix, *L'oeil blessé. Politiques de l'iconoclasme après la Révolution française*, Champ Vallon, Ceyzérieu, 2019.

29. On this topic, the observations by Maurice Agulhon remain important: see "Politics, Images and Symbols in Post-Revolutionary France", in *Rites of Power: Symbolism, Ritual and Politics since the Middle Age*, ed. by Sean Wilentz, Pennsylvania, University of Pennsylvania Press, 1985 (included with the title "Politique, images, symboles dans la France post-revolutionnaire" in Maurice Agulhon, *Histoire vagabonde*, vol. I, *Ethnologie etpolitique dans la France contemporaine*, Paris, Gallimard, 1988, pp. 283-318).

30. For a recent discussion on this topic, see *The Clothing of Politics (XIX-XX centuries)*, ed. by Carlotta Sorba, special issue of *Contemporanea* (2017). On Italy, see Carlotta Sorba, "'Ernani' Hats: Italian Opera as a Repertoire of Political Symbols during the Risorgimento", in *The Oxford Handbook of the New Cultural History of Music*, Oxford, Oxford University Press, 2011; Gabriella Romani, "Fashioning the Italian Nation: Risorgimento and Its *costume all'italiana*", *Journal of Modern Italian Studies*, 20/1 (2015), pp. 10-23; on Germany, see Isabelle Belting, *Mode und Revolution. Deutschland 1848-49*, Hildesheim, Georg Olms Verlag, 1997; on the Czech context, see Mirjam Moravocá, *Národní oděv roku 1848. Ke vzniku národne politického symbolu* (*National Clothing of 1848: The Origin of the National Political Symbol*), Prague, Academia, 1986; Jan Randak, "Symbolicke chovani v revoluci 1848: revolucni moda (Symbolic Behaviour in the Revolution of 1848: Revolutionary Fashion)", *Cesky Lid: etnologicky casopis*, 93/1 (2006), pp. 49-69.

it was political leaders such as Robert Peel and Richard Cobden, and then, in the central decades of the 19th century, figures such as William Gladstone and Benjamin Disraeli who were the subjects of great attention and popular public opinion. The reconstruction of what historians have observed in terms of their fame, celebrity and charisma[31] has also focused largely on the analysis of the visual and material aids that granted these figures extraordinary popularity, which was in some ways unprecedented and in many cases able to travel beyond the countries in which they operated.[32] During the 19th century, the use of political objects also took place within a context marked by the spread of consumer goods across broader sectors of society. As Manuel Charpy has shown, the 19th century marked a decisive turning point in the material culture-society relationship, thanks to a veritable explosion of personal objects and new forms of self-objectifying.[33]

The chapters in this volume fit within this historiographical debate and are an attempt to broaden and explore it further, capturing its many prompts and at the same time proposing new analytical reflections and insights through a number of case studies organised around three particularly important thematic strands: objects as instruments of political action; objects as forms of storytelling and narration; and, finally, objects as memorial and reliquary evidence.

3. *Objects in action*

In the conclusions to his chapter on the collection and re-use of the remains from the storming of the Bastille, Rolf Reichardt stresses how, during the French Revolution, objects operated above all on two fronts: namely, symbolic appropriation and propaganda. First, the possession and use of objects with political markings allowed individuals to visually demonstrate their adherence to the ideals and values that dominated the public scene. In the French Revolution, in the Spanish constitutional period or again in the Italian 1848 uprisings,

31. Fundamental texts are Antoine Lilti, *The Invention of Celebrity 1750-1850*, London, Polity Press, 2017, and David A. Bell, *Men on Horseback: The Power of Charisma in the Age of Revolution*, New York, Farrar, Stratus and Giroux, 2020.

32. See, for example, Philip Dwyer, "Napoleon Bonaparte as Hero and Saviour: Image, Rhetoric and Behaviour in the Construction of a Legend", *French History*, 18/4 (2004), pp. 379-403; Wayne Hanley, *The Genesis of Napoleonic Propaganda, 1796-1799*, New York, Columbia University Press, 2005; Alan Forrest, "Propaganda and the Legitimation of Power in Napoleonic France", *French History*, 18/4 (2004), pp. 426-445; Lucy Riall, *Garibaldi. L'invenzione di un eroe*, Rome-Bari, Laterza, 2007; Simon Morgan, "Material Culture and the Politics of Personality in Early Victorian England", *Journal of Victorian Culture*, 17/2 (2012), pp. 127-146.

33. Manuel Charpy, *Le théatre des objets. Espaces privés, culture matérielle et identité bourgeoise. Paris 1830-1914*, PhD thesis, Université François Rabelais de Tours, 2010; Manuel Charpy, "Le spectacle de la marchandise. Sorties au théatre et phénomèmes de mode à Paris, Londres et New York (1830-1914)", in *Au théâtre! La sortie au spectacle, XIXe-XXIe siècles*, ed. by Jean Claude Yon and Pascale Goeschel, Paris, Presses Universitaires Paris Sorbonne, 2014; *Usages de l'objet. Littérature, histoire, arts et techniques, XIXe-XXe siècles*, ed. by Marta Caraion, Champ Vallon, Seyssel, 2014; Deborah Cohen, *Household Gods: The British and their Possessions*, New Haven, Yale University Press, 2006.

wearing a rosette with the national colours or a button with evocative images (e.g. Commander Rafael de Riego, the Storming of the Bastille), seemed to place individuals within a political community, without the need to otherwise show their belonging. In fact, in some cases, it was precisely the wearing of objects with a strong symbolic connotation that allowed individuals who were usually silent, or barely entitled to speak, to have a leading role in the public arena. Thus, across the Italian cities that were shaken by patriotic demonstrations throughout 1847, women showed their allegiance to the national movement by wearing medals, pendants and headscarves with "the venerated image" of Pius IX, thereby becoming political actresses for the redemption of their nation. Through objects, politics was trivialised, but at the same time it invaded the private, even intimate, dimension of individuals: objects were not only worn and flaunted in public, but they populated domestic spaces and were thus evidence of the particular pervasiveness of political faith.

The symbolic appropriation achieved through the use or possession of an object with political connotations seems to be strengthened when there is no public dimension in which to make them operate. This was the case with the Napoleonic effigies that spread throughout Europe after the defeat of the French Emperor. Between 1815 and 1830, Europe was literally invaded by an impressive array of figurative objects of different kinds and shapes bearing the images of the former Emperor and members of his family, or with symbols (the letter N) and colours recalling their world.[34]

The extraordinary popularity of these objects represented the material and visual version of the great leader's legend which, in the aftermath of 1815, had left deep marks in Europe. This legend had a political version, when Napoleon was granted the role of the liberator of peoples, "Messiah of the Revolution" and, in Bourbon France, eponymous hero of a patriotism in which the Jacobin tradition merged with the cult of a dynasty that had been interrupted so abruptly.[35] But Napoleon's fame in the Europe of the 1820s and 1840s transcended his strictly political and military dimension and had much to do with the cult of celebrity and subsequent media coverage of the "illustrious men" that, precisely between the late 18th and the early decades of the 19th centuries, characterised Europe. In her chapter in this volume, Arianna Arisi Rota highlights not only the different types and iconographic models of Napoleonic objects, but above all the emotional ties that were established between the objects and their owners.[36] Memories and feelings of nostalgia were triggered in an audience made up largely of army veterans, former imperial officials and notables who had lived through that period.

34. Sudhir Hazareesingh, *The Legend of Napoleon*, London, Granta, 2004, ch. 3.

35. Sudhir Hazareesingh, "Napoleonic Memory in Nineteenth-Century France: The Making of a Liberal Legend", *MLN*, 120/4 (2005), pp. 747-773.

36. The topic of the relationship between objects and emotions is still under-researched but of great interest to reconstruct the complexity of affective – sensory – cognitive experience. A recent attempt to add materiality to the history of emotions is in *Feeling Things: Objects and Emotions through History*, ed. by Stephanie Downes, Sally Holloway and Sarah Randles, Oxford, Oxford University Press, 2018.

These feelings, however, were not without possible political implications, when they ended up becoming the basis of protests against the restored order.

The second front on which political objects operated is that of propaganda. The political re-semanticisation of everyday objects turned them, as París and Roca Vernet write in this volume, into "a crucial platform for the expression of political commitment to revolution and counter-revolution". In particular, consumer materials played an especially crucial role in making political ideals, characters and symbols familiar to those sectors of society that did not have easy access to written texts or that were distant from the canonical places of political debate (clubs, assemblies, etc). At the same time, the transfer of political images onto objects belongs to the process of the spectacularisation of politics that began to impose itself in those years. This is the case with the portraits of politicians who, from the French Revolution onwards, assumed a central role in the growing mediatic transformation of the political sphere, which also took place through the transfer of such personal images onto different types of objects.[37] Moreover, the presence of objects in the public space was not limited to a simple re-proposal – in other forms – of politically relevant images and symbols. It was precisely their material dimension that allowed them to play an important role in the staging of political action: for example, the busts of Pius IX, which were triumphantly carried at rallies in the Italian streets in 1848, helped define the character of the *Risorgimento*, i.e., the renaissance of the nation (the pope leading an orderly and approving people to its redemption).

The particular nature of these materials also placed them in contexts that were not only political. Before becoming vehicles of popular messages or actors in public performances, objects were above all consumer goods moving within a production and commercial chain. So there were artisans – for example, the figurine makers Sandro Morachioli discusses in his contribution – who adapted their production by adding political images, colours and symbols to their traditional products. In some cases, this choice was also dictated by their support of political ideals,[38] while in others it was mere "commercial speculation". This was the case of a merchant who, in Venice in 1848, proposed (unsuccessfully) to the revolutionary government that he exclusively produce items of clothing that made clear reference to the Republic, by placing a lion in the centre surrounded by the phrase "Italian Independence – Venetian Industry".[39]

37. See Amy Freund, *Portraiture and Politics in Revolutionary France*, University Park (PA), Pennsylvania State University Press, 2014; Gian Luca Fruci, "'Un contemporain célèbre'. Ritratti e immagini di Manin in Francia fra rivoluzione ed esilio", in *Fuori d'Italia: Manin e l'esilio*, ed. by Michele Gottardi, Venice, Ateneo Veneto, 2009, pp. 129-155 and 243-252 (iconographies); Henry Miller, *Politics Personified: Portraiture, Caricature and Visual Culture in Britain, c. 1830-80*, Manchester, Manchester University Press, 2015.

38. This is the case with one of the most important producers of popular prints in France, the Pellerins from Epinal, who were fervent supporters of Napoleon: see Barbara Day-Hickman, *Napoleonic Art: Nationalism and the Spirit of Rebellion in France (1815-1848)*, Newark, University of Delaware Press, 1999, pp. 21 ff.

39. As reported in Piero Brunello, *Colpi di scena. La rivoluzione del Quarantotto a Venezia*, Verona, Cierre, 2018, p. 315.

The commercial nature of these products also meant that, on the one hand, they were linked to changes in fashion and, on the other, that distribution circuits overlapped with those of other consumer goods. Thus, in constitutional Spain the fans and snuffboxes with the images of Rafael del Riego came from France, following the routes taken by fashionable goods. This intense transnational trade took on even clearer connotations in the case of objects with Napoleonic effigies, which also moved along smuggling routes, from Switzerland to Lombardy or from the German states to Bourbon France.[40] Manufacturers, artisans, merchants, *colporteurs*, smugglers: a variegated world lay behind what looked like the actual merchandising of politics. On the other hand, there were materials with such a symbolic load that they escaped this commercial dimension. This is what happened with objects made with stones and pieces of metal from the storming of the Bastille, which, as Rolf Reichardt has written, became "missionary relics intended to propagate revolutionary enthusiasm and symbolism, whereas the products of the milliners have, despite their decoration, a somewhat playful character". In short, the performative capacity of objects is not limited to the moment of political action in its strict sense, but is also manifest in what is configured as a narrative and memorial dimension.

4. *Objects and narration*

In fact, things tell a story, but again in their own way. That is to say, they incorporate political narratives of various kinds (which may even change over time) and do so in many different ways: at times more directly and immediately, and at other times more obliquely, but often no less effectively. In this sense, technical advances that make it possible to materialise messages in new ways can be decisive. This was the case with ceramic printing, which, from the end of the 18th century made it possible to combine texts and images in commonly used objects such as cups, plates and glasses. Simon Morgan has shown us this, focusing on the case of Peterloo pottery. The new technique was first used to celebrate some of the great national figures (Lord Nelson, the Duke of Wellington) or members of the royal family, but the radical tradition appropriated it quickly, in a particularly wide and varied way after the terrible massacre of 1819. They were objects (especially cups and glasses) which apparently circulated widely beyond Lancashire, telling a story of violence and innocent victims, "condensing" the story into a series of images and slogans and contributing very directly to an increasingly widespread political practice: subversive toasts wishing all harm to the "Manchester butchers" in an intertwining of memory, denunciation and a call to action.

However, the forms and modalities of the story could be different. In the *Risorgimento* Italy discussed by Sandro Morachioli, painting was filled with objects sometimes crucial to understanding the images and contexts represented. In fact, especially between the 1840s and 1850s, the most politically oriented

40. In 1823 the French police reported that 12,000 small busts of Napoleon were being produced in Württemberg for the French market: see Hazareesingh, *The Legend of Napoleon*, p. 54

artists frequently made militant use of objects, which were useful for narrating a character (the Napoleonic veteran, for example) or for connoting a situation. In this case, we are dealing with illustrated, two-dimensional objects that made up a rather lively transmedia story. They confirm the spread of their use but above all the poignancy of their evocative pull, which is the ability to immediately focus on a political belonging or experience.

However, this does not necessarily mean that objects contribute to building political narratives only by incorporating explicit political messages, whether figurative or textual. This was the case with Alessio Petrizzo's lost objects, which became the focus of a widespread recovery, collection and redistribution campaign by the pontifical authorities who returned to power after the dramatic fall of the Roman Republic in 1849. In this case, there were in fact the most disparate materials: kitchen crockery, mattresses, sheets, shirts, wood, poles, nails but also horses and carriages that had been requisitioned by the Republicans, especially in the months of the siege, to meet the needs of the wartime efforts and public health. The newly installed government intended to return them to their legitimate secular and religious owners, by means of a decidedly substantial symbolic operation. Immediately after the city was recaptured, a special Commission for the Recovery and Return of Items was charged with the task and accomplished it with meticulous and transparent determination, making it a key element in the process of restoring order. Through what happened to these objects, we thus get a taste of the rubble and upheavals in the post-revolutionary city, which had survived the long siege. In fact, the compensation received for these objects tells the story of a revolution run by thieves, swindlers and murderers, a "Garibaldi gang" capable only of requisitioning, looting and demolishing.

Finally, there are real story-objects such as those analysed by Roberto Balzani. These are things that do not represent but embody a figure and his adventures, accompanying a series of biographies in their making. Here the contexts are different and distant from each other (Greece, Mexico, the Habsburg Empire) but they share the dramatic struggle for the recognition of nationalities. In the strong identification between material objects and the fighting people we find in them, the role played by forms of mutilated physicality stands out, such as the leg of General Lopez di Sant'Anna, the hero of Mexican independence, or of Italian patriot Pietro Maroncelli, painfully amputated in the Spielberg prison and immediately afterwards described in Silvio Pellico's bestseller, *Le mie prigioni* (*My Ten Years' Imprisonment*). Long before becoming relics, materials of this type were heroic pieces of the self, telling and personifying a biographical journey. And they could find themselves experiencing unexpected and almost grotesque stories, as in the case of Sant'Anna's lost limb, for which a real funeral monument was erected.

5. *Objects as relics and memories*

Objects have a very peculiar relationship with time, which bears little resemblance to that of words and written texts. In them we find a sort of inextricable interweaving between persistence and changeability in uses and meanings. In fact, there are not many politically connoted or used objects that have managed to survive. In many cases they were made of ephemeral, fragile and not very durable materials, and they also often followed political fashions and died with them. But some still survive (not only as illustrations or descriptions in the documents) and represent a tangible and direct link with the past. When this happens, it is mostly because they were part of a process of memorialisation and then possibly of transformation into heritage, which in turn must be reconstructed and investigated in its many aspects. What is clear is that in their political life they tended to display a marked instability and changeability: they often changed hands, changed their uses and meanings, changed ownership and/or location.

It is well known how objects can be incorporated into the memorial building of the past, assuming the connotation of real relics. Relics – material remains of a celebrated body or objects owned by the latter – have long represented a central aspect of religious experience, and not only in the Western world; as corporeal testimony to the material life of "holy" figures, relics contribute to cult building, perpetuate the memory of saints and define their charismatic-magical power. In Christian Europe, relics and the devotional practices linked to them played a decisive role in shaping the relationship between religion and popular culture. Over the last thirty years, above all thanks to medieval and early modern historians,[41] studying relics has become the key to reconstructing religious practices, identifying the material and corporeal dimension of devotion and delineating the role of memory in legitimising religious belief. Scholarly attention to relics was not simply a matter of religious context. Within the historiographical tradition centred around an analysis of the consecration of politics and the religious dimension of public action, the existence of "profane" relics has been highlighted, as the expression of individuals with sacred connotations (the sovereign, the great leader, the patriot) and capable of activating some of the processes traditionally associated with religious experience (devotion, cult practices, memory). In the 18th and 19th centuries, the political phenomenon which acquired religious, holy connotations was the nation with its sacrificial and symbolic figures: heroes, warriors, patriots. Their deaths – frequently the result of "martyrdom" – were followed by a religious-cult construction process with reliquaries as one of its principal resources. In the absence of the magical-supranatural connotations of religious relics in the strictest sense, profane and political relics shared some of their foremost characteristics with the latter. As we can read in the final chapters by Silvia Cavicchioli and Marina Tesoro, they were capable of activating emotions and passions among the "faithful", they took the form of commemorative places and they managed to create legitimising links with the past. They were at the heart of intense promotional and popularising activities involving various individuals

41. Patrick J. Geary, *Furta Sacra: Thefts of Relics in the Central Middle Ages*, Princeton (NJ), Princeton University Press, 1978; Peter Brown, *The Cult of Saints: Its Rise and Function in Latin Christianity*, Chicago, University of Chicago Press, 1981; Caroline W. Bynum, *Christian Materiality: An Essay on Religion in Late Medieval Europe*, New York, Zone Books, 2011; Lindal Roper, "Luther Relics", in *Religion, the Supernatural and Visual Culture in Early Modern Europe*, ed. by Jennifer Spinks and Dagmar Eichberger, Leiden, Brill, 2015.

(the direct heirs of the "saints", public institutions, communities, museums), in some cases with an eye to their commercial dimensions as well.[42] The contributions that address these aspects do not simply analyse the symbolic capital of objects belonging to patriotic heroes, but also show how, in becoming "relics", they were transformed into political and relational capital. As has been suggested by anthropological studies, a relic becomes such only when it is capable of activating a context of practice and belief.

Investigating the collections of relics that filled the first museums of the *Risorgimento*, Silvia Cavicchioli has shown the complex path bringing the remains – both material and human – of those who rose to the role of martyrs, or in any case of notable figures in the *Risorgimento* epic, to a new role as relics, capable of linking a heroic past with the prosaic construction of the national state. The construction of this memorial system based on relics saw the active participation of disparate individuals (primarily family members, but also veterans, soldiers' associations, local history experts, doctors, parish priests), before public institutions intervened to include them within ceremonies and public places of remembrance. In this effort to collect and preserve material remains, women played an important role. The complex and varied relationships between gender and material culture, which has seen important developments in social and consumer history,[43] also appear significant from a political point of view. The subordinate and subsidiary position assigned to women within the national-patriotic discourse was partly subverted when they became real entrepreneurs of memory, active protagonists in the preservation and enhancement of a heroic family history. This was the case with Adelaide Bono Cairoli (mother of four patriots who had died for their homeland), and also with her daughter-in-law, Elena Sizzo Noris, who in Marina Tesoro's essay both appear as the priestesses of a patriotic memory capable of communicating with subsequent generations.

6. *Conclusions*

Speaking of political objects means, as we shall see in the chapters that follow, facing different things and situations and touching on many aspects of the relationship between culture and materiality. What we are interested in showing is that making the material and political dimensions interact in the reconstruction

42. Eva Giloi, *Monarchy, Myth, and Material Culture in Germany 1750-1950*, Cambridge, Cambridge University Press, 2011.

43. Out of the many investigations on this topic, see in particular *The Sex of Things: Gender and Consumption in Historical Pespective*, ed. by Victoria De Grazia and Ellen Furlough, Berkeley, University of California Press, 1996; *Oggetti*, ed. by Sandra Cavallo and Isabelle Chabot, *Genesis*, 1 (2006); *Gender, Taste, and Material Culture in Britain and North America, 1700-1830*, ed. by John Styles and Amanda Vickery, New Haven, Yale University Press, 2006; Leora Auslander, "Editorial", in *Objects et fabrication du genre*, ed. by Leora Auslander, Rebecca Rogers and Michelle Zancarini-Fournel, *Clio: Femmes, Genre, Histoire*, 40 (2014), pp. 6-14.

of the past can be interesting and fruitful on both sides. And it can therefore also allow a better understanding both of the functioning dynamics of the political sphere and of the role of materiality in the social world. From this point of view, the age of revolutions was a significant workshop for numerous reasons: its major traits included a political audience that was expanding and diversifying, the consolidation of forms of collective mobilisation that animated the public sphere with new voices and new expressions, a refinement of discourses and political practices that were not limited to revolutionary and subversive action, but also included counter-revolution and its communication strategies.

As we have said, objects can incorporate – and help generate – messages, narratives, ideas, emotions and plans of action and, in this sense, they must be adequately questioned. They can be mobile, in their meanings and also in the tangible circulation of artefacts and their iconographic and symbolic models. Their life, when it is possible to reconstruct it, can be varied, eventful, in many ways significant, as shown by the case studies included in this volume, which we hope further research will continue to investigate.

I

Objects in Action

Rolf Reichardt

Political Objects in the French Revolution: The Case of the Bastille

At the outset of "the long 19th century", the French Revolution represents an extremely fertile area for research concerning the production, spread and use of political objects on the small scale. Given the wealth of extant original documents and the wide diversity of objects, even historians of the Revolution have difficulties surveying the full range of the available material.[1]

On their own, the new "clothes of liberty" that conquered the public sphere in 1789 and over the following years constitute a complicated subject.[2] We can add the patriotic cockades and the red caps of liberty, objects that have survived in many different forms. At times they were objects of dispute and public struggle, like when anti-revolutionists dishonoured the national cockades, when royalists countered them with black or white cockades and when clubs of revolutionary women campaigned for the right to wear the *bonnet rouge* of the Jacobins.[3]

As concerns more solid materials, the profound cultural changes brought about by the Revolution manifested in the production of a wide variety of objects that were used privately in everyday life. On the one hand, there was the pottery distributed across the general populace: faience or earthenware dishes, cups, bowls, mugs, shaving bowls and more.[4] Their decoration with revolutionary symbols and inscriptions with the names of their owners testify to sincere political convictions. On the other hand, we find pocketwatches and other luxury products that were ordered and purchased by a more elitist clientele. In comparison to the faience, their patriotic decorations are rather cautious.[5]

And of course there are the various memorabilia devoted not only to the royal "martyr" and his family, but also to the "Martyrs of Liberty", notably Jean-Paul

1. Such a survey remains to be undertaken.

2. Nicole Pellegrin, *Les Vêtements de la Liberté*, Aix-en-Provence, Alinéa, 1989; *Modes & Révolutions, 1780-1804*, Paris, Musée de la mode et du costume, Palais Galliéra, 1989.

3. Bärbel Schmidt, "Freiheitsmütze", in *Lexikon der Revolutions-Ikonographie in der europäischen Druckgraphik* (hereafter *LRI*), ed. by Rolf Reichardt, Münster, Rhema, 2017, pp. 965-986; Bärbel Schmidt, "Kokarde", in *LRI*, pp. 1261-1280.

4. *Faïences révolutionnaires. Collections du Musée de la céramique de Rouen*, Paris, Varia, 1989; Edith Mannoni, *Les Faïences révolutionnaires*, Paris, Ch. Massin, 1989.

5. *La Révolution dans la mesure du temps: Calendrier républicain, heure décimale 1793-1805*, ed. by Catherine Cardinal, La Chaux-de-Fonds, Musée international d'Horlogerie, 1989.

Marat. Everything contributed to honouring and commemorating "the Friend of the People": his busts installed in the rooms of revolutionary clubs and republican schools, and his most popular portrait, transferred in small size on snuffboxes, medals, neck pendants, rings and many other revolutionary relics.[6]

But instead of continuing this *tour d'horizon* with the risk of enumerating single objects that have often lost their specific historical context, this article considers a special category of material, which was sufficiently detailed as to allow us to uncover "the social life of things"[7] – the numerous objects concerning the conquest and demolition of the Bastille.

1. *Badges of honour and fashion articles celebrating the conquest of the Bastille*

> The National Assembly, struck with a just admiration for the heroic fearlessness of the Vanquishers of the Bastille and wishing to give, in the name of the Nation, a public testimony to those who have risked and sacrificed their lives to shake off the yoke of slavery and make their homeland free, Decrees that it will be provided at the expense of the Public Treasury to each of the Vanquishers of the Bastille, so that they will be able to bear arms, a suit and full armament, according to the uniform of the Nation…; and that on the garment a mural crown will be applied either on the left arm, or next to the left lapel; that each of the said Vanquishers of the Bastille will be sent an honourable certificate to show their service and the Nation's recognition…

According to this diploma issued on 19 June 1790 – an illustrated etching printed on parchment and marked by two red seals[8] – 954 patriots who had truly participated in the conquest of the notorious state prison were being officially recognised as "soldier-citizens" ("soldats-citoyens"), or as national heroes of the new democratic era. They formed a special military corps named the "Vainqueurs de la Bastille", the "Vanquishers of the Bastille".[9] Their armament included a sabre with a hilt showing the falling towers of the Bastille.[10] As for the small symbols of honour awarded to them, the Musée Carnavalet in Paris keeps not only the "couronne murale" or civic crown mentioned in the diploma (Fig. 1), but also various pendants commemorating "July 1789" (Fig. 2) and even their seal stamp, which is a sculpture of the Bastille *en miniature* (Fig. 3).

6. *La mort de Marat*, ed. by Jean-Claude Bonnet, Paris, Flammarion, 1986; Guillaume Mazeau, *Corday contre Marat. Deux siècles d'images*, Vizille, Musée de la Révolution française, 2009; Alberto Milano, "Büsten, Figurenverkäufer", in *LRI*, pp. 608-623.

7. Fabio Dei, "La vita sociale delle cose, trent'anni dopo: quale 'svolta' negli studi di cultura materiale?", *Contemporanea*, 19/3 (2016), pp. 439-443.

8. Rolf Reichardt, *L'imagerie révolutionnaire de la Bastille. Collections du musée Carnavalet*, Paris, Paris musées/Nicolas Chaudun, 2009, cat. n. 18, p. 88.

9. Hans-Jürgen Lüsebrink, Rolf Reichardt, *The Bastille: A History of a Symbol of Despotism and Freedom*, Durham-London, Duke University Press, 1997, pp. 86-106; Hans-Jürgen Lüsebrink, "Die Vainqueurs de la Bastille: kollektiver Diskurs und individuelle 'Wortergreifungen'", in *Die Französische Revolution als Bruch des gesellschaftlichen Bewusstseins*, ed. by Reinhart Koselleck and Rolf Reichardt, Munich, Oldenbourg, 1988, pp. 321-357.

10. *Aux Armes Citoyens! Les Sabres à emblêmes de la Révolution*, Musée de la Révolution Française, Vizille, 1987, cat. nos 10-11, pp. 27 and 54-55.

In fact, the first and probably the largest production of small political objects during the Revolution coincides with the fall of the Bastille, the media event *par excellence*. Engravers, milliners and modists did not, however, attend the decree of the National Assembly, but started immediately bringing their patriotic goods to the market, as testified by the report of a Parisian correspondent that dates from August 1789 and which was published in a German fashion magazine:

> Our speculating manufacturers of knickknacks have had stones for rings and the like cut from the gray building stones of the Bastille, and have had them set as jewels. So now rings and ear-rings are worn *à la Liberté nationale*, buttons, fans and boxes *à la Bastille*…; the army makers of the frivolous and shopkeepers in the provinces… fabricate buttons *à la Bastille*.[11]

Those buttons were decorated with miniature images representing the conquest or demolition of the former state prison. Thus, a button in the manner of Wedgwood shows numerous workers on the towers of the Bastille; they are very busy breaking the walls of the monument in order to have its stones fall into the depth (Fig. 4). The handicraftsmen could draw their images from prints, as a single sheet offered a series of small medallions that visualised the same topic.[12] They could easily be either copied or cut out and applied on snuffboxes. Most of these *tabatières* presented the standard picture of the Bastille at the moment of its surrender, with the commander of the castle, de Launay, on the point of being arrested by two Vainqueurs (Fig. 5). Other boxes were adorned with allegorical scenes adopted from graphic satires, such as the personifications of the Three Estates dancing in front of the Bastille[13] or the figures of Liberty and France preparing the festival of the Federation.[14]

The fans *à la Bastille*, mentioned in the letter from Paris cited above, have also been preserved. Like the other folding fans from the Revolution, they were fabricated in a series for a wide audience, as the materials from which they were made – coloured etchings mounted on 14 or 16 wooden sticks – were much less expensive than those used for the luxury fans of the Old Regime (original paintings mounted on 20 or 22 sticks made of ivory and pearl). The *Prise de la Bastille* at the moment of surrender is one of their favourite themes. Repeatedly, the central image is accompanied on both sides by the texts of patriotic songs with their tunes (*air*) indicated at the beginning of each verse (Fig. 6). As these tunes were very popular and generally known, the fans facilitated the singing and memorisation of the verses. In our example, the verses were composed by the *chansonnier patriote* Déduit and copied from a print that schematically represented the capture of the

11. *Journal des Luxus und der Moden* 4, October/November 1789, 453 and 489; report is testified by the *Gazette d'Amsterdam*, 1st September 1789, 20.

12. *Prise des fusils aux Invalides...*, Twelve circular medallions representing the conquest and the demolition of the Bastille, colorated etching, 1789, Bibliothèque nationale de France (hereforth BnF), Est., coll. Smith-Lesouëf 2757.

13. Anonymous snuffbox without legend, lecquered paper-mache and painted paper, Ø 72, 1789, MC, OM 776.

14. Anonymous snuffbox without legend, painted ivory and gold-plated copper, Ø 85, 1790, MC, OM.0942.

fortress.[15] They evoke the historical context of collective emotions and symbolic acts: (1) the fear of an "ariscrat complot" preceding the 14th of July; (2) the heroism of the Vainqueurs embodied by the soldier Élie from the Gardes françaises; (3) the public execution of the "traitor" de Launay by the people; and finally, (4) the triumphal demolition of the "atrocious monument of tyranny".

1. "Air [:] *o ma tendre musette*
O jour immemorable,
Où nous devions périr,
Sans un trait admirable
Fait pour nous secourir
Des Faste [sic] de l'histoire
Tu seras l'ornement".

2. "Air [:] *regarde cette rose*
Eli rempli de zele,
Brave officier Français,
La couronne immortelle
Est due à tes succés.
Au bout de ton épée
Conserve cet écrit
Qui fait ta renommée
Que chacun applaudit".

3. "Air [:] *de mon berge volage*
Oublions les infames
Qui vouloient nous trahir.
La pitié dans nos ames
Ne peut s'épanouir.
Que du livre de vie
Leurs noms soient effacés.
Malgré leur perfidie
Tous nos maux sont passés".

4. "Air [:] *dans ma cabane onscure*
Cette affreuse Bastille
N'existe déjà plus,
D'ardeur chacun pétille,
Ses murs sont abattus.
Fuis honteux esclavage,
Fuis o ciecle [sic] de fer,
France reprends courage
Sous Louis et Necker".

2. *The debris of despotism converted into relics of liberty*

The highest number of revolutionary objects, however, was not dedicated to the conquest of the Bastille, but to the demolition of this "odious monument of despotism". In fact, the rubble from its destruction was transformed into thousands of revolutionary memorabilia endowed with a specific quality: as they were formed out of materials that had been quasi contaminated by their bad usage under the Old Regime, but that had now been converted into revolutionary symbols, they were seen to surpass objects manufactured from other materials in their historical and political authenticity.

This unique quantity of edited relics was the work of one and the same person, the rich building-contractor Pierre-François Palloy. Having been "electrified" by the storming of the Bastille, on 15 July he spontaneously dispatched his four hundred workers to begin razing the "infernal colossus". And some days later, when he was officially nominated director of its demolition, he understood his mission to be to promote revolutionary patriotism by disseminating memorabilia consisting of the materials of the monument.[16] As Richard Taws has illustrated,

15. *Prise de la Bastille*, anonymous coloured woodcut and printed characters, Orléans, Jean-Baptiste Letourmy, 1789, 270x364 mm; see Reichardt, *L'imagerie*, n. 7.

16. Lüsebrink, Reichardt, *The Bastille*, pp. 118-147; Richard Taws, *The Politics of the Provisional: Art and Ephemera in Revolutionary France*, University Park, Pennsylvania University Press, 2013, pp. 96-117.

Palloy provides "one of the most intriguing examples of how a strategic provisionality structured an engagement with both the material traces of the former regime and the revolution's new visual culture".[17]

The metals and stones from the Bastille were the main materials that the "patriote", as Palloy liked to be called, employed for his "relics of freedom", which were produced in large numbers. In summer 1790 his workshop began to construct miniature models of the Bastille, some of which were cut into stone blocks, while the majority were formed from a Bastille stone-dust paste (Fig. 7). He publicly announced his intention to cover the entire national territory with these "votive sculptures":

> It was not enough for me to have helped knock down the walls of this fortress. It was necessary to perpetuate the horror of its memory. Out of one Bastille I made 83, with which I paid homage to each of the departments, so that its ruins spread, so to speak, throughout France and will forever remind virtuous citizens of the atrocity of despots.[18]

In fact, Palloy founded the congregation of the "Apostles of Liberty", a group of confidants entrusted not only with transporting eighty-three miniature "Bastilles" to all the capitals of the new departments, at his expense, but also with organising their ritual public staging through inauguration ceremonies, patriotic speeches and civic processions in the city streets.[19] When, on 13 November 1790, the Bastille model of Dijon was inaugurated, the "apostle" Navier delivered a pathetic address probably worded by Palloy himself:

> In all places the Bastille threatened the eloquent and sensitive man…; its chains extended to the ends of the provinces, ready to overwhelm anyone who dared speak the language of philosophy and reason… Finally the Bastille is no longer… But we have before our eyes the image of all the evils of the old regime… At the sight of the model of the Bastille… our nephews will think they can see the dark dungeons; the sound of chains will strike their ears; the long moans of the victims will resound in their souls; a healthy horror will repel tyrants everywhere… Ah! may those who lament the old government come and meditate near these remains of the Bastille.[20]

Navier's address is a valuable document because it gives us some idea of how contemporaries imagined the impact of these models of the destroyed state dungeon. Seeing and touching them was supposed to awaken – all at once – their hatred of the cruelties of the Old Regime and their memory of the hour when this new freedom was born, and to give them strength and confidence. The cult of these "patriotic relics" had a semi-religious dimension rooted in the practices of popular piety.

Palloy pursued his self-chosen mission with an unwavering obsession and with great financial sacrifices. In order to extend the patriotic cult of the Bastille

17. *Ibid.*, p. 97.

18. *Journal de Versailles, des départemens de Paris, de Seine et de Oise*, n. 42, 12 July 1790, p. 172.

19. In addition to the models, the boxes Palloy sent to the departments contained books, pamphlets and prints that cannot be discussed here.

20. Records of the ceremony are edited in Georges Lecocq, *La prise de la Bastille et ses anniversaires d'après des documents inédits*, Paris, Charavay, 1881, p. 137.

even further, he had stone tablets of the prison decorated with prints and inscriptions and dedicated them to all of France's 544 districts. He therefore had some reason to be proud of his organisational performance when he gave an account of his activity to the deputies of the National Assembly on 7 October 1791:

> I have immortalised every epoch of the Revolution with trophies that I have dedicated to freedom… I have scattered the remains of despotism, which died in the ruins of Bastille, over the face of the earth, and especially throughout this empire. In addition, I have given out Bastille stones engraved with the Declaration of Rights and the dawn of freedom.[21]

Among the preserved stone tablets, some are decorated with a ground plan of the Bastille engraved by Jean-Baptiste Chapuy using one of Palloy's designs (Fig. 8), and others with a portrait of Lous XVI before his flight to Varennes.[22] But in each case there is an inscription that invokes the provenance of the stone from the underground dungeon cells ("cachots") of the Bastille where, according to rumours, the prisoners had suffered the cruelest tortures.

Indeed, during the first four years of the Revolution, Palloy's stones and models of the Bastille, many of which are still conserved in the depots of provincial archives,[23] were very present in the public arena. It appears that they inspired toymakers to construct miniature Bastilles made of cardboard, thereby allowing children the joy of reenacting the storming of the Bastille (Fig. 9).

In addition to the stones, the metals found in the ruins of the Bastille provided Palloy with another rich material for the production of smaller revolutionary objects, especially medals. These are remarkable in several aspects. First, in many statements Palloy explained repeatedly how he conceived of their creation, quality and suggestive power. For instance, when on 11 March 1792 he presented eight hundred copies of the medal bearing an image of the Freedom column planned for the Place de la Bastille (Fig. 10) to the National Assembly, he exclaimed:

> These medals, symbols of freedom, will be indissoluble bonds of brotherhood. I have had them cleaned and purified with fire. Placed on the hearts of the deputies, they will remind them of their former servitude and of the courage they need to resist the harassments of despots.[24]

Thus, thanks to the purifying effects of fire, the creation of the medals was imagined as a magical act that would convert the political substance of the material. More than the chisels of the stonemasons who modified the stones, it was the fire that melted the metals of the Bastille down that seemed most appropriate

21. Pierre-François Palloy, *Adresse à l'Assemblée Nationale Législative*, Paris 1791, p. 5.

22. Workshop of Palloy, *Ex Unitate Libertas, anno primo 1789/Cette pierre vient d'un des cachots de la Bastille*, stone plate decorated by an oval low-relief, 810x615 mm, MRF, D.1991.3.

23. Jean-Pierre Babelon, "Les maquettes et les pierres de la Bastille. Récolement des souvenirs lapidaires provenant de l'activité du patriote Palloy", *La Gazette des Archives*, 51/4 (1966), pp. 217-230.

24. *Procès-Verbaux du Comité d'instruction publique de l'Assemblée Législative*, ed. by James Guillaume, Paris, Impr. Nat., 1899, p. 311.

for explaining this metamorphosis. In this way, the medals were recharged with positive energy and, as most of them were sold with a ring by which they could be hung, they were to be used as amulets and talismans, stimulating the patriotism of those who wore them. And, as this magic symbolism was part of his credo, Palloy ensured that he only used metals from the Bastille.[25]

Second, Palloy's numerous papers, which are archived in the Bibliothèque Historique de la Ville de Paris (BHVP), grant fascinating insight into the production and distribution of his medals. Their manufacture required the cooperation of specialised craftsmen, like the metalworker Philippe Moisson. On 4 January 1792 the "architecte-entrepreneur" concluded a contract with Moisson for the production of 500 medals that were to be given to the Parisian Electors of 1789 on 28 January, together with the account of his demolition work. The long text of the contract is a characteristic mixture of revolutionary verbalism, an exact description of the material to be used and precise instructions:

> That I, Palloy, having lead that I removed from the old seals of the rings that were in the stones that emerged from the demolition of the Bastille, which were used to hold the chains of the unfortunate victims who were attached to it, I presumed to be able to use this material in a worthier manner by removing it from the stones where it had been poured and, having it recast, to strike it with a wedge that will mark the time of our Revolution. Consequently, I have determined to follow a project that an idea fixed in my mind and to make medals that will recall the first days of our freedom after the fall of despotism [...] I sent to Mr. Moisson [and] told him of my intentions..., begged him to make me a mould three inches in diameter in order to strike the said medals according to the design I gave him, representing the attack on the Bastille, further wishing that this design be in relief for a line and a half. On the first rim of each medal, a legend was thus conceived: This lead that sealed the rings that chained the victims of despotism traces the era of freedom conquered in the First Year. It is all engraved projecting from the band. At the bottom of the drawing will be this inscription: "Dedicated to the Electors of 1789, by Palloy, a patriot, during the redition of his account to the nation", also in relief...[26]

Moisson accepted all these details and promised to strike the medals within two weeks and to deliver the mint form (in order to avoid pirated copies), while Palloy committed to paying the handsome sum of 750 *livres*, the first third upon delivery and the other two-thirds in the two months after. Moisson fulfilled the contract.[27] The reverse of the medal is fitted with a small paper signed by Palloy and the Secretary of the Electeurs; the name of the receiver could be entered in the open space (Fig. 11). However, instead of having been invented by Palloy, the

25. Alain Weil, "Sur l'origine historique des métaux employés à la confection des médailles de Palloy", *Bulletin de la Société française de numismatique*, 29 (1974), pp. 692-694.

26. BHVP, Mss CP 5060, published by Alain Weil, *Histoire et numismatique du patriote Palloy, démolisseur de la Bastille*, Paris-Lyon, SPES, 1976, pp. 54-57.

27. Moisson after Pierre-François Palloy, *Ce plomb scellait les anneaux qui enchaînaient les victimes du despotisme. Retrace lépoque de la liberté conquise l'an premier* (circumscription)/*Siège de la Bastille* (legend)/*Dédié aux Electeurs de 1789 par Palloy patriote lors de la rendition de son com[p]te à la nation* (exergue), iron medal, Ø 82 mm, 1792, MC, ND.0594 (obverse). See Michel Hennin, *Histoire numismatique de la Révolution française*, Paris, J.S. Merlin, 1826, n. 26.

image on the obverse is copied from a popular iron medal of Bertrand Andrieu, which had already been published in January 1790.[28]

These few examples already indicate how important Palloy's editions of the coins were in terms of their numbers. Looking back to his activity as a "revolutionary medalist", he claimed in 1819 that:

> During the most remarkable periods of the revolution, I had sixty medals struck, a thousand each time, 1,200 for the members of the constituent assembly, 1,200 for the convention, which altogether makes 60,400 medals both in silver and copper, bronze, cast iron, iron, tin and lead, all material that was worked and manipulated that came in part from the famous Bastille and from the rags of the enemy armies which were sent to me by the generals to leave a mark on the French Revolution...[29]

As Alain Weil has argued, the "patriot" was exaggerating because there are only fifty medals that can be ascribed to him and because most of his medals are made of two plates of iron bound together by a copper rim. Therefore a total of about 25,000 medals appears more realistic,[30] although this is nevertheless a considerable amount.

Third, in distributing his medals Palloy ensured that he would address the gift individually to each recipient. For the medals produced in large quantities, he prepared printed letters autographically enlarged with his signature and the name of the recipient to accompany them. For instance, this was the case with the 1,200 copies of a medal representing a militant allegory of the city of Paris with the destruction of the Bastille in the background.[31] In early 1792 it was given to the former Constituents, including Anne-Louis-Henri de La Fare. In the letter addressed to him, Palloy once again explained his art of revolutionary metamorphosis:

> Monsieur... The irons that held and locked the victims, I had them purified by fire, and I reduced these appalling bars to medals struck with a wedge that represents the first beautiful days of our Freedom and which will mark our happy Revolution by recalling the famous Oath of the Jeu de Paume, of 20 June 1789... – So deign to receive this new homage of my Patriotism, and may this piece... remain with your descendants. It will teach them what their fathers did. They will know that they have conquered the Hydra of Despotism to free themselves from slavery. They will learn that it was given to them as a reward for their good civic-mindedness, by Patriot Palloy...[32]

We do not know if La Fare, a former archbishop and rather conservative deputy, was particularly pleased with this gift.

In any case, Palloy disseminated the medals on a large scale. The register of his consignments from 1790 to 1800 mentions a wide range of recipients: amongst others, numerous deputies of the departments of Hérault, Vienne and Vendée

28. BnF, Médailles, MR 125 and 126. See Hennin, *Histoire numismatique*, pp. 22-24.

29. Note by Palloy written in April 1819, cited in Weil, *Histoire numismatique*, p. 62.

30. *Ibid.*

31. Anonymus after Pierre-François Palloy, *A la gloire de la nation français. Epoque de la Liberté* (exergue), iron medal, Ø 37 mm, 1792, MC, ND.0598 (obverse). See Hennin, *Histoire numismatique*, n. 71.

32. Printed circular of Palloy with his manuscript additions, in BnF, Imprimés, Lb[39]10468.

(April-June 1792) and five "députés Tyrannicides" who voted for the death of Louis XVI (February 1793), along with influential politicians, such as Roederer, Charles Duval and Cambacérès (March 1793-February 1795), the Presidents of the Senate and Supreme Court (July 1800) and more. Besides attaching great importance to his gestures of patriotic generosity, Palloy was eager for a response and also for an acknowledgement to be noted in his register.[33]

On occasion, Palloy intensified the relationship with the recipients of his "relics" even more. When, in his capacity as President of the *Société populaire* of Sceaux near Paris, in November 1794 he organised a festival in honour of the "Martyrs of Liberty", he invited the 78 mayors of the Departement Hauts-de-Seine through a printed circular that adopted the republican "tu" with a commanding tone:

> [...] you will want to go there. For this purpose, I send you the republican oath, which you will sign, and you will give the duplicate to the commissioner of the festival, who is charged with giving you a civic medal made from the iron of the chains of the Bastille, and a roll of patriotic prints [...]. Keep this pledge, and each time you see it, remember your duty and your rights, so that you may meticulously fulfill the mission with which your fellow citizens have entrusted you [...].[34]

The significance of this passage lies not only in the mention of the "civic medal" itself (which cannot be identified), but also in the fact that it is accompanied by a printed poster of Palloy[35] and by some other revolutionary pamphlets. In this way, the distribution of the medals became part of multimedia propaganda knitting together a network of political communications. In a speech delivered in September 1792 at Epernay, Palloy himself described how his production of memorabilia created a process of patriotic exchange:

> Several men of letters and authors have sent me their works, among others Citizens Dussault, C. Villette, Collot d'Herbois, Cloost [sic], Manuel and others, which I accepted with great pleasure. Several patriotic journalists have visited me with their families, who I accepted with pleasure; artists have sent me paintings, engravings and diverse ornaments. I hurry to respond to them with pieces of stone, iron and fragments that I have metamorphosed, and in the different forms that I give them. They can be used to decorate their cabinets, as those that they send me augment my library.[36]

Fourth, among the different mediums Palloy employed, his medals constituted the most convenient objects for his project of imprinting a new political iconography on the material left by the Old Regime. Indeed, decorating the "purified" iron of the Bastille with revolutionary icons was an integral part of his art of political metamorphosis. He had no qualms about pirating pictorial models if they pleased him, as in the case of the coin made by Moisson (see

33. Papers of Palloy, BHVP, Mss C.P. 5249.

34. Printed circular of Palloy with his manuscript additions, dated "Du 5 frimaire, l'an 2 de la république française, une et indivisible" (26-11-1794), BnF, Imprimés, Lb^{40}2956.

35. Pierre-François Palloy, *Serment républicain*, Paris, 1794, in BnF, Imprimées, Fol. Lb^{41}292.

36. Pierre-François Palloy, *Discours prononcé en présence des bataillons de volontaires et citoyens d'Epernay le 23 septembre 1792*, [Paris, 1792], p. 57, cited by Taws, *The Politics of Provisional*, p. 112.

note 27). Palloy applied the same procedure to his *A la gloire immortelle de la nation française* medal (see note 31): his preliminary drawing for the obverse image,[37] provided to the medalist Férandine, was copied from an iron medal by Branche.[38] On the other hand, the Freedom column projected for the Place de la Bastille (see Fig. 10) was really one of Palloy's inventions.[39] When, on 17 July 1792, the first stone of the monument was laid,[40] the "architecte patriote" celebrated the event by presenting this medal to the public. The obverse legend emphasises the symbolic impact of the founding ceremony and of the image: "Liberty is standing upon the ruins of despotism". The column appears to be growing out of them.

Although the images on Palloy's medals are rather rough pieces of work, they stand out through their specific visual power, which resulted from a process of iconic condensation. We can observe this process in one medal devoted entirely to the fall of the Bastille (Fig. 12). The medalist used a drawing of the *Patriote* (Fig. 13) who, for his part, was inspired by a print of Laurent Guyot (Fig. 14). But, instead of simply copying this model, Palloy transformed Guyot's depiction of a spectacular historical event (*Démolition de la Bastille…*) into a general emblem symbolising the *Destruction du despotisme*.

Beyond this, the iconography of Palloy's medals connects the ruins of the Bastille with symbols of liberty. On the obverse of a medal probably struck at the end of 1789, it is the allegory of Liberty herself who, by the gesture of her right arm, effects the fall of the "monument of despotism" (Fig. 15).[41] While bearing her Phrygian cap placed on a stick, she is always ready to grasp the herculean club at her side, the symbol of sovereign power.

In April 1791 the festivities for the forty soldiers of the Châteauvieux regiment offered Palloy the opportunity to strike an even more expressive medal (Fig. 16).[42] Whereas in August 1790 the said soldiers had been sentenced to the galleys in Brest because of mutiny against their commander, General Bouillé, they were released a year later and hailed as heroes of liberty who fought against a secret leader of the counter-revolution. During their triumphal march from Brest to Paris, the green caps they wore as convicts were therefore replaced with red caps of liberty. The medal devoted to them shows a man with a Phrygian or red cap adopting a triumphal pose. Just as his nudity is all at once the nudity of the slave and the nudity of the hero, the broken chains in his hands suggest a double

37. See Palloy's autograph description with a drawing: BnF, Mss, Nafr 3241, fol. 154-155 and his drawing fol. 213.

38. Michel Hennin, *Histoire numismatique de la Révolution française*, Paris, J.S. Merlin, 1826, n. 72; BnF, MED. REVOL. 173 and 174.

39. Drawing of Palloy, BnF, Mss, Nafr 3241, fol. 213.

40. Lüsebrink, Reichardt, *The Bastille*, pp. 166-167.

41. Reverse: *Ce métal provient des verroux du despotisme* (legend), / L'Union fait la force (exergue), iron medal, Ø 40 mm, 1789/90, MC, ND.0605.

42. Reverse: *Ce fer vient d'un des carcans de la Bastille* (legend), *Donnée sur les décombres de la Bastille le 9 avril 1792 l'an 4 de la liberté par Palloy patriote aux soldats de Châteauvieux victimes du despotisme reconnus innocens par un décret du 30 décembre 1791 sollicité par Collot d'Herbois* (field), iron medal, Ø 43 mm, 1792, MC, ND.0607.

meaning: after having been burst open in 1789 in the Bastille, they were reforged by the counter-revolution and had now been broken apart for the second time. There was, indeed, no better material to carry this image than the iron from the chains of the destroyed "monument of despotism". Of course, the legend on the reverse emphasises that "this metal comes from the iron collars of the Bastille", while the exergue evokes the presentation of the medal in a symbolic act:

> Given on the ruins of the Bastille on 9 April 1792, year 4 of liberty, by Patriote Palloy to the soldiers of Châteauvieux, victims of despotism, recognised as innocent by a decree of 30 December 1791 requested by Collot d'Herbois.

3. *Appropriation and propaganda*

What the counter-revolutionary journalist Jacques-Marie Boyer-Brun (de Nîmes) uttered about the caricatures printed in his time is perhaps even more true of the small political objects of the French Revolution: they are the "thermometer that indicates the status of public opinion".[43] The wide range of objects related to the fall of the Bastille provides, in effect, outstanding evidence of this. It reflects a general patriotic enthusiasm surrounding the beginnings of the Revolution and its most sensational event.

Whereas the badges of honour awarded to the Vainqueurs de la Bastille were official signs of recognition, the wide range of fashionable accessories spontaneously offered by print shops, milliners and modists were not merely products of patriotism; to an even greater extent, they were merchandise that responded to the demands of customers. Wearing a coat with buttons *à la Bastille*, using a snuffbox decorated with an image of the fortress' conquest, unfolding a fan with the same topic – all of these external signs were designed to show that their wearer was fashionable and a friend of the Revolution. Aside from this public effect, these accessories had the more private function of memorabilia. With their decorations in miniature copied from prints,[44] they testified to their owners' desire to obtain and keep crucial revolutionary images in iconic condensation. In this, we can see acts of patriotic appropriation. This manifests most clearly when the object is rearranged by its owner, like in the case of a bronze image of the demolition of the Bastille attached to a *cocarde nationale* (Fig. 17). In this way, the accessory of furniture was turned into a patriotic souvenir.

What are the elements that defined the political character of the objects presented above? For the badges of honour, the buttons, the fans, the snuffboxes and other accessories, it is the image alone. To this, Palloy's stones and medals add a whole new dimension by applying the images to the politicised material of the Bastille regularly invoked by the *patriote*. It is primarily the fact that they

43. Jacques-Marie Boyer-Brun (de Nîmes), *Histoire des caricatures de la révolte des Français*, vol. I, Paris, Imprimerie du Journal du Peuple, 1792, p. 10.

44. For further details, see Rolf Reichardt, "Modèles graphiques circulant par copies à partir de la Révolution", in *Modes de circulation des images entre 1750 et 1848: représentation, politique et diffusion*, ed. by Pascal Dupuy, Rouen-Le Havre, PUGH, 2021 (in print).

were formed from the ruins of the most hated state prison that gave Palloy's memorabilia their special quality. They were missionary relics intended to propagate revolutionary enthusiasm and symbolism, whereas the products of the milliners, despite their decoration, had a somewhat playful character.

Furthermore, unlike the fashion articles, Palloy's patriotic objects were not merchandise to be sold, but "votive offerings of Liberty" distributed through extensive efforts, for propaganda purposes. As they were systematically directed to all of the administrative centres across France, as well as to revolutionary societies and many politicians, they spread a radical political imagery and also helped intensify the bonds of patriotic fraternity among patriots. The public staging of the models and stones from the Bastille especially functioned as a catalyst that strengthened the solidarity of revolutionary activists and radicals and provoked the political scepticism of their critics.

Symbolic appropriation and propaganda – it appears that most of the political objects left by the Revolution can be assigned to one of these two functions. Their decoration with iconic miniatures is a common characteristic. From this perspective, the case of the Bastille turns out to be exceptionally rich and typical at the same time.

1. Mural crown in the shape of the Bastille, pendant with a ring for suspension, gilded bronze, 20x31 mm, 1789, MC, OM.4222.
2. *Vainqueur de la Bastille / XIIII Juillet 1789 / Récompense Nationale*, enamel medallion surrounded by copper, 55x35 mm, 1789, MC, OM.637

3. *Comité des Vainqueurs de la Bastille*, seal stamp, gilded bronze, 44x42 mm, MC, OM.164.
4. Demolishing the Bastille, button, porcelain with blue dip surrounded by copper, Ø 42 mm, 1789, MC, B.0948bis.

5. Circular snuffbox representing the conquest of the Bastille, lacquered papier-mâché, painted paper and glass, Ø 83 mm, 1789, MC, OM.1323
6. *Prise de la Bastille par les Bourgeois et les Gardes Francaises le 14 Juillet 1789*, anonymous folding fan, anonymous colourated etching mounted on 14 rosewood sticks, 280x132 mm, 1789, MC, EV.992

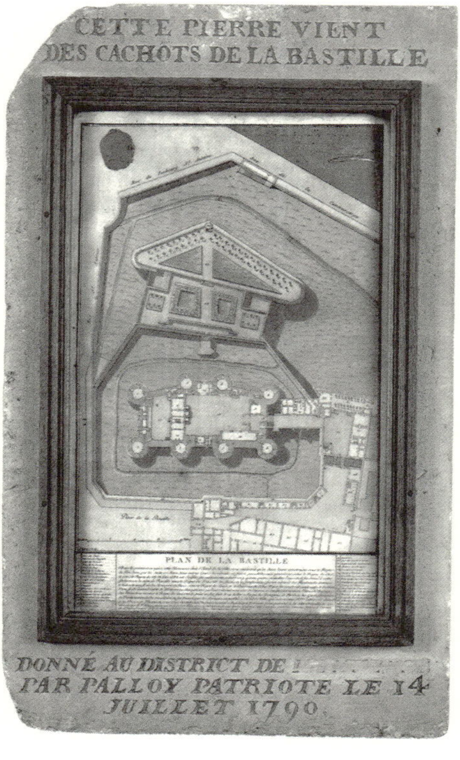

7. Model of the Bastille cut in a stone of the fortress, 380x970x550 mm 1790, MRF, D.1986.2.

8. *Cette pierre vient des cachots dela Bastille / Donné au District de* [name erased] *par Palloy patriote le 14 Juillet 1790*, stone from the Bastille with attached *Plan de la Bastille*, aquatint in colour by Jean-Baptiste Chapuy, 815x495 mm, 1790, MRF, D.1983.1.

9. Villeneuve, *Attaque de la Petite Bastille*, aquatint in colour, Ø 90 mm, Paris, Villeneuve, 1789, BnF, Est., coll. Qb1, M98979.
10. Férandine after Pierre-François Palloy, *Sur les ruines du despotisme s'est élevée la liberté* (legend) / *A la gloire de la nation française lan 3 de la liberté* (exergue), iron medal, Ø 41 mm, MC, ND.0638 (obverse).

11. Férrandine after Pierre-François Palloy, *Législateurs n'oubliez jamais le serment que vous prononçates de maintenir de tout votre pouvoir la constitution le 1er octobre 1791. Cette époque vous est réitirée par Palloy patriote*, iron medal, Ø 41 mm, 1792, MC, ND.0638 (reverse).
12. Anonymous after Pierre-François Palloy, *Destruction du despotisme* (legend) / *14 Jui. 1789* (exergue), iron medal, Ø 30 mm, 1789/90, MC, ND.1569 (obverse).

13. Pierre-François Palloy, *Destruction du despotisme*, etching, 70x93 mm, 1789/90, BnF, Est., coll. Qb1, M98853.
14. Laurent Guyot, *Démolition de la Bastille et Vue de la Porte qui conduisoit au Jardin*, coloured etching, 160x210 mm, Paris, L. Guyot, 1789, MC, G.4107.

15. Anonymous after Pierre-François Palloy, *La Liberté a détruit le despotisme* (legend), iron medal, Ø 40 mm, 1789/90, MC, ND.0605 (obverse).
16. Anonymous after Pierre-François Palloy, *La Liberté a rompu mes fers, l'Egalité m'a élevé* (legend), iron medal, Ø 43 mm, 1792, MC, ND.0607 (obverse).
17. *XIIII Juillet 1789 / Démolition de la Bastille*, punched bronze medallion attached to a tricolour cockade made of coloured wool, Ø 69 (bronze), Ø 90 (cockade), 1789, MC, OM.641(4).

Arianna Arisi Rota

The Violet, the Eagle and Beyond: Collecting, Touching and Wearing Napoleonic Nostalgia in the Italian *Risorgimento*

1. *Introduction*

> The peasants and relic-hunters about the place were scrambling around the pair as the soldier told his story, offering for sale all sorts of mementoes of the fight-crosses, and epaulets, and shattered cuirasses, and eagles.[1]

W. M. Thackeray's lines in *Vanity Fair* about a visit to the battlefield of Waterloo remind us that the collection relics of Napoleon's last adventure started at daybreak after 18 June 1815. Nor is it over yet: on June 2018 De Baecque and Associates' auction catalogue included as its most promising piece a two-cornered hat collected on that same battlefield and thought to have belonged to Napoleon, listed with a starting price of 30,000 euros and sold in the Lyon auction for around 350,000 euros. In November 2014 the dream of owning a similar hat, a better preserved one worn during the Battle of Marengo, came true for a Korean tycoon for the final price of 1.9 million euros. Stanley Kubrick's obsession with Napoleon and his never-filmed movie has recently-breathed life into a book documenting the director's incessant, monumental research on the subject.[2] Private collectors of Napoleonic memorabilia prove an endless source of inspiration for public exhibitions, such as *L'Empereur sous la verrière* in the Paris Grand Palais in September 2018, displaying objects from Pierre-Jean Chalençon's more-than-1,200-piece collection including portraits, marble busts, locks of hair, white silk socks, chinaware, cutlery, jewels and much more.[3]

But before becoming an obsession for evergreen, fetishist collecting, objects linked to the Napoleonic drama played a political role as evidence of, and vehicles for, individual and collective emotions such as nostalgia and longing.[4] Perhaps

1. W.M. Thackeray, *Vanity Fair: A Novel without a Hero*, Ware, Wordsworth Classics, 2001, p. 335.

2. *Stanley Kubrick's "Napoleon": The Greatest Movie Never Made*, Koln, Taschen, 2018.

3. At www.labiennaleparis.com, 8-16 September 2018. For an updated overview of Napoleonic collections, exhibitions and auction sales, see now Arianna Arisi Rota, *Il cappello dell'imperatore. Storia, memoria e mito di Napoleone Bonaparte attraverso due secoli di culto dei suoi oggetti*, Rome, Donzelli, 2021.

4. On the current challenges posed to historians by the history of emotions, see Rob Boddice, "The History of Emotions", in *New Directions in Social and Cultural History*, ed. by

the true essence of the 19th-century spirit is described in Chateaubriand's self-reflection on exile and absence:[5] these emotions, together with the hope of return, are precisely those that nurtured disguised Napoleonic propaganda. Both in the short-term – as masterfully investigated by Sudhir Hazareesingh in his Hundred Days "seditious objects" chapter[6] – and in the middle-run, as in the pre-1848 Italian *Risorgimento*, the narrative of political belonging experienced powerful fulfillment especially in private, domestic spaces and settings where material icons and relics of the glory shared in the Napoleonic army and administration could be admired, touched and shown in a safe, empathetic environment.

In recent years, scholarly investigation into material culture has shifted its focus from objects as repositories of meanings to objects in and of themselves. It is no coincidence that historians contributing to the authoritative 2013 *Oxford Handbook of the Archaeology of the Contemporary World* called for a shift away from history *through* things to the histories *of* things.[7] The biography of objects can in fact tell us much about their owners and, more to the point here, about the *political* relations between the owners' bodies and the objects themselves.[8] This is why, as happens in Stendhal's *Le Rouge et le Noir* when Julien Sorel keeps Napoleon's portrait in a paper box under his mattress, many two- or three-dimensional icons of the epic matching the Emperor with his son were hosted, or more frequently "hidden", in humble Italian houses as well as elegant villas, and circulated throughout the peninsula,[9] to share memories, hopes and feelings of

Sasha Handley, Rohan McWilliam and Lucy Noakes, London, Bloomsbury, 2018. Still useful regarding objects and memory is Susan Stewart, *On Longing: Narratives of the Miniature, the Gigantic, the Souvenir, the Collection*, Baltimore, Duke University Press, 1993, pp. 45-63. See also *Histoire des Emotions*, ed. by Alain Corbin, Jean-Jacques Courtine and Georges Vigarello, especially vol. II, *Des Lumières à la fin du XIXe siècle*, Paris, Seuil, 2016. On the case of Italy in the "long 19th century", see the collection of essays edited by Marco Manfredi and Emanuela Minuto, *La politica dei sentimenti. Linguaggi, spazi e canali della politicizzazione nell'Italia del lungo Ottocento,* Rome, Viella, 2018, which neverthless does not examine the Napoleonic experience.

5. Peter Fritzsche, "Specters of History: On Nostalgia, Exile and Modernity", *The American Historical Review*, 106/5 (Dec. 2001), pp. 1587-1618.

6. Sudhir Hazareesingh, *The Legend of Napoleon*, London, Granta Books, 2004. On the Italian Restoration, see Enrico Francia, "Oggetti sediziosi. Censura e cultura materiale nell'Italia della Restaurazione", *Mélanges de l'Ecole Française de Rome-Italie Méditerranée*, 130/1 (2018), pp. 31-41 (http://journals.openedition.org/mefrim//3624).

7. Tim Cole, "The Place of Things in Contemporary History", in *The Oxford Handbook of the Archaeology of the Contemporary World*, ed. by Paul Graves-Brown, Rodney Harrison and Angela Piccini, Oxford, Oxford University Press, 2013, p. 67. More generally, see also Frank Trentmann, *The Empire of Things: How We Became a World of Consumers, from the Fifteenth Century to the Twenty-First*, London, Allen Lane, 2016. Also very useful is the introductory essay and the collected essays in *Il lungo Ottocento e le sue immagini. Politica, media, spettacolo*, ed. by Vinzia Fiorino, Gian Luca Fruci and Alessio Petrizzo, Pisa, ETS, 2013.

8. Bjørnar Olsen, "Memory", in *The Oxford Handbook of the Archaeology of the Contemporary World*, p. 209.

9. Arianna Arisi Rota, "Tra desiderio e nostalgia. Declinazioni visive del culto napoleonico nell'Italia della Restaurazione", *Mélanges de l'Ecole Française de Rome-Italie Méditerranée*, 130/1 (2018), pp. 17-29 (http://journals.openedition.org/mefrim/3623).

militancy. Often produced in France, but sometimes re-produced by local artists and artisans, they repeatedly testified to the regenerative power of the myth (and of Bonapartist propaganda) around the times of the revivalist waves of 1814, 1815, 1821[10] and 1840, shaping that "narrative of loss"[11] that nourished the joint cult of father and son, of Napoleon I and Napoleon II.

The following pages comment upon a qualitative sample of objects of daily use as visual, tangible and portable documents of political memory and identity during the early decades of post-Napoleonic Italian society,[12] and beyond.

2. Le Printemps, *or the Violet is back*

The theme of Napoleon's return to power inspired the instant mass production of visual items for propaganda, consisting of caricatures and objects. Anti-Bourbon satirical prints soon sketched out what Napoleon had told his faithful followers upon abdicating in 1814: that he would be back in the springtime, with the blossoming of the violets.[13] The violet and the eagle thus became the icons and symbols for a handmade serial production, which endured in the form of nostalgic mementoes over the following years. *Le Printemps ou le retour de la Violette*, colour-printed in Paris by Mayer in Spring 1815,[14] is but one of the many images featuring animal-shaped characters showing the crowned eagle – Napoleon – with its fierce and grim look, coming from the sea holding in its beak the Legion of Honour decoration and with laurel and oak leaves in its claws. By its side, a little eagle – the King of Rome – flies, holding violets in its beak (*Père la Violette* being one of the code names given to Napoleon during the period of anti-Louis XVIII

10. On the so-called "1821 moment de mémoire", see Emmanuel Fureix's beautiful pages in his *La France des larmes. Deuils politiques à lâge romantique (1814-1840)*, Seyssel, Champ Vallon, 2009, pp. 415-428, and, more generally, ch. 10. On the iconoclastic anti-Bonaparte wave in the French Restoration, see Emmanuel Fureix, "Iconoclastia e Restaurazione. Epurare il passato, scongiurare la guerra civile (Francia, 1814-1830)", *Memoria e Ricerca*, 57/1 (2018), pp. 45-60, and Emmanuel Fureix, *L'oeil blessé. Politiques de l'iconoclasme après la Révolution française*, Ceyzérieu, Champ Vallon, 2019, ch. 2.

11. Cole, "The Place of Things in Contemporary History", p. 75.

12. Highly informative on this subject is Marco Meriggi, "State and Society in Post-Napoleonic Italy", in *Napoleon's Legacy: Problems of Government in Restoration Europe*, ed. by Lucy Riall and David Laven, Oxford-New York, Berg, 2000, pp. 49-64.

13. The violet as a Napoleonic symbol came back in the mourning fashion of wearing artificial black violets during the Summer of 1821, as happened with Napoleon's supporters in Lyon, the most pro-Napoleonic town of France (Thierry Lentz, *Bonaparte n'est plus! Le monde apprend la mort de Napoléon, Juillet-septembre 1821*, Paris, Perrin, 2019, ch. 18).

14. The caricature was on display in the Museo Glauco Lombardi, Parma, during the exhibition *Napoleone in caricatura*, April 18-October 4, 2015 and is now included in the catalogue *Napoleone in caricatura*, Quaderni del Museo n. 15, ed. by Francesca Sandrini, Parma, Museo Glauco Lombardi, 2015, pp. 29-30. I wish to thank Dr. Francesca Sandrini, Director of the Museo Glauco Lombardi, for allowing me to reproduce images and objects from the Museum collections and website: www.museolombardi.it. All the concerned images and objects are visible and described in the museum's online catalogue.

propaganda). Far in the distance, the popular image shows a sun rising above a lawn crowded with violets and bees, while a group of clumsy farm animals, frogs and snakes – the supporters of the restored Bourbon king – fly and throw themselves into the Channel at the sight of the returning eagle.

Chosen by Luciano Bonaparte as the family insignia, taken from ancient Roman military tradition, the powerful symbol of the eagle successfully opposed the parallel communication effort of the anti-Bonapartists – often showing Napoleon as an ugly mouse leading legions of mice[15] – and it soon became a suitable icon for objects of daily use. There are bronze and porcelain inkwells, for example, such as those of unknown latter-19th century manufacture in the Museo Glauco Lombardi collections, where the coloured porcelain piece is reinforced by the Legion of Honour decoration, the laurel leaves in the beak and the unmistakable hat. Inkwells, as well as snuffboxes – mass-produced objects apt to be charged with political meaning and allusions – were very popular in the 19th century, and are frequently found in private and public collections of the North-Central area of the Italian peninsula. Of course, it was the theme of Glory embodied by the eagle, that glory lived and lost, which might come to life again, that nurtured massive visual production during the Elba Island exile and the Hundred Days, but which was to continue until 1821 and beyond.

In this uncertain, transitional phase, Napoleonic iconography soon matched Napoleon's image with the image of his son, this latter being approached as a kind of "spin off" of the father's myth, which was to be expanded in the 1820s and 1830s, the time of his so-called "captivity" at his grandfather's court in Vienna.[16] Furthermore, the image of the child was probably meant as a vehicle for the "normalisation" of the figure of the father, a bourgeois approach in contrast with the "exceptionality" properly linked to the military context. Domestic sketches of family groups were often reproduced in illustrated volumes[17] as well as in widely printed engravings. As for political-object sets from the same period, the chubby yet pensive baby immortalised in François Gerard's painting while being shown by Napoleon to his officers and soldiers on the eve of the Battle of Moscova,[18]

15. Tim Clayton, Sheila O'Connell, *Bonaparte and the British: Prints and Propaganda in the Age of Napoleon*, London, The British Museum, 2015.

16. See Arisi Rota, "Tra desiderio e nostalgia" and its bibliography. During his teenager years in Vienna, Napoleon and Marie Louise's son, the King of Rome, now renamed as the Duke of Reichstadt, was forbidden to wear the decorations from his French childhood. In official portraits, such as the most famous one by Moritz Michael Daffinger, in miniatures and painted porcelain objects, the boy shows only the Habsburg Saint Stephen and Prefect of the Constantinian Order decorations.

17. As, for instance, the *Storia illustrata aneddotica e pittoresca di Napoleone e della Grande Armata scritta da Emilio Marco di St. Hilaire e tradotta in italiano da A. L., seguita da un compendio di storia militare italiana dal 1792 al 1815, dettata in italiano dallo stesso Traduttore*, Turin, 1844, p. 398. See also the engraving by Alexander Vincent Sixdeniers, from a painting by Charles de Steuben, *Napoleone I nel suo studio con il figlio*, Rome, Museo Napoleonico, inv. MN 609.

18. One version by Luis René Lucien Rollet, *Napoléon reçoit le portrait de son fils*, is on display in the Museo Glauco Lombardi in Parma.

or the curly-haired child reproduced by the skilled hand of Jean-Baptiste Isabey, could be transformed into products ranging from a gold-and-bronze pendulum clock to a paper-and-glass box, perhaps a candy box (Fig. 1).

The key point here is that the materiality of branded objects indicates a context of use that is far from the echoes of battlefields, and close to the bourgeois mood of nostalgia for a political dream that might yet come true (documented by the revival in March 1815 of watercolour engravings from Isabey's works) but which actually could not, as some famous "snapshots" of Napoleon's exile tell us. Antonio Marchi's engraving *Il ritratto del Duca di Reichstadt offerto a Napoleone dai compagni del suo esilio* and Gaetano Guadagnini's *Gli ultimi momenti del figlio di Napoleone*, both taken from paintings by Nicolas Eustache Maurin and dated to 1834 (two years after the *Aiglon*'s death) are good examples of such a production based on a "mirror effect" linking father and son and reviving the joint myth in the Italian peninsula, also.

3. *Fetishism, the materiality of power and the power of materiality*

As early as August 1815, one of the first visitors to the Waterloo battlefield, Walter Scott, was told by his publisher that the poem he had been asked to write about the battle would shortly be available at the cheap price of three shillings and six pence. Yet, much more than written words, it is the solidification and serialisation of the Napoleonic memory that we are interested in, with special attention to the things and icons guarded by nostalgic individuals and family groups in the Italian peninsula. Such objects have often been passed, by means of donation or commodate, into public collections: Casa Rognoni in Novara,[19] the Museo Glauco Lombardi in Parma and the Museo del Risorgimento in Milan are but a few of the precious locations where one can appreciate the creativity with which material devices and graphic synthesis were conceived for an enduring myth.

Besides chinaware, statuettes and medals, wearable objects are those that bring us closest to the bodily dimension of memory:[20] that same dimension stressed by Napoleon in his will in the passage dedicated to the objects he left to his son, including underwear, exactly because <u>it had been in contact with his own body</u>.[21] Among them can be found foulards, which were to enjoy a wave of fashion in the Italian 1848 revolutionary phase. In the Napoleonic case, those produced

19. *La memoria di Napoleone. Storia e collezionismo nella Novara dell'Ottocento*, ed. by Marco Albertario and Susanna Borlandelli, Novara, Interlinea, 2007.

20. See Judith A. Allen, "The Body and the Senses", in *New Directions in Social and Cultural History*, pp. 65-83. See also *Histoire du corps*, especially vol. II, *De la Révolution à la Grande Guerre*, ed. by Alain Corbin, Jean-Jacques Courtine and Georges Vigarello, Paris, Seuil, 2005.

21. Author's underlining. See *Testamento di Napoleone* in Giacomo Lombroso, *Vita privata di Napoleone e cenni storici sopra diversi de'primarj marescialli dell'Impero francese*, Milan, Tipografia Francesco di O. Manini, 1840 (but 1839), p. 217. Among the objects committed to his son are: the beloved snuffboxes collection, decorations, the camp bed, saddles, spurs, the chapel's pots and books.

after 1821 by the Heim et Fils manufacture in St Gallen, Switzerland, adopt the memorial-funeral pattern and the celebration-transfiguration pattern, as shown by the two pieces in the Museo Glauco Lombardi collections (Fig. 2), where Napoleon's head is centred before a bright cloud with rays and stars, encircled by the letters N A P O L É O N. In the ivory-colored silk "funeral" foulard, weeping willows as a symbol of mourning are placed at the four corners, while in the "heroic" foulard, the Emperor's transfigured face is surrounded by some twenty heads of Napoleonic celebrities. A further sample of unknown manufacture shows Napoleon on horse-back, surrounded by a golden-yellow frame with scenes from famous battles. Again, commemoration taffeta handkerchiefs reproducing famous portraits by David and others can be seen in the Museo del Risorgimento of Modena photo archive collections.[22]

The theme of the Emperor's transfiguration/deification is recurrent and resistant in the Italian environment, especially in the Parma area. Here, as late as 1830-1831, after the deep political crisis in Central Italy following the French July revolution, a former Napoleonic officer, Michele Varron, was able to commission Francesco Scaramuzza to paint *S. Napoleone martire.* The work is interesting visual evidence of both nostalgia for the Corsican and of liberal patriotic engagement (the Saint and the angel's draped clothes recall the green, white and red of the Italian flag). A similar subject was chosen around 1866 in the same area of Parma for Ferdinando Silvani and Toschi Studio's preliminary sketch for a painting entitled *Glorificazione di Napoleone*. Both works are located in the Museo Glauco Lombardi, in the room dedicated to Marie Louise. [23]

The theme of death and martyrdom inspired other objects in the post-1821 season of the Napoleonic cult, as well as in 1840 on the occasion of the return of Napoleon's remains from Saint Helena to *Les Invalides* in Paris. A kind of autonomous nostalgia-trend, it consisted of solid memorabilia of the earthly epic, like paperweights and inkwells in the shape of cenotaphs, as those in the Museo Glauco Lombardi collections, of unknown manufacture. In such cases, the monogram N, the hat and the sword, together with the powerfully evocative names of Marengo, Wagram and Austerlitz, add undoubted authority to heavy and austere handmade works of marble, bronze, brass and heavy glass.

Napoleonic nostalgia entered domestic spaces and daily life also in the shape of dinner-sets[24] and fire-fans bearing iconic symbols or scenes from

22. Costanza Bertolotti, Gian Luca Fruci, Alessio Petrizzo, *Icone politiche. Celebrità e nuovi media al tempo del Risorgimento*, Mantua, Istituto Mantovano di Storia Contemporanea, Istituto Superiore Carlo d'Arco e Isabella d'Este, 2018, p. 27.

23. A reproduction of Scaramuzza's painting is in the Guide of the *Museo Glauco Lombardi* ed. by Francesca Sandrini, Milan, Touring Club Italiano, 2003, p. 169. On the holy cult of Napoleon, now see Riccardo Benzoni, *San Napoleone. Un santo per l'Impero*, Brescia, Morcelliana, 2019. Further news on the painting is in "Napoleone 1821. La morte di Bonaparte: scenari, reazioni, conseguenze nel ducato di Parma", *Quaderni del Museo*, n. 20, ed. by Francesca Sandrini, Parma, Grafiche STEP, 2021.

24. One of the most active producers of dinner-sets was the Belgian Royal Boch, founded in 1841, which, according to the political and entrepreneurial sensibility of the Boch family, soon introduced into its catalogue a series decorated with Napoleonic battles and scenes from

battles, sometimes patiently embroidered by women's hands. Yet a lighter medium contributed to the fashionable visual heritage of the military, individual and collective adventures of General Bonaparte, of Emperor Napoleon I and of his "comrades". Paper was in fact the protagonist of some popular objects in the Lombardy area, such as fans,[25] but one of the most interesting versions of Napoleonic domestic "installations" on paper is to be found in the countryside near Brescia, in Villa Ferrante in Seniga. Its former owner, Luigi Ferrante – who made a fortune with the French and Napoleonic administration of Lombardy, which managed to survive under the Austrian Restoration also – chose to turn his country mansion into a political manifesto. In 1828 he ordered Paris Dufour et Leroy to manufacture some twenty metres of painted wallpaper[26] with black and white and sepia nuanced scenes from Bonaparte's Italian Campaign, from people welcoming the General and his soldiers during the passage of the Alps and the entrance to Milan, to the battle at Arcole and the glorious entrances to Rome and Naples, with their landscapes full of ruins and monumental highlights. Some thirty sheets of paper were thus installed by expert French hands in the main room of this villa by the river Oglio: as a result, a private panorama could surround the owner, his family and their visitors with a decorative device that was virtually unique in the peninsula, except for one other example in Ascoli Piceno, now lost, one in a villa near Treviso, and some twenty more worldwide. We can only imagine the emotions raised by immersion in such an unusual visual experience, testifying to the continuity of the myth as well as the sense of political belonging of the Napoleonic commercial and military elites in the gloomy days of the Austrian domination.

4. *Serialisation*

Apart from exceptional cases like Villa Ferrante, whose owner committed his visual nostalgia to wallpaper rather than to more classic painting, it is tangible nostalgia nurturing political identity and memory that objects perfectly satisfy. Due to their small size, not-immediate recognisability and great affordability, handmade serialised items like carved wooden snuffboxes or painted *papier-maché* ones had long lives in the pockets of veterans and on the writing desks

the Napoleonic epic. Boch-decorated ceramics were exported and purchased by wealthy Italian families also.

25. Alberto Milano, "Fogli per ventole e ventagli", in *Museo d'Arti applicate Raccolta Bertarelli. Ventole e ventagli*, ed. by Alberto Milano, Milan, E. Villani, 1995, p. 206, n. 687.

26. A specialist in the fashionable exotic-*animalier* variety of *papier peint*, Joseph Dufour also had some Napoleonic subjects specifically related to the Italian campaign in his catalogue. See the 1831 inventory of his prints on wood-die subjects in Bernard Jacqué, Georgette Pastiaux-Thriat (dir.), *Joseph Dufour. Manufacturier du papier peint*, Rennes, Presses Universitaires de Rennes, 2010, p. 84. See also Eric Arthur Entwisle, *French Scenic Wallpapers 1880-1860*, Leigh-on-Sea, F. Lewis, 1972, and Ulrich Lehmann, "Material Culture and Materialism: The French Revolution in Wallpaper", in *Writing Material Culture History*, ed. by Anne Gerritsen and Georges Riello, London, Bloomsbury, 2014, pp. 173-190.

of *notabili* who had often been ousted by the new regime. Moreover, they were frequently listed in the Lombardy-Venetia police reports after searches conducted in the houses of youths suspected of being militants in conspiracy networks: in fact, together with swords and decorations from the Italian corps of the *Grande Armée* (usually bequeathed by fathers and uncles), snuffboxes with Napoleonic subjects were immediately taken as evidence of political opposition.[27]

Aristocratic and bourgeois affection for the Napoleonic epic was better committed to precious materials such as brier, tortoise, ivory and bone items, with carved caps showing the miniaturised profiles of beloved heroes or evocative landscapes, such as the one with pyramids recalling Bonaparte's legendary and exotic battle, chosen for some snuffboxes. Among them we find one made of precious pearl, probably crafted by Antonio Turbiglio; or, soon after 1840, the famous and much-in-demand snuffbox showing Napoleon's funeral ceremony in Paris, with his sarcophagus carried by his men, one bone and bier specimen of which is included in the collections of the Musei Civici in Novara.[28]

A versatile and socially transversal object, often meant as a gift for loyal and clever officials, the Napoleonic snuffbox was able to live on in the peninsula and survive the iconic reset associated with the Restoration. Easier to carry than medals, swords and uniforms, it became a handy testimony of a past that could not be allowed to slip away. One important set, showing different subjects, sizes and materials, is on display in the first room of Milan's Museo del Risorgimento in the showcase dedicated to the Napoleonic Myth. Among the many items, the snuffbox created for the wedding of Napoleon and Marie Louise of Austria stands out, especially if we consider that it was to become a "cult" during the *Risorgimento* and circulated especially in the North-Central states of the peninsula: those same territories whose elites had played a leading role in the Napoleonic system (#2383 Museo Glauco Lombardi specimen).

As a parallel world for nostalgia on the writing desk,[29] the serial production of inkwells offers us a more unconventional narrative based on a friendly, almost playful Napoleon, whose features, thanks to polychromy and humorous attitudes, recall the *bon homme*, the jolly comrade and the soldier, more than the Emperor. An 18-piece collection from the Gerra commodate and donation, endowing the Museo Glauco Lombardi in Parma respectively in 2008 and in 2013, gives evidence of slight variations on a basic theme: full-length and half-length figures used as inkwells and pen-holders wear green, white and red colors, the Legion of Honour decoration on the breast, together with other iconic items from military life – such as drums and cannons – or from Napoleon's own iconography – his hat, or maps scattered on the table. In one case (Fig. 3), the tired, almost dejected attitude of Napoleon might be derived from Gustav Leybold's engraving dedicated to the eve of the Fontainebleau

27. For some cases in Giuseppe Mazzini's *Giovine Italia* conspiracy network in the Milan and Brescia areas, see Arianna Arisi Rota, *Il processo alla Giovine Italia in Lombardia, 1833-1835*, Milan, FrancoAngeli, 2003, pp. 63, 83.

28. *La memoria di Napoleone*, pp. 29, 43.

29. Gian Luca Fruci, "Il Risorgimento in tasca (e sul tavolo)", in *Una nazione da inventare*, ed. by Roberto Mancini and Marco Pignotti, Florence, Nerbini, 2011, pp. 92-102.

abdication (March 31, 1814), which was widely known in the Italian peninsula thanks to its inclusion in the best-selling volume *Lettere di famiglia* (Trieste, 1856), illustrated with steel engravings such as one by Gaspare Guzzi (Fig. 4). The pre-battle version, with a thoughtful and pensive Napoleon, a far cry from the jolly polychrome inkwells made of ceramics or china, also provided inspiration for a table decoration and a paperweight made of golden bronze, the same material used for the cenotaph-shaped inkwells of the mourning period.

5. *Durability*

Encompassing everything from the jolly comrade to the brilliant general, the gestures of the Emperor and those of the loving and protecting father, the character of Napoleon displays extraordinary versatility and yet perfect recognisability, even in different materials and more or less stylised shapes. The objects described in this chapter belong to a small portion of a large production of celebratory memorabilia created while the myth itself was in the making, a myth which proved capable of surviving throughout the decades of the 19th century as a model of remembrance and durability. Meaningful, apt to be worn and touched, objects could be easily passed down by the *passeurs* of the heroic time to their followers, those "children of the century" who in the post-Napoleonic peninsula were experiencing the frustrating search for their own glory and militancy.[30] Acting as memory clots in a sequenced, biographical and progressive narrative,[31] these objects acquired political value when kept close to the bodily interfaces of their owners, or when shown to an intimate circle of family members and friends inside the domestic environment.

A synthesis of this persistent myth, in a late Italian version, is offered by the painting *Il legionario napoleonico* by the Veronese *macchiaiolo*, Vincenzo Cabianca, in 1856, a precious piece in the collections of the Museo Revoltella in Trieste. Most probably inspired by Napoleon III's 1856 propaganda initiative of striking the Saint Helena medal, which surviving participants of the Napoleonic campaigns could apply for,[32] the subject presents a survey of all icons belonging to the tale of the heroic time, from a generational and gender perspective (Fig. 5). Captured in a humble domestic space, the aged veteran is standing wearing his old uniform and showing the medal on his breast, as well as maps on the table, while on his right side a group of three – a woman wearing a green ribbon placed under her chin on a red and white neck-handkerchief, a girl and an aged man on

30. On this subject, see Arianna Arisi Rota, *I piccoli cospiratori. Politica ed emozioni nei primi mazziniani*, Bologna, il Mulino, 2010.

31. Olsen, "Memory", pp. 210-211.

32. On this initiative in the late 1850s with Milan under Austrian control, when veterans left the municipal hospice and, wearing their medals, were caught by policemen while telling their stories in the streets around the Duomo square, see Arianna Arisi Rota, "Il linguaggio del controllo e della crisi: lo spirito pubblico lombardo nei rapporti dei delegati provinciali (1857-1859)", *Rivista storica italiana*, 119/1 (2007), pp. 112-141.

his knees – are religiously listening to him, while a child wearing a two-horned hat and carrying a sword on his shoulder is probably imagining himself on the battlefield. Even more important to our point, a statuette of Napoleon – probably a chalk one – is placed on a chest of drawers, and from nails in the wall iconic objects of military life – a stick, a rifle, a bag, a pot – add life to the plain wall and door. The presence of two- and three-dimensional objects in the background of domestic settings in order to reinforce the political message is a typical device for patriotic painting, such as that of the brothers Domenico and Gerolamo Induno.[33] Here, it comes under the shape of a paradigmatic private sanctuary for memory and personal identity. As the painter himself specified in a handwritten note on the back of the picture, this was the case of a mutilated veteran "telling his past adventures". Even though, as art historians claim, the painted scene might seem a bit too manneristic to an expert eye,[34] it still speaks to us of the durability and generational transmission of the Napoleonic myth as profoundly linked to the tale of the Nation.

33. On whose production see Sandro Morachioli, "La pittura e le cose. Gli Induno e l'oggettistica patriottica", in Manfredi, Minuto, *La politica dei sentimenti*, pp. 39-66.

34. *Arte e nazione. Dagli Induno a Fattori nelle collezioni del Museo Revoltella*, Trieste, Civico Museo Revoltella, 2015, pp. 55-56.

1. Candy box, with the kind permission of the Museo Glauco Lombardi, Parma, collection inventory # 2185.
2. Mourning *foulard*, with the kind permission of the Museo Glauco Lombardi, Parma, collection inventory # 2022B.

3. Inkwell, with the kind permission of the Museo Glauco Lombardi, Parma, collection inventory # 2559, Comodato Pierluigi Gerra.
4. *Napoleon at Fontainebleau*, 31 March 1814, Gaspare Guzzi engraver. Milan, private collection.

5. Vincenzo Cabianca, *Il Legionario napoleonico*, 1856, with the kind permission of the Archivio Fotografico del Museo Revoltella-Galleria d'arte moderna, Trieste, collection inventory # 1628.

Álvaro París, Jordi Roca Vernet

Green Ribbons and Red Berets: Political Objects and Clothing in Spain (1808-1843)*

> A handkerchief, a fan, a green or purple ribbon, in the preferred colours of the liberals, were enough to warrant the hatred of the masses.
>
> Modesto Lafuente, *Historia General de España* (1865)[1]

1. *Introduction*

The growing interest among historians in political objects stems from the material turn witnessed in the social sciences since the 1990s. The linguistic and cultural turns – which resulted in a boom of studies looking at discourse and representations – has run its course, and material culture has since returned to the centre of historiographical debate.[2] "Small" everyday objects, and their changing relationships with key social actors, are increasingly at the centre of attention. Far from being mere accessories or simply providing material evidence of historical transformations, everday objects played a central role in defining a new relationship with politics in the Age of Revolution. People's interaction with these artefacts contributed to the definition of new subjectivities and the construction of collective and national identities. Through their personal relationship with these items, consumers participated in a shared cultural horizon and used ordinary practices in the public and private spheres to establish a link with the political community.

* This research was conducted as part of the project "La dimensión popular de la política en la Europa Meridional y América Latina, 1789-1889", MICINN, PID2019-105071GB-I00.

1. Modesto Lafuente, *Historia General de España*, vol. XXVIII, Madrid, Imprenta del Banco Industrial y Mercantil, 1865, p. 294.

2. *Material Powers: Cultural Studies, History and the Material Turn*, ed. by Tony Bennett and Patrick Joyce, New York, Routledge, 2010; Katrina Navickas, "A Return to Materialism? Putting Social History Back into Place", in *New Directions in Cultural and Social History*, ed. by Sasha Handley, Rohan McWilliam and Lucy Noakes, London, Bloomsbury, 2018, pp. 87-108; Leora Auslander, "Beyond Words", *The American Historical Review*, 110/4 (2005), pp. 1015-1045.

The study of political objects began with pioneering works on the French Revolution and has since spread across Europe.[3] Spain has remained on the relative margins of this trend, however. Political historians remain more focussed on symbology, iconography and visual culture than on the material aspects of the media through which messages were conveyed,[4] while experts on material culture usually pay little attention to the political dimension of objects.[5]

This chapter constitutes an initial approach to what is an emerging field of research in Spain.[6] We focus on the first half of the 19th century (1808-1843) – a turbulent period characterised by the conflict between revolution and counter-revolution, during which new ways of doing politics were being trialled. Objects from foreign lands were increasingly adapted and turned into symbols of emerging political cultures.

In terms of sources, while objects destined for use by the elite have survived to the present day in museums, there is little trace of those objects geared towards the masses. Tracing these requires the collation of disperse references found in police reports, memoirs, *costumbrista* literature, engravings and press advertising. Moreover, we must adopt a transnational perspective when studying Spanish objects. The channels through which they were produced and distributed, and the ways in which fashions evolved, stemmed from European trends. French and British workshops anticipated the demand and adapted their formats to events in Spain in order to capture new markets. Likewise, key players under foreign influence learned to use new objects and adapted their uses and meanings to the dynamics of the local conflict.

Political objects have historically been unevenly distributed across Spain, owing to the rhythm of the changes experienced in the first half of the 19th century: periods of revolution characterised by the press freedom contrasted with absolutist reactions that restricted the distribution of objects and relegated them to more conventional formats (such as portraits of the king) or to the private sphere. Hence, most political objects that have survived to the present day focus on three well-

3. Richard Wrigley, *The Politics of Appearances: Representations of Dress in Revolutionary France*, Berg, Oxford, 2002; Richard Taws, *The Politics of the Provisional: Art and Ephemera in Revolutionary France*, University Park (PA), Pennsylvania State University, 2013; "Storia e cultura materiale: recenti traiettorie di ricerca. Interventi di Fabio Dei, Giorgio Riello, Beverly Lemire, Manuel Charpy, Leora Auslander", ed. by Alessio Petrizzo and Carlotta Sorba, *Contemporanea*, 3 (2016), pp. 439-482; "Culture visuali e forme di politicizzazione nel lungo '800 europeo", ed. by Gian Luca Fruci and Alessio Petrizzo, *Passato e presente*, 100 (2017), pp. 25-54.

4. *Historia de las Culturas Políticas en España y América Latina*, 6 vols, Madrid-Zaragoza, Marcial Pons-Prensas Universitarias de Zaragoza, 2014-2016.

5. Jesús Cruz, *El surgimiento de la cultura burguesa. Personas, hogares y ciudades en la España del siglo XIX*, Madrid, Siglo XXI, 2014; *Consumo, condiciones de vida y comercialización. Cataluña y Castilla, siglos XVII-XIX*, ed. by Bartolomé Yun Casalilla and Jaime Torras, Valladolid, Junta de Castilla y León, 1999; *Comprar, vender y consumir. Nuevas aportaciones a la historia del consumo en la España Moderna*, ed. by Daniel Muñoz Navarro, Valencia, Universidad de Valencia, 2011.

6. *Ciudadanos. El nacimiento de la política en España (1808-1869)*, ed. by Emilio La Parra, Madrid, Fundación Pablo Iglesias, 2010, pp. 144-351.

defined moments in Spanish history: the Peninsular War (known in Spain as the War of Independence) (1808-1814); the *Trienio Liberal* ("Liberal Triennium") (1820-1823); and the *Trienio Progresista* ("Progressive Triennium") (1840-1843). That said, outside of these periods when many such items emerged, and beyond museum display cases, there are objects that were shorter-lived and therefore more difficult to trace – coloured ribbons, garments and religious prints, for example – but nonetheless crucial to the more widespread politicisation.

In the first half of the 19th century, Spain was engaged in a civil war (whether outwardly declared or latent) in which conflicting sides attempted to gain dominance in the public sphere.[7] Patriots and *afrancesados*, liberals and royalists, and *carlistas* and *isabelinos*,[8] all deployed a new repertoire of symbols, colours, rituals and slogans, which were expressed materially in the form of objects that identified the warring sides. Certain items took on sacred connotations and became the targets of iconoclasm, bringing the appropriation of sovereignty and the "war of symbols" into the material realm.[9] The battle of symbols thus assumed a tangible aspect that enabled the conflict to be channelled into violence against material things. Iconoclasm was directed not only at objects with an explicitly political connotation but at those whose meaning depended on a context which is less clear (and often difficult to reconstruct). Quarrels in streets and taverns took on a political dimension when one of the parties attributed meaning to an everyday object, such as an item of clothing or an accessory in a certain colour. Consequently, objects were at the centre of the politicisation of daily life.

2. *The War of Independence (1808-1814)*

In the 18th century, everyday objects such as fans, boxes, snuffboxes, tableware and pendants typically bore *costumbrista* or mythological scenes, urban landscapes and portraits of the Royal Family. However, the French Revolution awoke Spaniards' interest in objects that reflected events in their neighbouring country. The cordon sanitaire established by Floridablanca in 1789 to prevent the spread of revolutionary ideas in Spain would affect not only printed material but the boxes, fans and all manner of artefacts that contained political messages. Because the Inquisition controlled borders and kept a close eye on merchants and fashion boutiques importing garments from France, we now have access to fans, snuffboxes, waistcoats bearing political markings, handkerchiefs hailing the guillotine or canes shaped like the

7. Jordi Canal, "Guerra civil y contrarrevolución en la Europa del sur en el siglo XIX: reflexiones a partir del caso español", *Ayer*, 55 (2004), pp. 37-60.

8. *Afrancesados* ("Frenchified"), i.e. those who supported Joseph Bonaparte (Napoleon's brother) during the War of Independence (1808-1814). From 1833 to 1840, a civil war pitted the *carlistas* (Carlists, i.e. those loyal to Carlos María Isidro, Ferdinand VII's brother) against the *isabelinos* or *cristinos* (those loyal to Isabella II of Spain and the Queen Mother, the Regent Maria Christina).

9. Emmanuel Fureix, *L'œil blessé: Politiques de l'iconoclasme après la Révolution française*, Paris, Champ Vallon, 2019.

Liberty Tree.[10] In Bilbao in the 1790s, the Inquisition confiscated 15 fans bearing scenes from the Storming of the Bastille and other revolutionary depictions.[11] A snuffbox with the inscription “Vive la Asemblée Nationale” was found in Vélez, and a watch fob engraved with “Vive la liberté” was found in Zaragoza.[12] Though anecdotal, these episodes demonstrate that the Spanish authorities were aware of the propagandist power of objects and feared that a penchant for French fashions could become a vehicle for spreading revolutionary ideas.

Censure could not stop French ideas from crossing the border. However, it was not the contagion effect that hastened the changes but the crisis at the very heart of the Spanish monarchy. The Revolt of Aranjuez on 17 March 1808 resulted in the fall of Godoy and the abdication of Charles IV of Spain in favour of his son, Ferdinand VII. Given the instability of the monarchy, Napoleon believed he could dethrone its corrupt head to take control of the body politic and place his brother Joseph on the Spanish throne. However, the Emperor had underestimated the ability of traditional bodies (the nobility, clergy and municipal councils) to channel widespread opposition against foreign invasion. Spanish resistance and British military support plunged the country into a spiral of war, popular armed uprisings, institutional collapse and clashing ideas, creating new space for politics.[13] Together with the press, propaganda, prints and proclamations, objects began to circulate, exalting patriotism and commemorating episodes of resistance against the French. Material culture played a crucial role in defining national heroes, spreading national sentiment and establishing a collective memory of military deeds.

In 1813, several fan models reached Spain from Great Britain depicting the events of the Peninsular War. British manufacturers exploited the opportunity to design models with political motifs based on prints circulating in Spain. Behrmann & Collmann in London was behind most political fans preserved from the period.[14] The fan-leaves were made from printed paper and sometimes mounted on wooden ribs. They could be mass produced and sold cheaply. Among the most widely reproduced images was the defence of the Monteleón artillery barracks during the Dos de Mayo Uprising of 1808 in Madrid, based on a print by Tomás López Enguídanos (see Fig. 1).[15] Another model by Behrmann & Collmann shows the moment when Godoy, the favourite of Charles IV of Spain, was arrested

10. Juan Francisco Fuentes, “Moda y lenguaje en la crisis social del antiguo régimen”, in *L’image de la France en Espagne pendant la seconde moitié du XVIIIe siècle*, ed. by Jean-René Aymes, Alicante, Instituto de cultura “Juan Gil-Albert”, 1996, pp. 85-95.

11. Archivo Histórico Nacional [AHN], Inquisición, 4429, exp. 6; Joaquín Ezquerra del Bayo, *Exposición del abanico en España. Catálogo general ilustrado*, Madrid, Imprenta Blass y Compañía, 1920, pp. 37-38.

12. Fuentes, “Moda y lenguaje”, p. 92; Philip Deacon, “Juan Meléndez Valdés en la Real Sociedad Económica Aragonesa, 1789-1791 (Con unos datos sobre Goya)”, *Dieciocho*, 15 (1995), pp. 95-148.

13. *Guerra de ideas: política y cultura en la España de la Guerra de la Independencia*, ed. by Pedro Rújula and Jordi Canal, Madrid, Marcial Pons, 2011.

14. Behrmann and Collmann, British Museum, https://www.britishmuseum.org/collection/term/BIOG144089.

15. Museo de Historia de Madrid [MHM], inv. 7624, inv. 2228 and inv. 2229.

following the Revolt of Aranjuez.[16] After his fall from grace, portraits of Godoy were burned and his image removed from books and printing plates, triggering a period of political iconoclasm that would intensify in the decades to come.[17]

Other themes on British fans included: the repression of rebels in Madrid by French soldiers on the Paseo del Prado; an allegory of the Spanish triumph in the Battle of Bailén; a portrait of the Duke of Wellington following victory in the Battle of Salamanca; and several depictions of the freeing of Ferdinand VII.[18] There was also a plethora of portraits of guerrillas on horseback including Julián Sánchez *El Charro*, Juan Martín Díez *El Empecinado* and Juan Palarea.[19] In addition to fans, snuffboxes were imported. One surviving example bears a portrait of the Duke of Wellington along with mention of his victories on the Peninsula.[20] These objects originated in London, mostly around 1813. They depict various aspects of patriotic and British propaganda during the war: the importance of the Madrid uprising; the exaltation of Ferdinand VII; the role of the British generals; and the guerrilla as the embodiment of popular resistance.

In addition to these examples from Great Britain, there are local items of more working-class origin. The most notable are ceramics from Talavera (Toledo), intended for everyday use. This style of ceramics could respond to changes in demand caused by the politicisation of society. Jugs, plates, bowls and pitchers adopted a new political repertoire that reflected patriotic and constitutional themes as well as absolutist perspectives.[21] Motifs from the period include allegorical scenes from the Constitution of 1812, crude depictions of generals and guerrillas from the patriotic side, satirical scenes ridiculing the French enemy and portraits of Ferdinand VII. One fine example is a jug with an equestrian image of the guerrilla Juan Palarea *El medico* ("The Doctor", Fig. 2). Spain was also the source of fans designed for the working classes, which owe their cruder aesthetic to having been produced in secret by anonymous printers.[22]

Most objects made in Spain were produced amid pressing circumstances and a climate of resistance. They were short-lived and designed for immediate use, and are therefore more difficult to track down in museums. We will look first at prints which, being cheaper, were the most accessible political object for the

16. MHM, inv. 7623 and 4621; Museo Nacional del Romanticismo [MNR], inv. CE2475.

17. Jesusa Vega, "Estampas de la crisis bélica contra Napoleón: escenarios, víctimas, héroes y gestas", in *El dominio de la realidad y la crisis del discurso. El nacimiento de la conciencia europea*, ed. by Concepción Camarero Bullón and Juan Carlos Gómez Alonso, Madrid, Polifemo, 2017, p. 131.

18. MHM, inv. 2230, 2003/17/642, 2003/17/643 and 4671; *Abanicos. La colección del Museo Municipal de Madrid*, ed. by Isabel Tuda and Maria Josefa Pastor, Madrid, Ayuntamiento de Madrid, 2002.

19. Museo de la Armería de Álava, inv. 0759; fans of *El Empecinado* and Palarea (Behrmann & Collmann) in the British Museum, inv. 1891,0713.396 and 1891,0713.366.

20. MHM, inv. 2.279.

21. Miguel Cabañas Bravo, "La imagen de Fernando VII y la Guerra de la Independencia en la cerámica de Talavera", *Archivo Español de Arte*, 267 (1994), pp. 243-256.

22. MHM, inv. 4925; Jesusa Vega, "Fernando VII: resistencia y deseo", *Journal of Spanish Cultural Studies*, 14/4 (2013), p. 358.

masses.[23] Prints formed a key part of the material culture and domestic equipment of the working classes. They were used as protective amulets, carried in pockets or hung on the walls of their homes.[24] The trade in prints took a turn from 1808 when engravers modified their plates to meet the growing demand for patriotic objects.[25] Among the most popular prints were portraits of Ferdinand VII, of Spanish and British generals and of guerrilla leaders, in addition to patriotic allegories and scenes of resistance in cities such as Madrid, Barcelona and Zaragoza. The engraver Juan Carrafa sold a successful line of calling cards illustrated with the most important episodes from the war (Fig. 3). There was also a proliferation of satirical prints and caricatures of Napoleon and Joseph I, the tone of which was adapted to suit popular taste. Joseph Bonaparte was portrayed as a drunken gambler with the nickname "Pepe Botella" (Pepe Bottle) or "Rey de copas" (King of Cups), depicted with his arms around a barrel or wearing clothes made from playing cards and wine glasses.[26]

While prints were made for people to look at and hang on their walls, they were also attached to clothing. In Barcelona, cockades were printed with the portrait of Ferdinand VII, patriotic slogans and "death to Napoleon". They were produced on paper, silk or Moroccan leather and worn on a lapel or hat as a symbol of support for the resistance.[27] Both Spain and America have a wide variety of cockades bearing portraits of the monarch, his initials ("FVII" or "F7º") or his motto ("Viva Fernando VII" ["Long Live Ferdinand VII"]). These could be worn alongside the red fabric cockade – the traditional emblem of the royal army adopted as a national insignia by the patriots. The *Diario de Madrid* advertised red satin cockades with a picture of the king and the inscription "Viva Fernando VII". These were sold for 4, 3 and 2 *reales* – an accessible sum for all members of society.[28] The red cockade became a symbol of patriotic resistance during uprisings against Napoleon. In Zaragoza, on 24 May 1808, the peasants – identified by a red cockade in their hat – rebelled against the Captain General, triggering hostilities against the French.[29] The same occurred in Sevilla, Valencia,

23. Juan Carrete Parrondo, "Estampas del Dos de Mayo de 1808 en Madrid. Entre la historia y la propaganda", in *Madrid. 1808: ciudad y protagonistas*, Madrid, Ayuntamiento de Madrid, 2008, pp. 159-170; Laura Corrales, "La iconografía de la guerra del Francès (1808-1814)", in *La Guerra del Francès: 200 anys desprès*, ed. by Ramon Arnabat, Tarragona, Universitat Rovira i Virgili, 2013, pp. 103-144.

24. Carmen Ortiz García, "Papeles para el pueblo. hojas sueltas y otros impresos de consumo masivo en la España de finales del siglo XIX", in *Palabras para el pueblo: Aproximación general a la literatura de cordel*, ed. by Luis Díaz G. Viana, Madrid, CSIC, pp. 145-190.

25. Vega, "Estampas de la crisis bélica contra Napoleón", pp. 129-312.

26. Emilio de Diego, "Medios de difusión: la calle", in *Guerra de ideas*, pp. 313-330.

27. Raymundo Ferrer, *Barcelona cautiva, o sea diario exacto de lo ocurrido en la misma ciudad mientras la oprimieron los franceses*, vol. III, Barcelona, Imprenta Antonio Brusi, 1816, pp. 314-315 and Appendix 2, pp. 51-52.

28. Vega, "Fernando VII", p. 375.

29. Pedro Rújula, "Zaragoza (1808-1809): El mito de la resistencia popular", in *Los sitios en la Guerra de la Independencia: la lucha en las ciudades*, ed. by Gonzalo Butrón Prida and Pedro Rújula, Cádiz, Universidad de Cádiz, 2011, p. 19.

Alicante and other cities that rose up against Napoleon that May.[30] There are also examples of satin ribbons bearing patriotic slogans, handkerchiefs with the image of the king, medallions, and portraits which were hung around the neck. Monarchical mottos were embroidered into garments, *mantillas* (shawls), hats and other accessories. As Jesusa Vega has shown, such objects were "quick to produce, could be carried discretely and, if need be, easy to hide and destroy".[31] Hence, they were perfectly suited to the climate of resistance and secrecy. Their short-lived nature (they had an immediate political use) has made it hard for us to track them down.

The portrait and motto of the monarch were the most effective way to arouse emotions and keep the resistance alive. The absent king became omnipresent through images; he was everywhere and nowhere at once. His orphaned people used objects to express their love and personal loyalty to the idealised king, himself now an object of longing.

In addition to the king, religion was also key to driving the resistance. Patriots carried religious prints and scapulars invoking divine protection during battle.[32] Defenders of the city of Zaragoza attached prints to their hats bearing images of the *Virgen del Pilar* (Our Lady of the Pillar), which were handed out by women.[33] At a time when civilians were fighters and religion was the great ideological weapon of the resistance, carrying a scapular or print of the Virgin could be taken as a sign of one's political leanings.

Images from the period enable us to reconstruct how patriotic objects were used in day-to-day life. One print depicts a Valencian vegetable farmer burning French soldiers at the stake (Fig. 4).[34] His hat bears a ribbon securing three prints and bearing the motto "Viva FVII", while a scapular hangs around his neck. This example shows how prints and ribbons became the political objects par excellence given their low cost and the ease with which they could be produced, distributed and hidden to evade suppression.

Lastly, engraving was used to personalise everyday objects and confer political meaning upon them. Merchants sold portraits of Ferdinand VII stamped on fabric for decorating snuffboxes, fans, medallions, belts, combs and other artefacts.[35] Silversmiths advertised decorated low-relief busts of the king carved in silver, intended for adorning snuffboxes, medallions, belts, cockades and combs.[36] Anyone was thus able to personalise an object to show their loyalty to the king, without having to acquire a costly imported item.

30. Rafael Pérez, *Madrid en 1808. El relato de un actor*, Madrid, Biblioteca Histórica, 2008, pp. 97, 102 and 104.

31. Vega, "Fernando VII", p. 357.

32. Pérez, *Madrid en 1808*, p. 134.

33. Francisco Javier Ramón, *La Virgen del Pilar dice... Usos políticos y nacionales de un culto mariano en la España contemporánea*, Zaragoza, Prensas de la Universidad de Zaragoza, 2014, p. 97.

34. *Viva España. Muera Napoleon*, printed anonymously (1808-1813), British Museum, 1878,0112.29; Vega, "Fernando VII", p. 368.

35. *Diario de Madrid*, 30/10/1812 and 13/10/1808.

36. *Diario de Madrid*, 4/11/1808.

In summary, during the War of Independence, objects were "active players in generating emotions" which helped create a common desire that motivated the masses to join the resistance and thus establish an interpersonal relationship with the king.[37] Patriotic artefacts embodied the wearer's commitment to the return of Ferdinand VII and were an outward display of the emotional ties (orphanhood, love and desire) that fuelled the fight against the invader. Objects were not simply lifeless evidence of events: they were weapons of war.

3. Trienio Liberal *(1820-1823), part one: fans, snuffboxes and tableware*

On 1 January 1820, Colonel Rafael del Riego proclaimed the Constitution of 1812 in Cabezas de San Juan in the presence of the troops that would be sent off to fight American insurgents. The wave of civilian and military movements triggered by the proclamation forced Ferdinand VII to swear allegiance to the Constitution in March 1820. This led to a period of political transformations that would resonate across Mediterranean Europe.[38] The *Trienio Liberal* was a first attempt to implement the Constitution effectively. It followed the brief yet turbulent experience during the War of Independence (1812-1814) when most of the country was occupied by French troops. The intense politicisation of society driven by the *Cortes* (Parliament), local council elections, the emergence of the press, public opinion, patriotic societies and the formation of the National Militia had an immediate impact on the proliferation of political objects.[39] The *Trienio Liberal* was a golden age for political objects in Spain resulting in an abundance and diversity of artefacts that would not be seen again until the last third of the 19th century. We will start by describing imported objects aimed principally at an elite audience (e.g., luxury fans, snuffboxes and ceramics) before looking at objects aimed at the working classes.

Fans

As was the case during the War of Independence, most fans commemorating Riego's proclamation came from abroad, in this case France. Most pieces were manufactured in factories in Paris and the department of Oise (Andeville-Méru).[40] They were exported to Spain and America, arriving a few months after the successful outcome of the revolution. They were purchased in cities such as Barcelona or Madrid by the middle and upper classes, who wanted to

37. Vega, "Fernando VII", p. 372.

38. Manuel Chust, Pedro Rújula, *El Trienio Liberal: Revolución e independencia (1820-1823)*, Madrid, Catarata, 2020.

39. *El Trienio Liberal (1820-1823). Una mirada política*, ed. by Pedro Rújula and Ivana Frasquet, Granada, Comares, 2020.

40. Musées des Arts Décoratifs, "Deux éventails de la période révolutionnaire", https://madparis.fr/francais/musees/musee-des-arts-decoratifs/collections/acquisitions/2019/deux-eventails-fin-xviiie-siecle (accessed 1/6/2020).

demonstrate their allegiance to the new regime.[41] The fans bear adaptations of the characteristic iconography of the French Revolution, such as the liberty cap, the Tablets of the Law and the dance around the Liberty Tree.[42] They mainly depicted the *pronunciamiento*[43] (military revolt) led by liberal military officers in 1820, the swearing of the Constitution by the king, and allegories that exalted the nation, monarchy and religion.[44] These themes were a reflection of the enshrinement of the Constitution and of the worship of symbols and national heroes. Abstract ideas were depicted through allegories that disseminated the principles of the new civic and political culture among the population.

The heroes of the *pronunciamiento* of 1820 included the officers Riego and Quiroga, who were either represented individually or together with Baños and Arco Agüero in a tetralogy of "immortal" heroes.[45] One of the most interesting depictions is the *Exaltation of Riego.* He is represented in the foreground as a liberator, leaning on a royal coat of arms and carrying a sword piercing a serpent (Fig. 5). In the background is a group of civilians dancing around a white and green (the colour of liberalism) flag, alongside a scene depicting the liberation of political prisoners from the absolutist period. In the *Homage to Colonel Quiroga*, a group comprising militiamen from the National Militia, civilians, women and a child dance a celebratory dance around a bust of the hero amid bucolic scenery.[46]

In contrast to the allegorical female figures embodying the Constitution and freedom are depictions of serpents and monstrous creatures representing reactionary forces and despotism.[47] Emancipation is represented by the breaking of chains, the ripping up of proscription lists, the freeing of prisoners or the destruction of the Inquisition Tribunal.[48] Several French fans condemn the Inquisition as an embodiment of fanaticism, oppression and anti-enlightenment.[49] The revolution of 1820 was followed by an assault on the Inquisition headquarters in several cities. However, the myth of the "Spanish Bastille" was soon dispelled

41. Manuel Rocamora, *Museo de indumentaria colección Rocamora*, Barcelona, Ayuntamiento de Barcelona, 1970.

42. Jean Starobinski, *1789. Los emblemas de la razón*, Madrid, Taurus, 1988; Georgina Letourmy-Bordier, "De Coriolan à la rosière de Salency. Les nouveaux héros et l'incarnation de la vertu representés sur les éventails au XVIIIe siècle", in *European Fans in the 17th and 18th Centuries: Images, Accessories, and Instruments of Gesture*, ed. by Miriam Volmert and Danijela Bucher, Berlin-Boston, Walter de Gruyter GmbH, 2020, pp. 76-94.

43. A *pronunciamiento* was an insurrection or coup d'état led by military officers, in this case proclaiming the Constitution.

44. Carlos Reyero, *Alegoría, nación y libertad. El Olimpo constitucional de 1812*, Madrid, Siglo XXI, 2010, p. 86. See figures 60, 61, 62 and 65.

45. Antonio Quiroga was the highest-ranking soldier to participate in the *pronunciamiento* of 1820, though Rafael del Riego was soon considered the driver of the revolutionary feat.

46. MHM, inv. 2.610.

47. Spelling errors allude to the pieces having originated in France: MHM, inv. 2.609 and 2.612; *Abanicos. La colección del Museo Municipal de Madrid*, pp. 154-155.

48. MHM, inv. 2.608, 2.611, 2.613 and 2.609.

49. Rocamora, *Museo de indumentaria*, see fans nos 88761, 88766, 88771, 88773 and 88766.

after inquisitorial prisons were found practically empty and with no evidence of the presumed atrocities.[50] Despite these attacks on the clergy and the Inquisition, many of the fans produced in Spain underscored the constitutional link between the monarchy and religion[51] and used Catholic symbolism.[52]

The vast majority of fans bearing constitutional motifs were produced during the first few months of the *Trienio* – not very successfully, it would seem, given the lack of continuity in subsequent years. In any case, the more than 20 different models that have been tracked down (ten times more than in subsequent periods) prove that the *Trienio Liberal* was a golden age for this political object.

The fan was a women's accessory that was also used as a domestic ornament. Fans were especially popular among the middle-to-upper classes, though some models manufactured with cheaper materials (wood and paper) were more affordable.[53] The proliferation of fans was connected to the widespread political engagement of women during the *Trienio*, both on the street and in social gatherings, patriotic societies, public opinion and even in the voluntary National Militia.[54] With these political fans, women erupted into the social sphere and publicly embodied the new liberal values. We are also aware of other objects – *mantillas* (shawls) with constitutional mottos, or green ribbons – that placed women from different levels of society at the centre of the new public sphere, though fewer examples of such objects have survived to the present day.[55]

With the coming of the second absolutist restoration (1823-1833), constitutional fans were hunted down. The domestic setting became a refuge for outlawed objects. In many cases, these posed a real threat to their owner's lives, and they were carefully stowed.[56] In 1824, the *Comisiones Militares Ejecutivas* (Executive Military Commissions) were established. These special tribunals passed summary judgements on political crimes, with the accused often being condemned to death or

50. Francisco Carantoña, "El difícil camino hacia la monarquía constitucional: 1820, del pronunciamiento a la revolución", in *Conspiraciones y pronunciamientos. El rescate de la libertad (1814-1820)*, ed. by Marieta Cantos and Alberto Ramos, Cádiz, Editorial de la Universidad de Cádiz, 2019, pp. 113-148; Luis Alonso Tejada, *Ocaso de la Inquisición en los últimos años de Fernando VII*, Madrid, ZYX, 1969, pp. 23-27; Emilio La Parra, María Ángeles Casado, *La Inquisición en España. Agonía y abolición*, Madrid, Catarata, 2013, pp. 153-171.

51. Rocamora, *Museo de indumentaria*, see fans nos 88762, 88775, 88774, 88777 and 88768.

52. Reyero, *Alegoría, nación y libertad*, p. 68. See figures 43, 69, 113 and pp. 96 and 173.

53. Richard Stites, *The Four Horsemen: Riding to Liberty in Post-Napoleonic Europe*, Oxford-New York, Oxford University Press, 2014, p. 86; *Abanicos de la colección del Museo de Historia de Madrid*, Madrid, Ayuntamiento de Madrid, 2002, p. 158.

54. Jordi Roca Vernet, "Emilia Duguermeur de Lacy, un liderazgo femenino en el liberalismo español", in *Las heroínas de la Guerra de la Independencia*, ed. by Irene Castells, Gloria Espigado and María Cruz Romeo, Madrid, Cátedra, 2009, pp. 371-397.

55. Juan Francisco Fuentes, Pilar Garí, *Amazonas de la libertad. Mujeres liberales contra Fernando VII*, Madrid, Marcial Pons, 2014, p. 194.

56. Enrico Francia, "Oggetti sediziosi. Censura e cultura materiale nell'Italia della Restaurazione", *Mélanges de l'École française de Rome*, 130 (2018), pp. 31-41.

military service.[57] Their victims included María Gutiérrez from Seville, who stood trial in 1824 after she was found to possess a constitutional fan.[58]

Given the risks that these objects posed, they were cleansed of their political references. The inscriptions on the fans of Riego and Quiroga mentioned previously have been rendered illegible (crossed out or painted over).[59] This suggests that words were considered more dangerous than images (the latter could be interpreted more ambiguously). It was likely the owners who removed the text from the fans so that they could still use them or hide them without running such great risk. Though the object was not destroyed, the threat it posed was eliminated by removing the most explicit political references.

Boxes, snuffboxes and ceramics

Whereas the female political object par excellence was the fan, in the case of men this role was played by the snuffbox. These small round boxes were designed to hold snuff (powdered tobacco that is sniffed up the nostril), though they also stored lozenges and powders. They were introduced in Spain in response to French fashions. The custom of inhaling snuff was adopted in the 18th century as a more civilised habit among distinguished society compared to the popular cigarette.[60] Most snuffboxes bearing political motifs were imported from France and replicated models distributed during the Revolution, the Napoleonic era and the Restoration.[61] They were illustrated with references to the proclamation of the Constitution of 1812, the constitutional oath taken by the monarch and the end of the Inquisition.[62] One of the most popular designs depicted the image of the king's oath as well as a list of important liberals including members of the *Cortes* (Parliament), military heroes, writers and scientists, interspersed with articles from the Constitution.

Another small box bears an image of the four heroes of the proclamation of 1820 (Riego, Quiroga, Baños and Arco Agüero) based on Motte's popular print titled *Les immortels*, which depicts them as a canonical foursome (Fig. 6).[63] Among the other surviving snuffboxes are examples honouring the delegation of French doctors that travelled to Barcelona to help combat the yellow fever epidemic that spread through the city in the summer of 1821.[64]

57. Álvaro París, *"Se susurra en los barrios bajos". Policía, opinión y política popular en Madrid (1825-1827)*, PhD dissertation, Universidad Autónoma de Madrid, 2016, ch. 5; Pedro Pegenaute, *Represión política en el reinado de Fernando VII. Las comisiones militares (1824-1825)*, Pamplona, Universidad de Navarra, 1974.

58. *Gaceta de Madrid*, 29/1/1825.

59. See Fig. 5. The inscription on the base of the stele has been crossed out.

60. Joaquín Álvarez de Barrientos, "La civilización como modelo de vida en el Madrid del siglo XVIII", *Revista de Dialectología y Tradiciones Populares*, 62/2 (2001), p. 160.

61. Rocamora, *Museo de indumentaria*, see box n. 103403. Museu Frederic Marès [MFM] Barcelona, collection of boxes depicting the Spanish royal family.

62. Rocamora, *Museo de indumentaria*, see boxes nos 103429, 103415 and 103410, all of them made in France.

63. Charles Étienne Pierre Motte, "Les immortels", 1820 (lithograph): MNR, inv. CE5723.

64. Rocamora, *Museo de indumentaria*, see box n. 103417.

As was the case with fans, snuffboxes did not manage to carve out a place in the Spanish market. Likewise, their iconography had strong ties to revolutionary and Napoleonic examples originating in France. The fact that snuffboxes were gradually replaced with cigarette boxes is testament to the emergence of intermediate social groups that preferred cigarettes to elitist snuff. In short, fans and snuffboxes were primarily aimed at an elite accustomed to consuming luxury products originating in other parts of Europe. These pieces have reached us through private collections which were incorporated into museums in Barcelona and Madrid in the 20th century. Despite their interest, in social terms they are not representative and reveal little information about how political objects circulated among the masses.

A variant of snuffboxes were the small circular boxes or "powder compacts" (*polveras*) containing foldable paper rounds printed with articles from the Constitution (Fig. 7).[65] The latter was also printed in miniature pocket versions decorated with luxury golden covers engraved with the swearing of the Constitution. The quality of the pieces highlights that these were luxury objects, not intended to be read daily, but rather tied to the sacred image attributed to the Constitution itself.

A citizen named Simón Ardit y Quer designed a set of constitutional playing cards which was manufactured in 1822 with funding from the Junta de Comercio (Trade Board) of Barcelona.[66] The cards had huge commemorative value, and many members of the *Cortes* received a set. Most strikingly, the deck makes symbolic references to the new regime, including portraits of the heroes of the War of Independence and of the *pronunciamiento* of 1820, as well as references to the Constitution. However, the monarch is not represented in any of the four suits. In place of kings are crowned lions (a symbol of Spain) holding up the Constitution, overthrowing despotism or stepping on an individual wearing aristocratic attire (Fig. 8).[67]

Next, we come to a somewhat more exclusive French porcelain coffee set decorated with motifs linked to the Constitution, and which likely belonged to someone from the liberal elite.[68] The scenes allude to the dissemination of constitutional culture among the working classes via the reading of printed material in groups. The depictions show soldiers reading aloud to an innkeeper, gentlemen arguing with a woman street vendor and a man giving newspapers to a lady. One cup shows a man in the traditional working-class dress (long cape and wide-brimmed hat)[69] reading some papers as two elegantly-attired fellows

65. MNR, inv. CE1192.

66. Arxiu Històric Ciutat de Barcelona [AHCB], n. 26035, "Colls Espanyols"; Museo Fournier de Naipes de Álava, inv. 44514.

67. Laura Corrales, "La imageria constitucional en el procés de la revolució liberal (1808-1840)", *Rubrica Contemporanea*, 1 (2012), pp. 61-62.

68. The complete set comprises two coffee pots, a milk jug, a sugar bowl, a platter and 12 cups with saucers.

69. The long cape (*capa larga*) and the wide-brimmed hat (*sombrero de ala ancha* or *chambergo*) were part of the popular male dress. The prohibition against wearing

watch (Fig. 9). The set, designed for someone from the elite, reflected the political nationalisation of liberal ideas and the desire to mobilise the working classes and women through their interactions with soldiers and the middle classes.

Contrasting this luxury porcelain set are the ceramics of Talavera. This trade tried to overcome the crisis and devastation caused by the war by adapting to the changing political circumstances. Patriotic messages from the War of Independence made way for constitutional messages throughout the *Trienio Liberal* and to anti-liberal messages during the absolutist restorations. In some cases, political inscriptions alternated with the name of the piece's owner. This may be a sign of the owner's personal support of the cause. One jug bears the motto "Constitución o muerte" ("Constitution or Death") together with the name of its owner, Bastiana Zamora.[70] On another, a portrait of Ferdinand VII sits above the inscription "viva mi dueño" ("Long live my master") in what is a devotional expression of unconditional love for the monarch (Fig. 2). The working-class nature of the pieces is inherent not only in their aesthetic but in the use of humorous and scatological themes that were somewhat distinct from the solemn images used on fans.

4. Trienio Liberal *(1820-1823), part two: prints, ribbons and cockades*

Prints and engravings

French iconography had a decisive influence over how the Spanish revolutionary process was depicted in France and Europe and even on how Spanish liberals depicted themselves. French political propaganda turned Spain into the new heart of the revolution from the early months of the *Trienio Liberal* onwards. A testament to this is the series of lithographs by Godefroy Engelmann based on drawings by Hippolyte Lecomte, which used three ideas to represent the political changes. First was the leading role of the figure of the military commander, as though there were a new Napoleon. Lithographs were dedicated to the two main leaders of the proclamation of 1820: Antonio Quiroga and Rafael del Riego.[71] Second were the images of the occupation of the palace of the Inquisition in Barcelona,[72] which imitated the Storming of the Bastille.[73] Third was the proclamation of the Constitution in Madrid's Plaza Mayor, which

these garments in Madrid in 1766 was seen as an assault on popular customs and led to the Esquilache Riots. See José Miguel López García, *El motín contra Esquilache*, Madrid, Alianza, 2006.

70. Cabañas Bravo, "La imagen de Fernando VII", p. 249, n. 20.

71. Jordi Roca Vernet, "Las imágenes en la cultura política liberal durante el trienio constitucional (1820-1823): El caso de Barcelona", *Cuadernos de Ilustración y Romanticismo*, 10 (2002), pp. 185-220.

72. "Atac a la seu del tribunal de la Inquisició a Barcelona", 1820, AHCB, n. 07825.

73. *La Prise de la Bastilla* (1793), Charles Thévenin, Musée Carnavalet, http://parismuseescollections.paris.fr/fr/musee-carnavalet/oeuvres/prise-de-la-bastille-le-14-juillet-1789-10 (accessed 1/6/2020).

put soldiers almost exclusively at the centre of events.[74] The author depicted the beginning of the revolution using stereotypes of the Spanish liberals and their goals. For example, the image of the Inquisition in Barcelona bears no likeness to the location and features of the actual building.

Political prints were widely circulated among the popular classes, as was the case during the War of Independence. The most significant was the image of Riego, elevated above the other heroes and the object of popular worship. His portrait was carried along the streets in defiance of the moderate authorities,[75] causing clashes between the army and the crowds.[76] Riego was depicted on all manner of everyday objects, from fan and snuffboxes to medallions and common items such as straight razors and hair combs.[77] However, prints were the most widely held political objects among the popular classes. Prints of the liberal heroes Riego, Lacy, Torrijos and Mina hung on the walls of working-class homes dwellings. The writer Ayguals de Izco used these words to describe the room of a liberal day labourer (*jornalero*) from Madrid enlisted in the Urban Militia in 1834:

> a small vase with flowers on the table, two small painted plaster birds sat sideways symmetrically, six prints or portraits, namely Riego, Mina, Lacy, el Empecinado, Torrijos and Manzanares, along with a broken mirror, a crucifix and a virgin, were the adornments in the labourer's room.[78]

Plaster figurines, crucifixes and images of virgins and saints sat alongside new, political prints in working-class homes. Portraits of liberal heroes were placed in prominent places in the home, where they were worshipped and lit by candles, much like religious images would have been. Revolutionary worship was persecuted by absolutists as sacrilegious. In 1824, a shoemaker from Madrid named Francisco de la Torre was sentenced by the Military Commission for having a portrait of Riego hanging in his home.[79] His wife was also sentenced on account of "irreligious behaviour", since the portrait was allegedly hidden in a frame behind a print of the Virgin. According to the person who informed on the family, the accused would light candles before the image of the hero. The sentence against the shoemaker reflects the desire of the absolutists to exorcise political objects of their power. Francisco was forced to carry the portrait around

74. Jesusa Vega, "Estampas del Trienio Liberal", *Villa de Madrid: revista del Excmo. Ayuntamiento*, 94 (1987), pp. 28-52.

75. Liberals were soon divided into radicals (*exaltados*) and moderates *(moderados)*. The former sought to broaden political participation. The latter wanted to strengthen order and obedience to the authorities.

76. Sebastián de Miñano, *Relación Histórica de la batalla de las platerías*, Biblioteca Nacional (Madrid), BN R/C 775-69.

77. Víctor Sánchez Martín, *Rafael de Riego: símbolo de la Revolución liberal*, PhD dissertation, Universidad de Alicante, 2016, p. 712; Stites, *The Four Horsemen*, pp. 85-88.

78. Wenceslao Ayguals de Izco, *María o la hija de un jornalero*, Madrid, Imprenta Ayguals de Izco, 1845, p. 28.

79. *Gaceta de Madrid*, 20/11/1824; Francisco Morales Sánchez, *Páginas de sangre. Historia del Saladero*, vol. II, Madrid, Manuel Rodríguez, 1870, pp. 582-585.

his neck to the Plazuela de la Cebada (the site of public executions). There, the object was burned at the stake by an executioner in the presence of onlookers. Francisco was sentenced to ten years in prison, his wife to two years in the *galera* (a female prison) and his older son to two years. The couple died during their imprisonment, and the son was hung in 1831 for crying "Viva la libertad y mueran los realistas" ("Long live freedom and down with the royalists").[80]

Aleluyas

The Liberal Revolution saw the politicisation of popular forms of entertainment which originated in religious propaganda – catechisms, credos and songs – all to disseminate revolutionary symbology and discourse among the largely illiterate working people. Printed broadsheets known as *aleluyas* were among those objects that made the greatest contribution to the politicisation of the masses. *Aleluyas* were sheets of paper (usually low quality), typically 30-40 cm in size and printed on one side (Fig. 10). They used images (usually 48 vignettes or scenes distributed in 8 rows of 6) and a small subordinate text (mostly written in rhyming verse) to depict an important historical, social or political event, a biography, or the story from a *romance*[81] or a well-known work of literature. They also commented on diverse figures (saints, soldiers, literary characters, animals) or described leisure, *costumbrista* or educational games and activities, all using a broad, varied and essentially visual thematic repertoire. They had religious origins: during Corpus Christi processions and Easter Sunday, small printed squares called *aleluyas* bearing religious imagery were thrown into the air. The squares were sold as a leaflet and cut up before being tossed during ceremonies.[82] In the 18th century, their content became more secular, sometimes even playful, with the incorporation of all manner of games, arts and trades along with natural history, animals, fables and the trope of the "world turned upside down".

From the 1820s, *aleluyas* turned political, reaching their zenith mid-century due to low production costs. In 1838, the traveller Charles Dembowski described a scene during *Semana Santa* or Holy Week (preceding Easter) in Madrid, when children scrambled to collect the *aleluyas* thrown from windows during a procession.[83] Along with prints of saints, "since politics has spread everywhere over the last three years", *aleluyas* depicted episodes from the Carlist War and from victories by liberal generals such as Espartero.[84] Religious media was used

80. *Ibid.*, pp. 586-588.

81. A *romance* was a short poem to be memorised and recited or sung in public. It was part of a tradition of popular literature in Spanish-speaking countries.

82. *Aleluyas. Juegos y literatura infantil en los pliegos de aleluyas españoles y europeos del siglo XIX*, ed. by Pedro C. Cerrillo and Jesús Maria Martínez González, Cuenca, Ediciones de la Universidad de Castilla-La Mancha, 2012, p. 15. See also the *Colección de aleluyas de la Fundación Joaquín Díaz* (https://funjdiaz.net/aleluyas1.php).

83. The custom remains alive during *Semana Santa* in Elche.

84. Charles Dembowski, *Dos años en España y Portugal durante la Guerra Civil, 1838-1840*, vol. I, Madrid, Espasa Calpe, 1931, p. 84. Adrian Shubert, *Espartero, el Pacificador*,

to depict political themes in the context of sacred rituals – such as *Semana Santa* – and to confer an air of divinity upon the liberal heroes.

The process originated during the *Trienio Liberal*. After all, this was a period characterised by innovation and experimentation around forms of propaganda aimed at the popular classes. Up to that point, the only explicitly political *aleluyas* were those in honour of royal ceremonies – in particular, the journey made by the monarchs to Barcelona in 1804 – or of military achievements during the War of Independence. The new paradigm of the *aleluya* dedicated to the Constitution was printed by Joan Noguera and published by the printer Ignacio Estivill in 1822 (Fig. 10).[85] This *aleluya* narrated the history of the Constitution, from its enactment in the *Cortes de Cádiz* through to its proclamation in 1820. Various editions were printed, some with titles (e.g., *Viva la Pepa*)[86] and some without, some in black and white and others in colour. The iconography on *aleluyas* was clearly distinct from that used on fans and snuffboxes, which highlights the existence of a form of popular iconography based on a specific tradition with close ties to religious practices and references. Other striking images are scenes depicting the absolutist repression and the failed liberal insurrections that took place between 1814 and 1820. General Luis Lacy would be given extraordinary protagonism, even becoming a martyr. Some eight vignettes – more than for any of the other protagonists of the proclamation of Cádiz – were created in his honour. Reverence for Lacy took hold among the working people of Barcelona, who turned him into a local martyr of freedom.[87]

Ribbons and cockades: political colours

Red was adopted as the national colour during the War of Independence. However, the splitting of the patriotic side along both liberal and royalist lines sparked the use of new colours. The army that was at the centre of the *pronunciamiento* of 1820 (known as the *Ejército de la Isla* or Island Army) began adding a green trim to the red cockade. In the *Cortes*, Quiroga proposed that green be added to red in all army units – a request that was denied.[88] Green became the colour of radical (*exaltado*) liberalism that (in contrast to the moderates) supported a deepening of the revolutionary process. Green ribbons were worn on hats or sewn onto cockades and often bore the motto

Madrid, Galaxia Gutenberg, 2018, photo 16; Joan Amades, Joan Colominas, Pep Vila, *Les auques*, Barcelona, editorial Orbis, 1931; Begoña Torres, *La col·lecció d'Auques del CESC*, vol. I, Sant Cebrià de Vallalta, Centre d'Estudis de Sant Cebrià, 2017.

85. Roca Vernet, "Las imágenes en la cultura política liberal", pp. 185-220.

86. The Cádiz Constitution was known as *La Pepa* because it was enacted on San Joseph's Day (*Pepe*, in Spanish), on March 19, 1812.

87. Jordi Roca Vernet, "La Revolución Liberal en España en clave trasnacional a través de la Amazona Emilia du Guermeur, viuda de la Luis Lacy", *Lacy, Revista de Estudios Sanroqueños*, 5 (2017), pp. 67-86.

88. *Diario de las actas y discusiones de las Cortes, Legislatura de 1820 y 1821*, vol. V, Madrid, Imprenta de las Cortes, 1820, pp. 177-179, from the session of 10/09/1820.

"Constitución o muerte".[89] As internal liberal divisions became wider, the most radical sectors began using purple ribbons in reference to the secret society of the *Comunería* (Confederación de los Caballeros Comuneros) (Fig. 11).[90] The *Comuneros* took their name from the revolt of the Communities of Castile against Charles I of Spain in 1520 and constituted the most radical shade of liberalism. They were opposed to the Freemasons, who were still identified by green. Much like the Italian *Carbonería*, Spanish liberal secret societies battled for political hegemony in the *Cortes* as well as in the press, the streets and the National Militia. Different coloured ribbons thus symbolised internal liberal divisions, such that the constitutionalists "were at war over a miserable ribbon at a time when everyone should only be warring with the enemies of the [liberal] system".[91]

Coloured ribbons were versatile and cheap and therefore became the political badge of choice. Green was sometimes complemented with yellow and red. Among the inscriptions are "Constitución por Riego" ("Constitution by Riego"), "Libertad o Muerte" ("Liberty or Death"), "Religión, Cortes, Libertad, Constitución o Muerte" ("Religion, Parliament, Liberty, Constitution or Death") and "Constitución o venganza y nunca alianza" ("Constitution or vengeance and never alliance").[92] During the second absolutist restoration (1823-1833), royalists adopted the white ribbon, whereas green or purple garments were considered tell-tale signs of liberalism.

The *Trienio Liberal* was a golden age for political objects in Spain. There were three parallel processes behind this. Firstly, the importation of political objects which were significantly influenced by French iconography and aimed at the elite. Secondly, experimentation with popular formats, such as crude pottery, portraits and *aleluyas*. These pieces are more difficult to track down but nonetheless had a decisive impact on everyday politicisation and the popular appropriation of liberal iconography. Some of these objects were linked to syncretic practices stemming from the religious uses to which prints had traditionally been put. Lastly, the use of certain colours and mottos embroidered on garments or accessories (ribbons, shawls or hats) led to the politicisation of clothing and the use of appearances to manifest a clear taking of sides in the public arena.

89. Antonio Alcalá Galiano, *Memorias de D. Antonio Alcalá Galiano, publicadas por su hijo*, Madrid, Vision Net, 2009 [1886], p. 359.

90. Marta Ruiz Jiménez, *El liberalismo exaltado. La confederación de comuneros españoles durante el Trienio Liberal*, Madrid, Fundamentos, 2007.

91. *El Diablo*, n. 24. Cited in Vicente León Navarro, "El Trienio Liberal (1820-1823) a través de la prensa valenciana", *El Argonauta español*, 17 (2020), at http://journals.openedition.org/argonauta/4035.

92. Pedro Rújula, *Constitución o muerte. El trienio liberal en Aragón y los levantamientos realistas. 1820-1823*, Zaragoza, Rolde de Estudios Aragoneses, 2000, p. 59; Sánchez Martín, *Rafael de Riego*, p. 752; Ramon Arnabat Mata, *Revolució i Contrarevolució a Catalunya durant el Trienni Liberal (1820-1823)*, PhD dissertation, Barcelona, Universitat Pompeu Fabra, 1999, p. 950, n. 191; Antonio Moliner Prada, "En torno al Trienio Constitucional (1820-1823)", *Rubrica Contemporánea*, 1 (2012), p. 36; AHN, leg. 12.271, exp. 5, 24/8/1823.

5. *Counter-revolutionary and royalist political objects during the absolutist restorations (1814-1820 and 1823-1833)*

The circulation of political objects diminished drastically during the absolutist restorations. The iconography on fans, snuffboxes and ceramic containers was limited to representations of Ferdinand VII, the Royal Family and commemorations of the monarchy.[93] French manufacturers adapted to the situation from 1823 and produced fans and snuffboxes with images of Ferdinand VII and the Duke of Angoulême. However, most of these pieces were designed for the French market, which demanded products commemorating victories by the French expedition sent to Spain to overthrow the liberal regime.[94] All manner of decorative objects were made depicting Spanish defeats in Madrid, Cádiz and Logroño. They include a fan showing the arrival of the Duke of Angoulême in Barcelona.[95]

Once again, the ceramics of Talavera are the exception. Most pieces from the period bore portraits of the king, though one jug shows royalist soldiers administering an enema to a liberal as punishment for his "impassioned love of the accursed Constitution [*su amor exaltado a la rea Constitución*]".[96] The iconography on prints was also more aligned with popular tastes by means of an aggressive anti-liberal discourse. One such piece portrayed the Constitution as the "monster of Cádiz", a diabolical figure that trod on symbols of the monarchy and the church, reflecting the eschatological nature of anti-liberal discourse.[97] The advertisement published in the press indicated that it should be purchased by "all faithful Christians", while "all liberals or *negros*"[98] should have one at home so as to remind them of their miserable situation "when getting out of bed, while eating and when going to sleep".[99] Other widespread prints represented the murder of the priest Vinuesa (an absolutist martyr killed in prison by a liberal mob in 1821), scenes from the secret societies of the *comuneros* and *carbonarios*, and Riego's imprisonment.[100]

After absolutism was restored in 1814 and 1823, a visual battle was undertaken to remove the memory of liberalism from the public realm.[101] The central roles of the king and religion in absolutist iconography were not the result of mere inertia or a lack of originality. The royalists attempted to appropriate the legitimacy of the monarchy and turned universal political references (God, King and Homeland

93. MHM, inv. 3.253; *Abanicos Rocamora*, n. 19, p. 21.

94. Emmanuel Larroche, *L'expédition d'Espagne. 1823: de la guerre selon la Charte*, Rennes, PUR, 2013.

95. Rocamora, *Museo de indumentaria*, see fan n. 88748.

96. Cabañas Bravo, "La imagen de Fernando VII", p. 249.

97. *El monstruo gaditano*, c. 1820, Real Biblioteca de Palacio, ARCH2/CART/2 (71).

98. *Negro* (black) was a derogatory term to refer to the liberals, as opposed to the royalist white (the colour of the Bourbon dynasty).

99. *El Procurador General del Rey*, n. 20, 17/6/1823, p. 100.

100. *El Procurador General del Rey*, supplement to n. 23, p. 118; *Diario de Madrid*, 25/11/1823, p. 6; *Diario de Madrid*, 19/10/1824, p. 3.

101. Carlos Reyero, "Absolutismo frente a liberalismo doceañista. El contraataque visual", *Hispania*, 256 (2017), pp. 407-436.

[*patria*]) into projectile weapons against the liberals.[102] The new "reactionary canon" tried to set itself apart from the visual vocabulary of liberalism by reinterpreting tradition in a partisan manner, in which the monarchy exclusively pertained to the counter-revolution.[103] The lack of new symbols stems from the fact that absolutism was not conceived as a new regime but as the restoration of a natural order that had been altered by the revolutionary catastrophe.

For normality to be restored, liberal objects had to be erased from the face of the Earth, as though they had never existed at all. Destroying them was a form of catharsis that re-sacralised the public space. Material evidence of liberalism had to be purged of its power using an iconoclasm driven by two forces: royalist crowds and the restored State. In the anti-liberal riots of 1814 and 1823, the constitutional plaques were dragged through the streets, allegorical statues were toppled and reminders of the overthrown regime were destroyed.[104] Copies of the Constitution, portraits of Riego and other liberal objects were publicly burned, and ceremonies were held to bury the Constitution in a parody of the traditional "Burial of the Sardine" after Carnival.[105] To hide constitutional objects was a sign of resistance, and repression created a new generation of liberal martyrs. The most famous example is Mariana Pineda, who was executed after a constitutional flag she was embroidering was found in her home.[106]

Portraits of Ferdinand VII became the political objects par excellence – as happened during the War of Independence – and were reproduced in all manner of everyday formats. In this case, however, they were used not as a unifying image against invading forces but as a weapon hurled against a domestic enemy: the liberals. Royalists tried to capitalise on the political legitimacy of the portraits, using traditional monarchical symbols against liberals who were excluded from the political community. Hence, restored absolutism "does not formulate a new visual language but redirects it using the prestige of memory".[107]

Religion, together with the figure of the king, was the glue of royalism. Anti-liberal guerrilla fighters carried crucifixes, scapulars and prints of the Virgin. One liberal caricature shows the guerrilla monk Antonio Marañón *el Trapense* ("the Trappist") carrying a rosary, a cross and a scapular around his neck. According to the monk, these protective amulets would make him impervious to enemy fire.[108]

102. *Ibid.*, p. 409.

103. Pedro Rújula, "Realismo y contrarrevolución en la Guerra de la Independencia", *Ayer*, 86 (2012), pp. 64-65.

104. Constitutional plaques were installed in every main town square to rename the latter the "Square of the Constitution". Royalists tore these plaques down, smashed them into pieces and dragged them through the streets to symbolically humiliate the liberal regime. Álvaro París, "La entrada de Fernando VII en Madrid", in *El viaje del rey. Fernando VII desde Valençay a Madrid*, ed. by Pedro Rújula, Zaragoza, Fundación Ibercaja, 2019, pp. 137-155.

105. On 24/4/1823; see Faustino Casamayor, *Años políticos e históricos de las cosas más particulares ocurridas en la imperial, augusta y siempre heroica ciudad de Zaragoza, 1822-1823* (ed. by Pedro Rújula), Zaragoza, Comuniter-Institución Fernando el Católico, forthcoming.

106. Juan Francisco Fuentes, Pilar Garí, *Amazonas de la libertad*, pp. 271-280.

107. Reyero, "Absolutismo frente a liberalismo", p. 431

108. Emmanuel Larroche, *L'expedition,* p. 239. Gérard Dufour, "'Roucouler la guerre; vociférer la paix': les événements d'Espagne de 1820 à 1823 dans les poèmes publiés par la

White cockades and ribbons were adopted as royalist symbols towards the end of the *Trienio Liberal*. White was traditionally the colour of the Bourbon Dynasty and was also used by the liberals on most military flags and standards.[109] In France, however, opposition to the Republican and Napoleonic tricolour flag had turned white into the colour of the royalists. In 1814, news reached Spain of white cockades and flags being raised in towns in the south of France saluting Napoleon's abdication.[110] French influence led Spain to begin associating white with royalism. However, this would not manifest itself clearly until the *Trienio Liberal*, when the royalists began using white cockades and ribbons to defy the regime.[111] On 13 June 1822, "various men" appeared in the main square of Almagro (Ciudad Real), "self-proclaimed defenders of the faith, wearing white cockades and urging others to wear them".[112] In May 1823, when General Bessières' royalist troops entered Madrid, working women took to the streets wearing white ribbons, singing royalist songs and chasing after liberals.[113]

The liberals began to be referred to pejoratively as *negros* (blacks), in opposition to the white of the royalists.[114] The name evoked the impure and heretical nature of supporters of the Constitution; they were to be expelled from the community like Jews.[115] Opposition between blacks and whites dominated the political language of the absolutist decade (1823-1833). The "blacks and whites nicknames" stoked street violence between the sides, while supporters of reconciliation called for the "disappearance of the dictates by blacks and whites which are so poisonous to the spirit".[116]

presse française de l'époque", *El Argonauta español*, 13 (2016), at http://journals.openedition.org/argonauta/2311.

109. Pedro Rújula, "Blanco: un color en el extremo de la política", in *Los colores de la política*, ed. by Jordi Canal, Zaragoza, Prensas Universitarias de Zaragoza (forthcoming); Luis Sorando Muzás, "Las banderas de las Guerras Carlistas", in *Las guerras carlistas*, ed. by Alfonso Bullón de Mendoza, Madrid, Ayuntamiento, Madrid, 2010, p. 210.

110. The *Gaceta de Madrid* makes as many as 12 references to the French white cockades over just two months – 9 April to 26 May 1814. Pierre Triomphe, *1815: La Terreur blanche*, Toulouse, Privat, 2017; Emmanuel Fureix, "Police des signes, ordre et désordre urbains en temps de crise (1814-1816)", *Histoire urbaine*, 43 (2015), pp. 157-176.

111. Rújula, "Blanco".

112. Juan Díaz Pintado, "Reacción absolutista y desórdenes en La Mancha (1814-1822)", *Cuadernos de Historia Contemporánea*, 16 (1994), p. 59.

113. *Nuevo diario de Madrid*, 21/05/1823; Estanislao de Kostka Bayo, *Historia de la vida y reinado de Fernando VII*, vol. III, Madrid, Repullés, 1842, p. 88.

114. Jordi Canal, "Matar negros, hacer blancos: Los colores y los nombres del enemigo en las guerras civiles de la España contemporánea", *Espacio, Tiempo y Forma, Historia Contemporánea*, 20 (2008), pp. 19-36.

115. Álvaro París, "Porque le olía a negro: vestimenta, costumbres y politización popular en Madrid (1750-1840)", in *Procesos de civilización: culturas de élites, culturas populares. Una historia de contrastes y tensiones (siglos XVI-XIX)*, ed. by José María Imízcoz, Máximo García and Javier Esteban, Bilbao, Universidad del País Vasco, 2019, pp. 99-132.

116. AHN, Consejos, leg. 12.292, police reports 14/7/1825 and 27/7/1825, celador [secret agent] 3 and AHN, Consejos, leg. 12.312, police report 27/06/1825, celador 5.

Throughout the persecution of liberals during the absolutist restorations of 1814 and 1823, clothing and accessories also took on political meaning. In Madrid, royalist crowds attacked those wearing certain types of hats, ties and accessories, such as beret caps or shoe straps (known as *galgas*) worn by women.[117] Such garments were considered signs of liberalism. These foreign fashions, adopted by the middle and upper classes, transgressed traditional attire and popular customs. From the late 18th century, the working people of Madrid began identifying the new types of clothing as a French-influenced innovation. Those who adopted them were called *petimetres*, *currutacos* or *lechuguinos* (all roughly translating as "dandies").[118] The widespread image of the liberal individual was built upon these stereotypes. Elegant men sporting frock coats (*levitas*), or women wearing fashionable hats, were labelled as *negros* (blacks). Liberals were identified not only by their ideas or political expression but by their dress and manners. Royalist crowds pulled off people's hats and ties because "they were, as was said, signs of freemasonry".[119] Dionisio Chaulié tells of a "screaming crowd" of royalists running through the working-class neighbourhood of Barquillo (Madrid). Elegant gentlemen ripped the tassels from their shoes while women removed their shoe straps, so as to not be exposed to "that savage horde hunting down the constitutionalists".[120] The wearers of such items did not necessarily think of them as being explicitly political, unlike green and purple ribbons. However, one sector of the working people identified foreign fashions with liberal ideas, associating them with new cultural customs and habits promoted by merchants, liberal professionals and the middle and upper classes.[121]

During the absolutist restorations, a green or purple ribbon, a hat or a cap were sufficient grounds for a street fight that could have mortal consequences. The codes that governed the politicisation of everyday clothing are complex, though police sources are helpful in reconstructing them. One person from Madrid was almost beaten in a café for wearing "an otter skin cap",[122] while royalists stated that the *negros* (blacks) "have begun wearing little low-crown hats, in the Portuguese style, and we must therefore declare war and strike them down".[123] A black ribbon on a watch triggered a quarrel in a billiard hall. Another subject walking through a working-class district sporting a hat and a handkerchief was beaten because he "smelled liberal [*olía a negro*]".[124] Pedestrians were chased "for adorning their clothing with anything green or purple, or for wearing caps or *cachuchas*, a sort of beret that many liberals used

117. París, "Porque le olía a negro", pp. 100-105.

118. Rebecca Haidt, *Women, Work and Clothing in Eighteenth-Century Spain*, Oxford, SVEC, 2011.

119. Ramón de Mesonero Romanos, *Memorias de un setentón*, Barcelona, Crítica, 2008, p. 160.

120. Chaulié, *Cosas de Madrid*, p. 167.

121. París, "*Se susurra en los barrios bajos*".

122. AHN, Consejos, leg. 12.335, police report 30/12/1825, celador 3

123. AHN, Consejos, leg. 12.335, police report 24/12/1825, celador 6.

124. AHN, Consejos, leg. 12.317, police report April 1827, and AHN, Consejos, leg. 12.342, police report 27/6/1825.

at that time".[125] According to Kostka Bayo, a group of civilians walking around Santander wearing caps were beaten by royalist volunteers who "destroyed" the caps and left their wearers gravely wounded.[126]

Aggression was also aimed in the opposite political direction. In 1835, a bakery boy from Madrid was injured with a sabre by a member of the Urban Militia who told him that "the *chambergo* [wide-brimmed hat] he wore was used by many others in the neighbourhood with the same ideas".[127] Carlist ideas were the problem on this occasion, though the boy insisted that "he wore the hat for work".

6. *The regency of Maria Christina and the* Trienio Progresista *(1833-1843)*

During the regency of Maria Christina (1833-1840), the foundations were put in place for a constitutional system that sought to distance itself from its revolutionary origins. The regent tried to appeal to moderate liberals while retaining the loyalty of the absolutist elites and public servants. She enacted a charter – the Royal Statute of 1834 – and sought to establish a "middle ground". These reforms caused unrest among the ultra-royalist sectors, which rallied around the Infante Don Carlos (Ferdinad VII's brother) to support his claim to the throne. This led to a seven-year civil war (1833-1840) fought between the *carlistas* (loyal to the pretender Charles V) and the *isabelinos* or *cristinos* (loyal to Isabella II). During this period, the monarchy's priority was to reinforce its legitimacy against Carlism. Therefore, political objects were less abundant and more conventional than in the preceding and subsequent liberal periods. The monarchy was placed at the centre of political iconography and was depicted as the guarantor of Spanish reconciliation in the face of the instability created by the civil war.

Propaganda during the *Trienio Liberal* was notably novel and focused on the Constitution. During the regency of Maria Christina, however, the monarchy regained its pre-eminence in political representations of the liberal regime. The most common political objects commemorated royal events (weddings and baptisms) and the queen's travels to the provinces.[128] The few fans that we have been able to track down extol the figure of the regent as the author of Spanish reconciliation and union, as well as the Royal Family, the enactment of the amnesty decree of 1834, the Constitution of 1837 and the Convention of Vergara, which put an end to the Carlist War in 1839.[129] Other items include two commemorative

125. Vicente de la Fuente, *Historia de las sociedades secretas antiguas y modernas de España, especialmente de la Franc-Masonería*, vol. I, Lugo, Soto Freire, 1870, p. 424; Chaulié, *Cosas de Madrid*, p. 212.

126. Kostka Bayo, *Historia de la vida y reinado*, vol. III, p. 246.

127. AHN, Consejos, leg. 12.349, 24/3/1835.

128. Rocamora, *Museo de indumentaria*, see handkerchiefs nos 89246, 89247, 88807 and 88808.

129. Rocamora, *Museo de indumentaria*, see fans nos 88806, 88778, 88770 and 88806. The fan depicting the Convention of Vergara is in Manuel Rocamora, *Abanicos históricos*, 1956, p. 32. MFM Fan Collection, one of them dedicated to the Constitution of 1837.

handkerchiefs – one dedicated to the amnesty decree of 1834, and the other to the opening of the new *Cortes* under the Royal Statute.[130]

Fans and handkerchiefs alike were made in Spanish factories, though production levels and circulation were considerably lower compared to the 1820s. All of this is evidence of the decline of this type of production, which was transitioning towards new forms of representation and new objects, as the subsequent period shows. The thematic variety and complex symbology of fans from the *Trienio Liberal* also disappeared. What this shows is that the iconography that was closely tied to the French revolutionary process did not take root in Spain, and in later stages of the Liberal process would not be reused. The reduction in the number of fans may also suggest that the political engagement of middle- and upper-class women – significant during the *Trienio* – was limited in later stages of the Liberal Revolution.

Prints for the masses, on the other hand, boasted more novel and varied content. Along with *aleluyas* are a multitude of *romances*, calendars, flyers, prints and cordel literature with political motives. One of the most interesting formats were *ventalls*, the popular and affordable version of fans designed for the elites. *Ventalls* were loose quarto sheets bearing an illustration along with a short text written in verse that could be memorised and sung. They were folded around a cane to create a rigid fan (see Fig. 12). They cost a mere quarter[131] and, in addition to being practical, provided information on the current political situation and enabled the exchange of information by reciting it aloud. The acid wit of the texts and images, which catered to working-class tastes, also provided entertainment.[132] Early examples had conventional images of the monarchy, including Maria Christina approving decrees or of Queen Isabella II. As the political conflict worsened, propaganda emerged against the Carlists (*facciosos* or rebels), the moderates (*pasteleros* or turncoats) and the reactionary clergy, as well as tributes to the Constitution of 1837 and to Espartero. *Ventalls* were a simplified version of *romances* containing much less text and putting the image at centre stage. They were suited to an almost illiterate audience and could be adapted to the latest political events.

The end of the Carlist War generated a new phase of the Liberal Revolution with the exile of Maria Christina and the ascent of General Baldomero Espartero – who capitalised on the liberal victory – to the regency. The politicisation of society throughout the *Trienio Progresista* (1840-1843) went hand in hand with a new proliferation of political objects. The Isabelline monarchy was relegated to the background in favour of the popular General Espartero. Two handkerchiefs were created in his honour (this form of political propaganda had been reserved until then for the Royal Family).[133] Handkerchiefs bearing images of Espartero were

130. Rocamora, *Museo de indumentaria*, see handkerchiefs nos 89235 and 89305.

131. A *real* was equal to 8 and a half quarters. The average wage of a labourer could be up to 5 or 6 *reales* per day.

132. Corrales, "La imageria constitucional", pp. 47-77, and Laura Corrales, *L'estampa i la primera guerra carlina a Catalunya (1833-1840)*, PhD dissertation, Universitat de Barcelona, 2014.

133. Some exceptions include the handkerchief dedicated to the Constitution of 1812 produced in France: Rocamora, *Museo de indumentaria*, see handkerchief n. 89233.

produced in the "Bouquet à Deville"[134] factory in Rouen. There are no traces of any being produced in Spain. He was also honoured with fans that depicted him signing the Convention of Vergara with Carlist general Maroto, or proclaiming the Constitution of 1837 amid public acclaim. As happened with the image of Riego, that of Espartero was circulated on all manner of personal objects (tobacco cases [*petacas*], cigarette cases, paperweights and portraits) primarily aimed at men.[135] The regent was always depicted in military dress, though sometimes wearing different uniforms and in different positions (on horseback, looking straight ahead, to one side, etc.). These objects highlight how widespread Espartero-worship was among liberals. Until then, tobacco and cigarette cases were not typically used for political propaganda. The politicisation of this personal object is also testament to the exploration of new and innovative propaganda formats connected to tobacco and alcohol consumption. This particular political object was designed for a largely male audience. In turn, the object itself came to reinforce a model of masculinity based on military heroism, tobacco and alcohol consumption, and exaltation of the regent's plebeian origins.

Espartero was also depicted on more popular and affordable items including printed portraits, *aleluyas*, pottery, tile inscriptions and more.[136] One pottery dish from Manises (Valencia) shows the general swearing the Constitution of 1837, along with the inscription "Constitución o muerte" that directly referenced the final year of the *Trienio Liberal*, when this motto became widespread (Fig. 13).[137]

Prints with his portrait were widely circulated among the working people, who eventually erected small altars in their homes where they worshipped, lit candles and honoured his saint (San Baldomero, celebrated on the 27th of February).[138] Writing to him was a widespread custom and his letters of reply were exhibited as heirlooms in people's homes. One follower of Espartero wrote to him in 1869 to tell him that they had celebrated his saint since 1836 and that they kept his letter behind glass with the print of his portrait, which they illuminated with candles on special occasions.[139] Much like events during the *Trienio Liberal*, the politicisation of the working classes led to the emergence of new objects that moved away from languages exclusively focused on the monarchy and royal commemorations. Depictions of constitutional heroes (such as Lacy, Riego and Espartero) in affordable formats for mass consumption reflected not only the prestige these leaders held among the working people but the emergence of a new form of popular liberalism. Worship of their portraits in the domestic setting

134. Rocamora, *Museo de indumentaria*, see handkerchiefs nos 89248 and 89249, the latter with a portrait of Espartero.

135. Collection of objects in the Museu d'Història in Barcelona [MUHBA]: cigarette cases nos 830, 828, 826, 848 and 827; snuffbox n. 832; glass paperweight with portrait of Espartero n. 848; and miniature portrait with registration number nos 831, 829 and 845.

136. Adrian Shubert, *Espartero, el Pacificador*, see figures 8 and 9.

137. Museo Nacional de Cerámica y Artes Suntuarias González Martín, inv. CE1/01939.

138. Adrian Shubert, "Being – and Staying – Famous in 19th-Century Spain: Baldomero Espartero and the Birth of Political Celebrity", *Historia y Política*, 34 (2015), pp. 211-237.

139. *Ibid.*, pp. 220-221. Daniel Aquillué, *Armas y votos. Politización y conflictividad política en España, 1833-1843*, Zaragoza, Institución "Fernando el Católico", 2020, pp. 214-215.

demonstrates the connection that everyday life and popular religious repertoires had with the civic and political culture of the liberal masses.

7. *Carlist objects (1833-1840)*

Research into political objects has generally looked at the construction of revolutionary identities, with a focus on objects linked to ideas from the French Revolution, Bonapartism and nationalism. What is clear is that counter-revolutionaries, royalists and legitimists contributed just as much as their enemies to the circulation of political objects. Not only did they imitate revolutionary models but used specific formats, including anagrams and symbols representing legitimate dynasties, or made political use of scapulars of the Sacred Heart and other religious artefacts.[140] Counter-revolutionary irredentism gave rise to a panoply of objects which were used all throughout the 19th and 20th centuries to carry memory of the "lost cause".[141] Successive defeats drove the legitimists to cling to the idea of continuity, and they established material links between the various stages of the resistance and the different candidates for the throne.

Carlist objects were primarily inspired by French counter-revolutionary objects that circulated during the *Vendée*, the *Chouannerie* and the Restoration. Among the most representative objects are white cockades, scapulars of the Sacred Heart with the motto "Dieu et Roi", crosses bearing royalist slogans and all manner of pendants and broches with the Bourbon Fleur de Lis. Carlist objects also inherited Spanish royalist iconography. Like the royalists from 1820 to 1833, the Carlists were considered the true defenders of the monarchy and religion, hence their political objects were designed to reinforce these pillars of traditional legitimacy. The main goal of Carlist propaganda was to fight with the liberals over the traditional principles embodied by the "God, King and Homeland" trinity rather than to create new symbols.[142] The declaration of these familiar and well-known principles was enough to ensure that Carlist objectives reached a broad audience. In fact, their vagueness and universality were the keys to their effectiveness. Carlist flags were similar to those flown by the liberal army and bore additional inscriptions such as "Carlos V" ("Charles V") or "Dios, Patria, Rey, legitimidad" ("God, King, Homeland, legitimacy") along with religious images, particularly of the Immaculate Conception.[143]

140. Katrina Navickas, "The 'Spirit of Loyalty': Material Culture, Space and the Construction of an English Loyalist Memory", in *Loyalism and the Formation of the British World, 1775-1914*, ed. by Allan Blackstock and Frank O'Gorman, Woodbridge, Boydell & Brewer, 2014, pp. 43-60.

141. Eduardo González Calleja and Carmine Pinto (eds.), special issue, "Cause perdute. Memorie, rappresentazioni e miti dei vinti", *Meridiana*, 88 (2017); Jordi Canal, *Banderas blancas, boinas rojas. Una historia política del carlismo*, Madrid, Marcial Pons, 2006.

142. Jordi Canal, *El carlismo. Dos siglos de contrarrevolución en España*, Madrid, Alianza, 2000, pp. 19-22.

143. Ramón Guirao Larrañaga, Luis Sorando Muzas, "Banderas carlistas de la primera guerra (1833-1840)", *Aportes*, 25 (2004), pp. 29-40; Luis Sorando Muzás, "Las banderas de las Guerras Carlistas", in *Las guerras carlistas*, pp. 206-217.

During the Carlist War, images of the pretender Charles V circulated on prints and portraits alongside those of his most popular generals, including Zumalacárregui and Cabrera. There are also examples of boxes and other objects engraved with the motto "Dios, Patria y Rey" and the initials CV (Charles V). One fine example is a silver lighter with the initials CV and the motto "un Dios, una Ley, un Rey" ("one God, one Law, one King")(Fig. 14).[144]

Scapulars and religious prints proliferated much like in the preceding periods. The most original variants of these were called "detentes". These scapulars of the Sacred Heart were manufactured on fabric and sewn onto clothing as a talisman to protect fighters from enemy fire. They typically bore the inscriptions "detente bala, el sagrado corazón de Jesús está conmigo" ("stop, bullet, the Sacred Heart of Jesus is with me"), hence their name.[145] Carlist women were responsible for making the scapulars in the rear guard.[146]

The Carlist object *par excellence* was undoubtedly the beret. It was adopted by the Carlist battalions and became a symbol steeped in mythology that persists today. Berets began being used in the Basque Country and Navarre during the First Carlist War (1833-1840) as an alternative to the flamboyant and cumbersome shako (a cylindrical military hat). Berets were comfortable, cheap and versatile and were adopted as the regulation headgear both by the Carlists and by some liberal regiments in the north. The Carlists wore different coloured berets (red, blue or white) and their use soon spread to the army of the Maestrazgo region (Aragon and Valencia).[147] The beret gradually came to be identified as a Carlist symbol – an image that entered the popular imagination through prints and illustrations in the press. A garment that was likely adopted for practical reasons (lack of uniforms and comfort) thus came to be a symbol that Carlist sympathisers sported in civilian life. In 1838, Espartero (then Supreme Commander of the Northern Army) made a proclamation prohibiting the wearing of berets, which he considered the "particular emblem of those who make war against the legitimate rights of our august Queen Isabella".[148] In his memoirs, the Italian Pietro Bubani says that he was arrested in 1844 in Pamplona by a police officer convinced he was a Carlist because he wore the typical beret of the Basque lands.[149] Red slowly became the dominant colour, though the red beret as the movement's emblem of choice did not become widespread until the second half of the 19th century.

144. Javier Urcelay Alonso, "El Museo Carlista de Madrid", *Aportes*, 34 (2019), p. 251.

145. Pedro Rújula, "Carlismo", in *Los símbolos de la política*, ed. by Francisco Fuentes Aragonés (forthcoming).

146. Gloria Martínez Dorado, *Estado y acción colectiva: España y la primera guerra carlista*, PhD dissertation, Universidad Autónoma de Madrid, 2017, p. 116.

147. Carlos Canales Torres, "Los uniformes de las Guerras Carlistas", in *Las guerras carlistas*, pp. 185-205.

148. Logroño, 27 November 1838.

149. Mikel Alberdi Sagardia, *Txapela. La boina en el siglo XIX*, Museo Zumalakarregi, 2019, https://www.zumalakarregimuseoa.eus/es/actividades/investigacion-y-documentacion/txapena-la-boina-en-el-siglo-xix; Francisco Fuentes Aragonés, Isabel Martín Sánchez, "Boina/sombrero: una dicotomía social y simbólica en la España del siglo XIX", *Historia y Política*, 43 (2020), pp. 225-254.

Lastly, coins minted during the war in regions controlled by the Carlists would become amulets throughout subsequent decades.[150] The ability to mint money was one essential attribute of sovereignty. It enabled Carlism to position itself as the embodiment of a legitimate State with effective control over the territory. Stamps and medallions handed down from generation to generation to keep tradition and collective memory alive also played an important symbolic role.[151] In short, the Carlists did not stop at copying models used by the liberals but used objects in a novel way to drive their propaganda campaigns.[152]

8. *Conclusion*

Political objects in Spain can be divided into three main categories. Firstly, we found artefacts created in France and Britain following foreign models, aimed at the middle and upper classes. Secondly, there were objects produced locally, with a simpler design and lower cost and bearing iconography more aligned with the taste of the working classes. Finally, there were those garments and accessories which lacked an explicit political message but were "politicised" in specific social contexts.

During the War of Independence and the *Trienio Liberal*, French workshops produced fans, snuffboxes and tableware for both the Spanish and French markets, inspired by models from the French Revolution but adapted to national peculiarities. Some of these objects fed into a transnational revolutionary material culture in which portraits of Napoleon, Riego and Kitsos Tzavellas (hero of the Greek War of Independence) circulated widely throughout southern Europe. Political propaganda became transnational, and it had the potential to turn every day-to-day object into a political object.[153]

Some objects such as fans, handkerchiefs, gloves and shawls were specifically aimed at women. Others, like tableware and jugs, had a domestic decorative function. Thus, political objects became a channel for the politicisation of women, allowing the latter to build a direct relationship with the symbolic aspects of politics. The images of international revolutionary heroines – such as the Eleonora Pimentel Fonseca and Luisa Sanfelice from Italy, Manto Mavrogenous from Greece or the Anne-Josèphe Théroigne de Méricourt from France – circulated in Spain during the *Trienio Liberal.* These female exemplars, along with national examples including Maria Pineda, contributed to stimulating the political engagement of Spanish women. Liberal women from Barcelona drew

150. Fausto Antonio Moya Cendán, "Breve tratado de la moneda carlista", *Aportes*, 25 (1994), pp. 9-27.

151. Eduardo Escalada-Goicoechea, "Los sellos carlistas", *Aportes*, 25 (1994), pp. 41-51.

152. Canal, *Banderas blancas*, pp. 131-135; Julio Nombela, *Detrás de las trincheras. Páginas íntimas de la guerra y la paz desde 1868 hasta 1876*, Madrid, Imprenta de Manuel Hernández, 1876, pp. 230-231.

153. Angélique Amandry, "Le philhellénisme en Frances à travers les étiquettes Comerciales", *Revue de la Bibliothèque Nationale*, 9 (1983), pp. 12-21.

inspiration from Girondin Théroigne de Méricourt of France when designing the attire for local militiawomen.

The years of the *Trienio Liberal* were the golden age for political fans and handkerchiefs. However, these items declined during the regency of Maria Christina (1833-1840), creating space for objects dedicated to the Royal Family and the commemoration of royal events. The 1840s marked a new era for political objects. The number and diversity of the artefacts aimed at the elites decreased, while those aimed at the working classes flourished. Prints in different formats – portraits, *aleluyas* and *ventalls* – played a crucial role. These affordable and versatile objects could be used either in a domestic context or attached to clothing. The political use of prints was linked to religious practices. Moreover, their motifs reflected the existence of different forms of popular iconography to those found on objects aimed at the middle and upper classes.

The proliferation of political objects devoted to the regent Baldomero Espartero (1840-1843) led to a cult of his personality, taking the fame previously reached by Riego to a new level. Espartero became the most popular person in Spain after the Queen herself. His humble origins and his military victories against the Carlists earnt him an unprecedented level of popularity which was translated into the proliferation of all manner of objects for all social groups. During this period, political objects became a very profitable business. The Espartero cult became a model for subsequent progressive liberal leaders such as Juan Prim.

Finally, along with iconography, colours (green, purple, black or white) were associated with opposing political projects. Wearing a ribbon or a hat was sufficient grounds for a quarrel in the streets and in public houses. Political objects and their wearers were chased and harassed, so that everyday life became stepped in political conflict.

In conclusion, from the War of Independence onwards, political objects became a crucial platform for the expression of political commitment to revolution and counter-revolution. The study of these artefacts allows us to explore new paths for politicisation which complemented the press, public speeches and official symbols. Everyday objects reveal the ordinary ways in which political discourses and collective identities were appropriated. Through these objects, normal people identified themselves with new political projects, and endorsed and translated these to align with their own experiences. The traditional focus on formal and institutional politics, on written statements and on parliamentary life tend to conceal the everyday aspects of politics "from below". Political objects opened the door to a broader conception of politics, in which ordinary people adopted new discourses and practices not by passively absorbing them, but by interpreting them on their own terms.

1. Fan with scene from the Dos de Mayo Uprising in Madrid, Behrmann & Collmann (London), 1813. Museo de armería de Álava, inv. 0771.
2 a-b. Ceramic jugs from Talavera de la Reina. On the left, portrait of the guerrilla and general Juan Palarea, *El Médico*, c. 1815. Museo Nacional del Romanticismo, inv. CE0359, photographer: Pablo Linés Viñuales. On the right, portrait of Ferdinand VII. Museo Ruiz de Luna de Talavera de la Reina, CE3493, Ministerio de Cultura y Deporte.

3. Patriotic calling cards (1814). Juan Carrafa, sheet of calling cards illustrated with episodes from the War of Independence. Ayuntamiento de Madrid, Museo de Historia de Madrid, inv. 2223.

4. Depiction of a vegetable farmer with prints, patriotic ribbon and scapular. *Viva España. Muera Napoleon*, printed anonymously (1808-1813). British Museum, 1878,0112.29, 331346001, ©The Trustees of the British Museum. All rights reserved.
5. Fan depicting the *Exaltation of Riego*. Ayuntamiento de Madrid, Museo de Historia de Madrid, inv. 5154.

6 a-b. Snuffboxes, c. 1820. On the left, portraits of the four heroes of the proclamation of 1820: Quiroga, Riego, Baños and Arco Agüero. Ayuntamiento de Madrid, Museo de Historia de Madrid, inv. 2616. On the right, scene depicting the King's constitutional oath. Ayuntamiento de Madrid, Museo de Historia de Madrid, inv. 2605-A.

7. "Compacts powders" containing examples of the Constitution of 1812, c. 1820. Creator: F. Henrionnet. Museo Nacional del Romanticismo, inv. CE1192, photographer: Pablo Linés. Viñuales.

8. Deck of constitutional playing cards. Museo Fournier de Naipes de Álava, inv. 44514.
9 a-b. Constitutional coffee set and coffee cups. On the left, a man in working-class dress reads as two gentlemen watch. On the right, a man hands out newspapers or leaflets to a lady. Ayuntamiento de Madrid, Museo de Historia de Madrid, inv. 2583 and inv. 2571.

10. Constitutional aleluya. Ayuntamiento de Madrid, Museo de Historia de Madrid, inv. 4949.
11 a-b. (above, opposite page) Green, red and purple ribbons. Ayuntamiento de Valencia, Biblioteca Serrano Morales, box 7286/82. Green ribbon (with the motto "Constitución o muerte") and red ribbon ("Constitución y orden"). The inscriptions on the purple ribbon read "Vivan los hijos de Padilla" and "Viva Riego sin mandil".

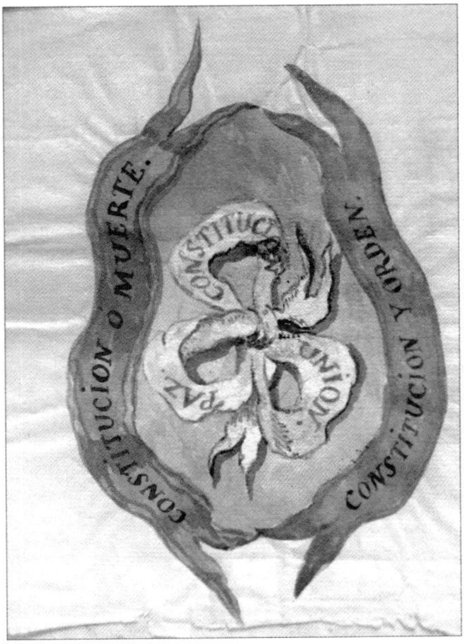

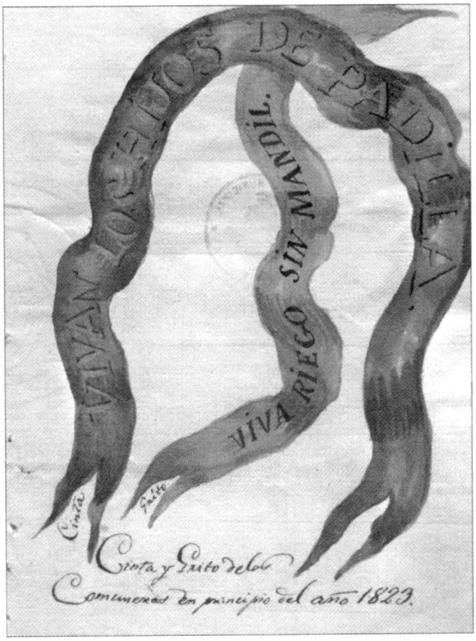

12 a-b. *Ventalls*.On the left, *ventall* of *El faccioso rendido*; Biblioteca de Catalunya, Barcelona, Ms. 1086/18 (f. 259). On the right, examples of assembled *ventalls*, Colección Domènech-Ballester, photo courtesy of Albert Domènech, http://librorum.piscolabis.cat.

13. Dish with portrait of Espartero. Museo Nacional de Cerámica "González Martí", inv. CE1/01939, photographer: Javier Rodríguez Barrera.
14. Silver Carlist lighter. Museo Carlista de Madrid. Photo courtesy of Javier Urcelay.

Simon Morgan

Material Radicalism: Commemorative Ceramics and Political Narratives in the Age of Peterloo

In the 18th and 19th centuries, commemorative ceramics were used to convey political messages of all kinds. Some were specific to a particular time or place, commemorating individual contested elections, for example; others had national significance. The advent of transfer printing in the 1760s, by which two-dimensional images could be transferred to three-dimensional pots, jugs and plates, allowed for more accurate depictions of individuals than could be achieved through hand-painting, and it also facilitated the reproduction of sophisticated satires to be spread through pottery. The combination of words and images, each serving to inform and enhance the meaning of the other, meant that political pots functioned as "iconotexts".[1] Political pottery therefore became an extension of print culture, contributing to the wider political discourse conducted in pamphlets, newspapers and broadsides. However, the constraints of the form limited the amount of information that could be conveyed. As with political images, meaning was inferred through the use of easily recognisable tropes and simple iconography. Political ceramics therefore aided the process of simplifying, fixing and popularising political narratives around specific events and personalities.[2]

This chapter focuses on the ceramic legacy of the British Peterloo massacre of 1819. Unlike previous treatments of Peterloo objects, it places this pottery into its broader context, which included not only earlier radical ceramics, but also the flourishing production of loyalist commemoratives during the long years of war against France. Moreover, by interpreting the pottery in the context of contemporary visual and print media, the aim is to highlight the distinctive role of ceramics within the broader coalescence of a radical narrative of the events of 16 August 1819 and their aftermath. It argues that the various radical or sympathetic representations of Peterloo came to focus on three elements: the indiscriminate and cowardly violence of the yeomanry; the plight of the defenceless victims, especially women and children; and the heroic role of Henry Hunt, the man whose arrest had been the ostensible objective of the soldiery, and whose trial and subsequent imprisonment became the focus of attempts to obtain justice for the

1. Peter Wagner, *Reading Iconotexts: From Swift to the French Revolution*, London, Reaktion Books, 1995.

2. Simon Morgan, "Material Culture and the Politics of Personality in Early Victorian England", *Journal of Victorian Culture*, 17/2 (2012), pp. 127-146.

murdered and maimed. By combining two or more of those elements, the pottery helped to construct meaningful narratives of the event, with a discernible shift from the anger of the immediate aftermath, focused on the brutality of the cavalry and the innocence of their victims, to the search for justice and legal redress, which ultimately centred on Hunt's trial.

In August 1819, the United Kingdom was shocked by the sudden, violent dispersal of a peaceful reform meeting at St Peter's Fields in Manchester, which led to the deaths of ten men, four women and one child, and the injury of over 650 others.[3] The event has come down to posterity as "Peterloo": a name coined in bitter mockery of the Manchester and Cheshire yeomanry cavalry, implicitly contrasting their actions with the heroics of the British Army and its allies at Waterloo, just four years prior. As an event that seared itself into the national consciousness, Peterloo generated a substantial material legacy. This ranged from relics purporting to be from the field itself, including truncheons, cavalry sabres and radical symbols, to the myriad prints and artefacts produced after the event to condemn or commemorate it.[4] In the first wave came the biting print satires produced by the likes of S.W. Fores and George Cruickshank, which were quickly reproduced in cheap editions or translated onto other media such as calico handkerchiefs, soon circulating as far afield as Ireland, and a wide assortment of ceramic mugs and jugs.[5]

By 1819, there was an established tradition of public events being exploited as commercial opportunities by British potters. In the 18th century, occasions ranging from contested elections to military victories had been commemorated in this way.[6] Moreover, the faces of public figures were frequently depicted, from admirals and generals to the Methodist preacher John Wesley, making ceramics a key, if under-appreciated, medium in the spread of a nascent culture of celebrity.[7] Transfer printing allowed mass-produced popular prints to be reproduced on three-dimensional surfaces with little loss of quality, establishing a close connection between the print trade and the potters.[8] The shift towards mass production in

3. The definitive account of the massacre is now Robert Poole, *Peterloo: The English Uprising*, Oxford, Oxford University Press, 2019. For counts of the dead and estimates of the wounded, I have relied on Michael L. Bush, *The Casualties of Peterloo*, Lancaster, Carnegie, 2005. While the basic facts of the day are mostly undisputed, the causes of the massacre have been hotly debated. See Robert Poole, "'By the Law or the Sword': Peterloo Revisited", *History*, 91/302 (2006), pp. 254-276.

4. Chris Burgess, "The Objects of Peterloo", in Robert Poole (ed.), "Return to Peterloo", *Manchester Region History Review*, 23 (2012), pp. 159-167; Eric Taplin, "Peterloo Artefacts", *Manchester Region History Review*, 3/1 (1989), pp. 91-94.

5. See Diana Donald, "The Power of Print: Graphic Images of Peterloo", *Manchester Region History Review*, 3/1 (1989), pp. 21-30.

6. John May, Jennifer May, *Commemorative Pottery 1780-1900: A Guide for Collectors*, London, Heinemann, 1972.

7. Antoine Lilti, *The Invention of Celebrity*, trans. by Lynn Jeffress, Cambridge, Polity Press, 2017.

8. David Drakard, *Printed English Pottery: History and Humour in the Reign of George III, 1760-1820*, London, Johnathan Horne, 1992.

the 18th century saw the industry become concentrated and organised. However, commemorative pottery should not be seen simply as a kind of three-dimensional print. As John Brewer noted in relation to the Wilkesite teapots produced during the 1760s, the fact that many of them took the form of practical objects such as jugs, bowls, teapots and cups meant that they could potentially play a rather more active role in the performance of political identity and ritual than a two-dimensional image hanging passively on the wall.[9]

The identity being performed was not always radical or subversive. The majority of ceramic objects turned out in the 1780s, 1790s and 1800s were loyalist and patriotic in nature: ranging from simple respectful depictions of Nelson, Wellington or members of the Royal Family, to more satirical commentaries on such enemies of the status quo as Tom Paine, Charles James Fox and Napoleon Bonaparte.[10] There was even a good trade in (presumably decorative) ceramic chamber-pots enclosing a miniature bust of "Boney", inviting observers to envisage venting their coprological contempt upon the Corsican corporal.[11] Indeed, the prevalence of loyalist pottery in these years has led one recent commentator to conclude that Peterloo represented the first use of ceramics to commemorate a radical political event.[12]

In fact, there was a long tradition of subversive ceramics in the British Isles, going back to the Jacobite artefacts of the late 17th and early 18th centuries.[13] One of the earliest recognisably radical outpourings came via the teapots and other artefacts produced to commemorate John Wilkes' elections for Westminster and his persecution by the authorities over the infamous "Number 45" of the *North Briton* in the 1760s.[14] The so-called "Pittite terror" encouraged radicals to greater circumspection after 1793, but as the Napoleonic Wars ground on, and Pitt himself was succeeded by lesser men, criticism of the government became increasingly open, with some notable events leaving their mark in the material record. In 1809, the scandal around the Duke of York's dalliance with Mrs Clarke and allegations of the corrupt disposal of army commissions saw the whistle-blowers Miss Mary Taylor and Col. Wardle MP fêted in the capital. Consequently, commemorative medals and jugs were produced bearing their portraits, alongside satires of Clarke and the Duke.[15] In 1812, ceramics appeared carrying non-caricatured images of

9. Neil McKendrick, John Brewer, J.H. Plumb, *The Birth of a Consumer Society: The Commercialization of Eighteenth-Century England*, London, Europa Publications, 1982, pp. 197-262.

10. Examples of all of these can be found in the Willett Collection, Brighton Museum (hereafter Willett Collection).

11. For example, Willett Collection, R4554/7.

12. Alison Morgan, "Starving Mothers and Murdered Children in Cultural Representations of Peterloo", in Poole (ed.), "Return to Peterloo", pp. 65-78, 71.

13. Neil Guthrie, *The Material Culture of the Jacobites*, Cambridge, Cambridge University Press, 2014; Murray Pittock, *Material Culture and Sedition, 1688-1760: Treacherous Objects, Secret Places*, Basingstoke, Palgrave Macmillan, 2013.

14. Examples can be found at the People's History Museum, Manchester and the Willett Collection.

15. Drakard, *Printed English Pottery*, plates 616, 617, 619a, b and c.

John Bellingham, the assassin of the Prime Minister Spencer Perceval, hinting at subversion.[16] One jug reproduced a print of the murder scene in which Bellingham appears to be showing instant remorse, and where lookers-on seem more to be comforting than apprehending him.[17] All this seems innocuous enough, but in the febrile atmosphere of 1812, with the economy suffering the ramifications of Perceval's notorious "Orders in Council" and news of his death greeted with bonfires and bell-ringing in some major towns, such ambiguities could take on potentially seditious meanings.[18]

A more direct successor to Wilkes as a victim of official persecution and rallying point for popular discontent can be found in the apotheosis of the radical baronet Sir Francis Burdett M.P., following his arrest and committal to the Tower of London on the warrant of the House of Commons in 1810. Burdett was already a popular figure in London, having won elections for Middlesex in 1804 and Westminster in 1807, both parliamentary constituencies with large electorates including high numbers of artisans. His radicalism was of a relatively modest sort, based on what he saw as the "restoration" of a more perfect historic constitution rather than root and branch reform. In Middlesex, Burdett's campaign slogan had been the distinctly constitutional "Burdett and Independence", encapsulating his critique of attempts by a corrupt government to pervert the democratic process through the undue use of influence over voters and their representatives. In 1810, Burdett's "crime" had been to publish a letter in William Cobbett's *Political Register* criticising the arbitrary arrest of the radical John Gale Jones. Initially prevented by the mob that gathered outside his house, his eventual apprehension turned into a classic piece of Georgian political theatre, as the arresting party burst in to find Burdett apparently in the process of listening to his son translate the *Magna Carta* from the original Latin.[19] Burdett's arrest catapulted him to new heights of popularity. Toasts to Burdett were being drunk in London taverns, while pro-Burdett graffiti appeared in provincial towns and supportive public addresses poured in from as far afield as Liverpool.[20]

Burdett fever reached its height on 21 June 1810, the day Jones and Burdett were released from the Tower. Their radical supporters had planned a gala occasion, with processions of London liverymen, bands of music, flags and banners. Commemorative medals were struck, bearing Burdett's portrait and carrying the slogan: "The Intrepid Champion of Freedom, the Enlightened Advocate of the Rights and Liberties of the People".[21] Newspapers reported that

16. Willett Collection, 606.

17. *Ibid.*, 605.

18. Denis Gray, *Spencer Perceval: The Evangelical Prime Minister, 1762-1812*, Manchester, Manchester University Press, 1963, pp. 459, 462.

19. Anne Hone, *For the Cause of Truth: Radicalism in London 1796-1821*, Oxford, Clarendon Press, 1982, pp. 181-190. For this "hastily arranged scene", see Francis Place Papers, British Library Add. MS 27850, f. 197.

20. John Rowland Dinwiddy, *Radicalism and Reform in Britain, 1780-1850*, London, Hambledon Press, 1992, pp. 112-113; for the Liverpool address, Burdett Papers, Bodleian Library, MS Eng.hist.b.199, fos 52-71.

21. British Museum, BNK, EngM.286.

the streets on the procession route "were soon full of people wearing silvered and gilt medals, and blue favours, the windows were crowded with female beauty, decorated with insignia and colours of the Honourable Baronet... The hackney and stage-coaches bore the same testimonials of the popular feeling".[22] However, when Burdett's liberation party finally set off from the Tower, it was missing one crucial element. To the chagrin of his supporters, particularly Place, who never forgave him, the hero of the hour was absent: he had been spirited away from the Tower by boat and was already rumoured to be *en route* for Wimbledon.[23]

It is likely that much of the Burdett pottery produced in 1810 was intended for sale as a commemorative of his release, taking advantage of the vast crowds who amassed for the occasion and the huge publicity that had accompanied the affair over the previous two months in the form of press reports, broadsides and caricatures. Respectful portraits of Burdett were quickly reproduced on pottery, much of it cheap earthenware and most putting Burdett's image over the slogan "The determined enemy of corruption & the / constitutional friend of his SOVEREIGN" (see Fig. 1). The loyal sentiments were partly tactical. George III was still at a high point of popularity following his jubilee the previous year and Burdett's supporters were anxious not to revive the accusations of Republicanism which had dogged the radical cause since the days of the French Revolution: after all, Britain was still at war with France. Just as importantly, stressing loyalty to the monarchy emphasised that it was the unreformed House of Commons, not the King, that had so flagrantly abused the spirit of the *Magna Carta* by consigning Burdett and Jones to the Tower without trial. Some of the larger items also included specific detail, such as this from a creamware jug: "Sir FRANCIS BURDETT / Bart M.P. / Committed to the Tower / 6th April, 1810 / By the house of Commons for firmly / and disinterestedly asserting / the legal rights of the / British People".

There was some variation in the text, other examples harking back to Burdett's election campaigns with slogans such as "Sir Francis Burdett the Independent Champion of British Freedom" and "Burdett and Independence". However, the overall stability of this message contrasts with the greater variety of images and texts produced on the Peterloo pottery and supports Drakard's conclusion that the Burdett pottery was all produced within a relatively compressed timeframe.[24]

Burdett commemoratives carried a relatively straightforward message about an apparently straightforward incident: the persecution by the House of Commons of one of its own members for standing up for the rights of a private citizen and, by extension, the liberties of the English people. Burdett's case was therefore a relatively simple cipher for the plight of an England misgoverned by a narrowly elected and inherently corrupt legislature. Ceramic commemoratives were particularly effective at conveying such clear narratives, leaving the satirical prints of the day, with their complex iconography and proliferating speech bubbles, to elaborate on the specifics. The challenge of Peterloo was rather more difficult. Here was an event which was uglier and messier, and a hero, in the form of Hunt, with

22. *The Times*, 22 June 1810, 3b.
23. Place Papers BL Add. MS 27850 fos 156-240, esp. 236-240.
24. Drakard, *Printed English Pottery*, pp. 222-224.

a rather more chequered reputation, whom loyalists were determined to cast as the real villain of the piece. Despite these efforts, it was the radical version of Peterloo that soon held the field: this had been a peaceful demonstration of popular support for reform; the drilling that had preceded it and the supposedly "military" formation of the marchers had been intended to demonstrate the orderliness of the people, not to intimidate property owners or as the prelude to an uprising; above all, the charge of the yeomanry and regular cavalry units had been an unprovoked assault on a defenceless crowd. The radicals were aided by the presence of neutral journalists at the meeting, including Edward Baines junior of the *Leeds Mercury* and John Tyas of *The Times*, whose papers were in favour of moderate reform, but who were no friends of Hunt's demands for universal suffrage.[25] Similarly, public outrage ensured that usually hostile caricaturists such as Fores and Cruikshank were readily recruited to the cause. It was their images, cropped, abstracted and simplified, that frequently came to adorn the mugs and jugs that commemorated Peterloo.

Out of the chaos of the Manchester meeting, the Peterloo ceramics moulded a coherent narrative from three key elements: the innocence of the victims, as symbolised by the presence of women and children; the violence of the yeomanry; and the heroism of Hunt. In each element there was a complex interplay between the symbolic language of pre-photographic illustration and the actual events that those symbols represented. For instance, contemporary audiences would have been familiar with the appearance of women in art and illustration to symbolise abstract virtues: sometimes feminine ones, as in the case of Renaissance Madonnas; sometimes masculine ones, as in the use of female figures to represent classical male virtues such as Justice, which was often the case in statuary.[26] At Peterloo, though, real women had not only been present, but had taken an active role in marching, bearing flags and even appearing on the hustings. Moreover, those terrifying minutes after the yeomanry charged had been inscribed, sometimes permanently, on real female bodies through the sabre, bayonet and truncheon wounds that many carried, and which came to be described, displayed and debated at trials and inquests and in the print media. Four women and one child of two years of age were among the dead. As Michael Bush has argued, the disproportionate number of women killed and seriously injured at Peterloo suggests that they were deliberately singled out, and some were certainly the victims of frenzied violence from their assailants.[27]

There was an instant propagandic value to the radicals and their sympathisers in emphasising the victimhood of women at Peterloo. A powerful strand of the gender consensus of the day constructed women, particularly mothers, as bearers of moral virtue in need of masculine protection. Men had a duty to provide this protection, making the actions of the military power all the more reprehensible.

25. See reports in *Leeds Mercury*, 21 August 1819, and *The Times*, 19 August 1819.

26. See Marina Warner, *Monuments and Maidens: The Allegory of the Female Form*, London, Athenaeum, 1985.

27. Michael L. Bush, "The Women at Peterloo: The Impact of Female Reform on the Manchester Meeting of 16 August 1819", *History*, 89/294 (2004), pp. 209-232; Bush, *The Casualties of Peterloo*, pp. 30-35.

Loyalist commentators did their best to deny feminine virtue, and therefore the right to such protection, to those women present: a tactic that would routinely be employed against women reformers in the 1830s and 1840s. Nonetheless, the most characteristic image of Peterloo was that of the innocent woman, usually with a child, being ridden down by a corpulent yeoman. It had its origin in George Cruikshank's angry satires *Manchester Heroes* and *Massacre at St Peter's or "Britons Strike Home"*, and was reproduced in various permutations, including on several types of Peterloo pottery, sometimes accompanied by the slogan "Murdered on the plains of Peterloo". Along with the innocent victims, the yeomanry were depicted trampling flags bearing radical slogans such as "No Corn Bill" and "Liberty or Death" (Fig. 2). It is clear from this juxtaposition that the portrayal of women victims was meant to be interpreted both in a literal and an allegorical sense, the assumption of feminine innocence standing for the purity and justice of the cause itself. Arguably this message was undercut by the inclusion of slogans such as "Liberty or Death", which were used on flags at Peterloo and seen by hostile observers as proof of the meeting's insurrectionary intent.[28] Like the role of women at Peterloo itself, its significance here is ambiguous. The Peterloo victims had gathered to demand liberty, and the authorities had given them death; but at a time when feelings were running high and much of the country was in a febrile state, it could also be interpreted as a call to arms. Other Peterloo pottery called more explicitly for revenge, as in the case of a pearlware jug that bore a depiction of the massacre entwined with a scroll emblazoned with the word "MURDER" above the following verse:

> The scripture crys out life for life
> And God ordain'd it so
> We'll not forget to pay the debt
> Incurr'd at PETERLOO[29]

On the one hand, this is a reminder that radicalism itself was divided at this time between constitutionalists like Hunt and those such as Arthur Thistlewood, the Cato Street conspirator, who favoured more violent solutions. On the other, it is indicative of the anger elicited by Peterloo, which manifested itself in arming and drilling in some localities, and in poems such as "A Song of Slaughter" written in Ilchester gaol by the radical leader Samuel Bamford, which later appeared as a street ballad.[30]

Bush surmises that women were targeted at Peterloo because their attendance at a radical political meeting was a threat to the established gender order. He further speculates that this gender rage had been sharpened by the pre-Peterloo practice

28. Matthew Roberts, "Radical Banners from Peterloo to Chartism", in Poole (ed.), "Return to Peterloo", pp. 93-109, esp. 96-98.

29. See at https://www.worthpoint.com/worthopedia/19thc-pearlware-sunderland-1793141066, accessed 7 Feb. 2021.

30. John Gardner, *Poetry and Popular Protest: Peterloo, Cato Street and the Queen Caroline Controversy*, Basingstoke, Palgrave Macmillan, 2011, pp. 30-31; Samuel Bamford "Song of the Slaughterd [sic]" (Manchester: Wheeler, n.d.), *Broadside Ballads Online*, http://ballads.bodleian.ox.ac.uk/, Roud Number V34391.

of having women formally present caps of liberty, flags and other radical symbols to contingents of male radicals: a direct inversion of the Napoleonic practice whereby prominent gentry women presented "colours" to volunteer regiments as a chivalric endorsement.[31] The inversion of loyalist rituals and symbolism was a characteristic part of radical culture, and the role of the yeomanry at Peterloo, the successors to the Napoleonic volunteers, gave an unrivalled opportunity to attack the hypocrisy and violence of these part-time patriots. Pottery proved a particularly apt vehicle for this. During the Napoleonic period, the invasion scares of 1798 and 1803-1805 led to the formation of large numbers of local volunteer regiments, often with some form of aristocratic sponsorship.[32] The volunteer movement generated its own ceramic heritage, ranging from jugs and pots bearing the generic slogan "Success to the Volunteers" to more specific pieces relating to the formation of local regiments. For example, Okehampton museum contains a creamware jug inscribed with "Success to the Volunteers of Spreyton", probably dating from the formation of this Devon volunteer regiment in April 1798.[33] The collection of Susan Rees includes a delicate and skilfully decorated mug inscribed "Success to the Bury Volunteers" (see Fig. 3), a unit formed in 1803 under the command of the first Sir Robert Peel, father of the future Prime Minister. The mug, bearing the monogram of its owner, is richly illustrated with images of regimental paraphernalia including flags, drums, tambourines, bugles, and the characteristic Tarleton hat worn by many mounted units during the Napoleonic wars. On the reverse, it bears the legend "To protect our families and property", illustrating the local and even personal motivations underpinning the creation of such bodies.[34] These items were grounded in earlier precedents, attested by the survival of a number of ceramics commemorating the foundation of Irish Volunteer regiments during the American War of Independence, also using the formula of "success to the… Volunteers".[35]

Presumably, the presence of the slogan "Success to the Volunteers" on jugs and drinking vessels was intended to act as the prompt for a loyal toast from those using them. If we accept this assumption, then the juxtaposition in 1819 of murderous yeomanry soldiers and the phrase "Bad Luck to the Manchester Butchers" on some pottery – as was the case on the pearlware jug mentioned above – becomes more intelligible, both as an inversion of the traditional loyal sentiment and as an invitation to multiple individual and collective acts of subversion and protest. Manchester, along with the other large Lancashire towns, had been a major centre of volunteering

31. Bush, *Casualties of Peterloo*, p. 33.

32. John Ernest Cookson, *The British Armed Nation, 1793-1815*, Oxford, Clarendon Press, 1997; Austin Gee, *The British Volunteer Movement, 1794-1815*, Oxford, Clarendon Press, 2003.

33. At http://www.spreytonvillage.co.uk/the-history-of-spreyton/the-spreyton-volunteers, accessed 7 Feb. 2021.

34. Susan Rees collection at www.commemorativeceramics.co.uk. By coincidence, George Greenhalgh, who was one of those arrested after Peterloo and charged with instructing the protestors in military drill, claimed to have gained his military experience in the Bury Volunteers. *Hansard*, XLI, 24 November 1819, col. 245.

35. See examples in the Willett Collection.

in the Napoleonic period, and at Peterloo it was the part-time yeomanry, like the volunteers officered by local notables and manned by local men, who became the focus of radical ire in the wake of the massacre.[36] The significance of the slogan "Bad Luck to the Manchester Butchers" would have been as obvious to yeomanry soldiers and citizens alike as the deliberate double meaning in Cruikshank's "Britons Strike *Home*!". One example, a creamware jug in the collection of the National Army Museum, provides an even more obvious subversion of traditional loyalist sentiment, reproducing on its opposite side Nelson's famous communication before Trafalgar, "England expects every man to do his duty", followed by the savage qualification: "But none of your butchering cavalry".[37]

It is striking that the radical narrative of Peterloo tended to foreground the actions of the yeomanry, while downplaying the role of the regular cavalry who were sent in to extract them from the crowd, or the infantry units with fixed bayonets who blocked lines of escape from the field.[38] This, despite evidence that these soldiers were also culpable for injuries and deaths, may reflect the concern of radicals not to be seen as attacking a national institution, the British Army, which had gained a new place in the nation's affections following Wellington's victory at Waterloo.[39] More likely, it sprang from a desire to concentrate fire on a force viewed by many radicals as intended for domestic repression as much as national defence, and which, unlike the regular army, was perceived to be drawn specifically from the gentry and other property-owners rather than "the people".[40] Similarly, responsibility for ordering in the military power was placed firmly on the heads of the local justices, with at least one type of Peterloo mug bearing the slogan "None of your butchering magistrates" below a portrait of Henry Hunt.[41] In the ensuing months, as men and women around the country sought locally available subjects for their anger, yeomanry regiments became targets for reprisals and popular insult, with the phrase "Manchester Butchers" often the epithet of choice. On 4 October 1819, members of the Warwickshire Yeomanry were confronted by a large, belligerent group of men armed with bludgeons who made an unprovoked assault on one of their number. According to witnesses, members of the mob, initially more than fifty strong and swelling to over a hundred, had frequently yelled "Manchester Butchers" as a provocation.[42] The following June it was reported that the Yorkshire Hussars, another yeomanry regiment, had been "exposed to daily and repeated insults" in the streets of York: "Cries of '*No b----y*

36. Katrina Navickas, *Loyalism and Radicalism in Lancashire 1798-1815*, Oxford, Oxford University Press, 2009.

37. National Army Museum collection, NAM 2015-03-8-1 (https://collection.nam.ac.uk/detail.php?acc=2015-03-8-1), accessed 7 Feb. 2021.

38. For instance, see Samuel Bamford, *Passages in the Life of a Radical*, Oxford, Oxford University Press, 1984, p. 153.

39. Bush, *The Casualties of Peterloo*, pp. 50-55.

40. Gardner, *Poetry and Popular Protest*, pp. 89-92.

41. Yellow earthenware mug, collection of Susan Rees.

42. *Birmingham Chronicle*, 14 October 1819; *Coventry Herald*, 14 April 1820. For the unpopularity of the yeomanry after Peterloo, see Malcolm Chase, *1820: Disorder and Stability in the United Kingdom*, Manchester, Manchester University Press, 2013, p. 121.

Manchester Butchers', with other opprobrious epithets, as well as hooting and hissing, were frequent".[43] The slogan was one of a number (others including "Hunt and Liberty", "Liberty or Death" and "Blast the Oppressor") reportedly being used as copying exercises for boys at so-called "Reform Schools", an unsubstantiated allegation that was widely reprinted.[44] When Queen Caroline arrived for the opening of her "trial" at the House of Lords on 17 August 1820, a year and a day after the massacre, it was used by the assembled pro-Caroline crowd as an insult for the City Light Horse.[45] As the phrase "Manchester butchers" seems to be particularly connected to Peterloo pottery, these examples may give some indication as to the impact of ceramics in spreading the radical narrative of Peterloo beyond Lancashire, as well as the extent to which the items themselves may have circulated.

The third element of the radical Peterloo narrative was the figure of Henry Hunt. In the immediate aftermath of the Peterloo meeting, a number of earthenware and creamware pots and jugs were rushed out with the words "Henry Hunt Esq." over portraits purporting to be of Hunt but actually depicting Commodore Bainbridge, an American naval commander. Bainbridge was one of a number of American heroes of the War of 1812 honoured in Staffordshire pottery: evidence of the potters' dominance in American markets, which manifested itself again in the production of commemoratives for Lafayette's American tour, a few years after Peterloo.[46] The appearance of Hunt's name on mass-produced pots over transferred images of Bainbridge suggests, first, that the onset of demand for Peterloo-ware was rapid, and second, that the potters took advantage of the situation to shift old stock. While the portraits were often dubious, the captions were significant elements of the radical narrative. Hunt was a "gentleman radical", one of a line including Major Cartwright and Sir Francis Burdett, who supposedly stooped from their superior social status to become the champions of the oppressed people. The type remained a key feature of popular politics in Britain until the Chartist period, with late examples including Feargus O'Connor and Ernest Jones.[47] The caption "Henry Hunt Esq." above respectful portraits of a well-dressed man (whether it happened to be Hunt or not), reinforced Hunt's

43. *Public Ledger and Daily Advertiser*, 10 June 1820.

44. *Northampton Mercury*, 3 June 1820; *Leeds Intelligencer*, 5 June 1820; *Hereford Journal*, 7 June 1820; *Stamford Mercury*, 9 June 1820; *Durham County Advertiser*, 10 June 1820; *Yorkshire Gazette*, 17 June 1820.

45. *Suffolk Chronicle*, 19 August 1820. The phrase had a long half-life as an abusive term for cavalry soldiers, being used during disturbances in Boston, Lincolnshire, in 1832: *The Times*, 9 August 1832, 2e.

46. Drakard, *Printed English Pottery*; May, May, *Commemorative Pottery*, pp. 136-410; Marian Klamkin, *The Return of Lafayette 1824-1825*, New York, Charles Scribner's Sons, 1975, pp. 53-56.

47. John Belchem, James Epstein, "The Nineteenth-Century Gentleman Leader Revisited", *Social History*, 22 (1997), pp. 174-193; James Epstein, *The Lion of Freedom: Feargus O'Connor and the Chartist Movement, 1832-1842*, London, Croom Helm, 1982; Miles Taylor, *Ernest Jones, Chartism and the Romance of Politics, 1819-1869*, Oxford, Oxford University Press, 2003.

gentlemanly credentials and gave him a crucial air of respectability. Given the popularity of ceramics depicting Nelson and other military heroes during the Napoleonic period, the images of Hunt can also be read as a further inversion of loyalist tropes.

Other pots carried portraits of Hunt (or Bainbridge) under the slogan "Hunt and Liberty", which again may well have been the prompt to a radical toast.[48] "Hunt and Liberty" was an established radical cry, long before the yeomanry brandished their sabres on the 16th of August. It appeared on a banner at a meeting in Manchester in January 1819, and on a cap of liberty at Stockport the following month.[49] Hunt's partisans had chanted it during their hero's attendance at the Manchester theatre in January, prompting a confrontation with local loyalists.[50] It was again in evidence at St Peter's Field, while Bamford recalled shouting it to his wife to rouse her spirits when he was arrested after Peterloo.[51] The cry echoed the earlier "Wilkes and Liberty" and had its roots in the traditional radical rhetoric of the defence of "English liberties".[52] However, as with the cap of liberty itself, the French Revolution had given it a more threatening edge, contrasting with the cautiously constitutional "Burdett and Independence".[53] Both were political slogans that became catch phrases, a form of shorthand at once identifying the named individual with a set of radical values and political positions, but vague and open-ended enough for individuals to imbue them with their own hopes and aspirations.

Hunt had, in many respects, supplanted Burdett as a popular hero by the time of Peterloo, as the baronet's caution alienated his more radical supporters. Hunt stood against him at Westminster in 1818, where he won the show of hands at the electoral nomination: a sign that Burdett was losing the sympathies of the non-electors.[54] Though the decline in Burdett's metropolitan popularity can be exaggerated, by the summer of 1819 Hunt was already ensconced as the darling of many provincial radicals, particularly in the textile districts of Lancashire and northern Cheshire. Peterloo, however, made Hunt the centre of national attention. His was the identifiable face of the radical movement, and the fact that it was the order for his arrest which had been the catalyst for the Manchester tragedy placed him, for a moment, at the fulcrum of confrontation between a suffering people and the coercive power of a corrupt state.

In the days and weeks after Peterloo, many of the industrial districts teetered on the brink of insurrection, arming being reported from many localities, with

48. There are two examples in the Willett Collection.

49. *Morning Post*, 21 January 1819; *The Times*, 21 January 1819, p. 3, col. a; *Morning Post*, 23 February 1819.

50. *The Times*, 26 January 1819, p. 3, col. b.

51. "Objects of Peterloo"; Bamford, *Passages in the Life of a Radical*, p. 167.

52. George Rudé, *Wilkes & Liberty: A Social Study of 1763-1774*, Oxford, Clarendon Press, 1962, p. 27.

53. James Epstein, "Understanding the Cap of Liberty: Symbolic Practice and Social Conflict in Early Nineteenth-Century England", *Past and Present*, 122 (1989), pp. 75-118.

54. John Belchem, *"Orator" Hunt: Henry Hunt and English Working-Class Radicalism*, Oxford, Clarendon Press, 1985, pp. 78-90.

much loose talk of revenge. Some of the more violent Peterloo-ware may date from this early period, a hypothesis supported by the fact that it was often associated with the Hunt/Bainbridge portrait. However, as the initial shock subsided and funds were gathered to support the wounded, attention came to focus on Hunt's trial at York the following March. Almost all of the Peterloo ceramics bore Hunt's portrait, the single contrary example discovered by the author being a small earthenware mug depicting a cavalryman riding down a woman carrying a banner inscribed "Liberty or Death": even here, one of the other banners the rider is trampling carries the slogan "Hunt and Liberty".[55] Hunt is therefore a constant of Peterloo pottery, indicating his central place in the radical narrative of the massacre and its aftermath.

As champion of the people, Hunt's persecution by the authorities represented a figurative "martyrdom", in turn symbolising the literal blood sacrifice of St Peter's Fields.[56] Moreover, it was Hunt who carried the hope of some form of justice for the victims, following the abandoned inquest into the death of John Lees, who died of his wounds several days after the massacre, and the open support of Lord Liverpool's government for the magistrates' actions.[57] The magnitude of Hunt's support can be gauged from his entry into London after the massacre, where *The Times* estimated the crowds at not less than 300,000, and the triumphal progress to his trial at York, where he was hailed as a hero at every stop.[58] Earlier sedition trials, such as those of Wooler and William Hone, had established the courtroom as a key site of radical theatre.[59] In the prescribed fashion of such radical melodramas, Hunt took charge of his own defence, but his efforts to use the trial as a platform to mount a general attack on the authorities and their tools were stymied by the judge. Despite the acknowledgment, even by pro-government observers, that the defence had the best of the argument, and the judge's summing up for an acquittal, Hunt was found guilty on one count and sentenced to two and a half years imprisonment in Ilchester gaol.[60]

The narrative tying Hunt to the campaign for redress is most eloquently expressed through one of the more elaborate pieces of "Peterloo-ware". This takes the form of a blue lustre-ware jug, carrying on one side the image of a black catafalque or plinth that supports a roundel containing an image of Hunt (see Fig. 4). The latter is flanked by a portrait of Thomas Wooler, editor of the radical *Black Dwarf*, and a weeping figure of Britannia carrying a banner inscribed "Hunt and

55. Willett Collection, 507.

56. For the matyrology of Peterloo, see Joseph Cozens, "The Making of the Peterloo Martyrs, 1819 to the Present", in *Secular Martyrdom in Britain and Ireland*, ed. by Quentin Outram and Keith Laybourn, Basingstoke, Palgrave Macmillan, 2018, pp. 31-58.

57. Joseph August Dowling, *The whole proceedings before the Coroners' Inquest at Oldham... on the body of John Lees, who died of sabre wounds at Manchester, August 16, 1819*, London, 1820.

58. *The Times*, 14 September 1819, p. 3, col. a.

59. Kevin Gilmartin, *Print Politics: The Press and Radical Opposition in Early Nineteenth-Century England*, Cambridge, Cambridge University Press, 1996, pp. 121-127.

60. Belchem, *"Orator" Hunt*, pp. 112-121.

Liberty".[61] The plinth is inscribed "To the Memory of the Unfortunate Sufferers at Manchester". The opposite side of the jug carries a further portrait of Hunt, above the following lines of verse:

> May the Rose of England never blow
> Nor the Thistle of Scotland never grow
> Nor the Harp of Ireland never play
> Till Henry Hunt has won the day.

Unlike other pieces, there is no depiction of violence or references to "Manchester butchers": female agency is limited to the firmly allegorical Britannia, and the victims are now "sufferers". The quality and sophistication of the piece suggests it was aimed at a higher-class market than the earthenware mugs and jugs, and it is almost certainly later in date, after the initial outrage had begun to cool and emphasis turned to the upcoming trials.[62] Wooler's inclusion was a reference to his arrest for the part he played at a radical meeting in Birmingham, shortly before Peterloo, at which Sir Charles Wolesley had been elected as a "legislatorial attorney", a proceeding deemed illegal by the government. Depicting Wooler and Hunt together may have been intended to link Peterloo and Hunt back to the wider constitutional movement for radical reform, symbolised by the "No Corn Laws" flag stretching between the two men, and a distancing from the more violent wing of the radical movement.

The excitement of Hunt's trial had barely subsided when a new opportunity presented itself to the manufacturers of commemorative pottery in the form of the Queen Caroline affair. As with Peterloo, the events have been extensively treated elsewhere.[63] They had their roots in the efforts of George IV to divorce his estranged wife, Caroline of Brunswick, by means of a bill of "Pains and Penalties". Caroline had other ideas, arriving in England in June 1820 and immediately becoming the focus of a wave of popular adulation. The sheer quantity and variety of pro-Caroline ceramics leaves all previous oppositional and radical outpourings in the shade. Malcolm Chase identified at least 40 separate "lines" of pottery.[64] As well as the ubiquitous jugs, other items of crockery bearing Caroline's portrait included plates, bowls, cups and saucers and teapots. In addition, there were several types of wall-plaque, and even a small figurine.[65] This variety is an indication of the tremendous interest in Caroline's case, and the fact that it was not just the lower classes who were primarily concerned, as was the case with Peterloo, but the whole nation.

Pottery captured the whole narrative arc of Caroline's "journey": from her physical arrival at Dover in June to her eventual death the following year,

61. Examples may be found in the collection of Susan Rees, and at the People's History Museum in Manchester.

62. Though a cruder and more down-market version also exists, still bearing the Bainbridge transfer on the reverse: Marx Memorial Library, Klugman Collection, OB. 11.

63. Chase, *1820*, chs 5-6; Roger Fulford, *The Trial of Queen Caroline*, London, B.T. Batsford, 1967; Ernest A. Smith, *A Queen on Trial: The Affair of Queen Caroline*, Stroud, Sutton, 1993.

64. Chase, *1820*, p. 176.

65. Willett Collection, 58 and 59.

following the ignominy of her exclusion from the Coronation ceremony.[66] As with many Peterloo pieces, feminine innocence was a key theme, but the emphasis now was on the suffering of the wronged wife, giving the potters an opportunity to wax lyrical in defence of domestic felicity, as in the case of a lustre-ware jug inscribed:

> When man presumes to chuse [sic] a wife,
> He takes his lovely spouse for life
> Who can Judge and not repine
> The wofull [sic] case of CAROLINE[67]

Most items, however, were content to reproduce Caroline's portrait, their subversive intent residing in the use of her proscribed royal title, and occasionally the reproduction of the royal coat of arms. Unlike Peterloo's emphasis on Hunt, references to Caroline's male "protectors" were relatively few, though some items did reproduce images of Caroline's legal counsel, Henry Brougham and Thomas Denman.[68] It has been suggested that the Queen's affair acted as a relatively harmless safety valve for popular discontent after twelve months marred by potential and actual attempts at popular insurrection and conspiracy, and certainly its material productions are a long way from the visceral response to the bloodshed of St Peter's fields the previous year.[69]

Peterloo occurred at a time when pottery was at its height as a medium for political communication. The ceramics analysed in this essay played their role in the dissemination of images of Peterloo, and of political slogans. Together with the print media, these slogans and images helped to forge a narrative of the massacre that emphasised the brutality of the authorities and their military tools, the innocence of the victims and the justice of their cause, and the heroism of Hunt as the champion of the people. Particularly in the earlier phase immediately following the massacre, these ceramic effusions were the most radical and subversive of the productions of British potteries in the whole period, certainly when compared to the loyal references to the monarchy in the Burdett-ware and the respectable tone of most pro-Caroline material. This is testimony to the shock of Peterloo, and its widespread interpretation as a desecration of basic English liberties. However, questions remain. While we can make inferences about how these ceramics were used or displayed, there is precious little reference to them in the written record of the time. Similarly, their longer-term biographies remain obscure. Their survival in reasonable numbers is testament not only to their widespread distribution, but also to the durable properties of pottery compared to other political ephemera, such as cheap prints or textiles. What significance did they continue to hold after the immediate circumstances of their production had passed from memory into

66. For a jug depicting her landing at Dover, see the collection of Susan Rees at www.commemorativeceramics.co.uk. Other examples of Caroline commemoratives can be found in the Willett Collection. See Stella Bedoe, *A Potted History: Henry Willett's Ceramic Chronicle of Britain*, Woodbridge, ACC Art Books, 2015, pp. 24-25.

67. Willett Collection, 63. See Anna Clark, "Queen Caroline and the Sexual Politics of Popular Culture in London, 1820", *Representations*, 31 (1990), pp. 47-68.

68. Jug in the private collection of Susan Rees, at www.commemorativeceramics.co.uk.

69. Chase, *1820*, p. 213.

myth? What pride of place did they retain within a household, what stories and memories attached to them and how long did they remain in use or on display? Such questions are tantalising but usually unanswerable. Nevertheless, Peterloo ceramics were once more at the fore during the 2019 commemorations of Peterloo in Manchester and elsewhere: condemning the brutality of the "Manchester butchers", memorialising the innocence of the victims, celebrating the heroism of Hunt and demanding justice that never came.

1. Sir Francis Burdett: yellow earthenware jug from the collection of Susan Rees (www.commemorativeceramics.co.uk).
2. "Murderd [sic] on the Plains of Peterloo", creamware jug, Manchester Art Gallery, Acc. No. 1967.127. Manchester Art Gallery/Bridgeman Images.

3. *Success to the Bury Volunteers*, from the collection of Susan Rees (www.commemorativeceramics.co.uk).
4. Peterloo jug from the collection of Susan Rees (www.commemorativeceramics.co.uk).

II

Objects and Narration

Sandro Morachioli

Not Just Print Culture: Small-Size Sculptures and Street Vendors in the Visual Culture of the *Risorgimento*

Era un Lucchese, uno di quei Lucchesi
Che con un po' di gesso e due stampini,
Girando innumerabili paesi,
Stampan Santi, testiere, burattini,
Pii Noni, Carli Alberti e Leopoldi,
E ritornano a casa con de'soldi

Antonio Guadagnoli, *Il figurinaio*[1]

1. *Public consumption of the* Risorgimento

As he struggles with his transformation into an accessory to be opened and closed, the Prime Minister of the Kingdom of Sardinia appears perplexed, as he says: "And now they will say I am not useful to Piedmont, me! There are even daily *speculations* on my terracotta and papier-mâché belly". In this cartoon from *Il Fischietto*, the caricatured statuettes with Cavour's features were not the caricaturist's creation, but actual coloured jewellery boxes sold in Piedmont in the mid-1850s (Figs 1-2). With the minister's sizeable belly, these statuettes alluded to his frequent speculations on the stock exchange and the voraciousness of his fiscal policy.[2] However, they were also "speculations" – and the success of the cartoon played on this dual meaning – which are fully inscribed in the history of iconographic consumption triggered by the *Risorgimento* uprisings.

Giuseppe Augusto Cesana, a journalist working in Milan and Turin halfway through the century, recalled how, in the streets of Milan, the enthusiasm for the election of Pius IX to the papacy had produced a great display of patriotic scarves by men and medallions with the Pope's portrait by women, while plaster busts or paintings of the "national" Pope began to appear in people's homes. In short, the

1. Antonio Guadagnoli, *Poesie giocose di Antonio Guadagnoli*, Florence, G. Barbera, 1888, pp. 557-561: "He was from Lucca, one of those Lucchesi / Who with a bit of plaster and a couple of moulds, / Touring endless villages, / Reproduce Saints, busts, puppets / Of Pius IX, Charles Albert and Leopold, / Returning home with a few *soldi*".

2. See *Museo del Risorgimento: catalogo*, ed. by Leo Morabito, Genoa, 1987, pp. 230-231.

Pope's election had fostered the development of a whole commercial sector where "speculation [...] wonderfully indulged" the public's taste with a varied range of objects made by "trinket-makers, goldsmiths, silk workers, photographers, plaster figurine makers from Lucca and lithographers".[3]

The thriving market of political images partly used the same effective channels – which were booming around 1848 – of the so-called "print culture", but it was not limited to them: not only two-dimensional images, but a vast typology of figurative objects began to play a new role in the building of patriotic identities, which the historiography has only recently started to investigate.[4] In this context, some ordinarily used objects were politicised: the so-called "national snuffboxes" given as gifts by various newspapers in 1848 to their subscribers, for example, were normal snuffboxes with lithographic prints pasted on them, "representing on one side the busts of the three Sovereigns who had promoted the Italian Risorgimento, Pius IX, Charles Albert of Savoy and Leopold II of Lorraine, and on the other the busts of three distinguished Italian writers, Vincenzo Gioberti, Cesare Balbo and Massimo D'Azeglio".[5] They were certainly not the gold snuffbox that Napoleon had given to Vincenzo Monti as a reward for his epic poem *Il Bardo della Selva Nera* ("The Bard of the Black Forest"), but a new and more inclusive way to involve readers, aimed at the material sharing of a pocket pantheon, in which political celebrities took on the forms and material characteristics of everyday objects.[6] Like it or not, to enter into people's daily lives, great politicians were in fact reduced, trivialised and multiplied: from Cavour's jewellery box to Napoleon's matchboxes, to Garibaldi-decorated pipes or handkerchiefs, up to Victor Emanuel II turned into a walking stick.[7] But there is more. Not only were these objects reproduced and multiplied, sold or given away, confiscated or flaunted, they were also drawn, painted and sometimes even carved, arousing a decidedly intense visual interest. Worthy successors of the medieval halberds and armour of historical painters, they became indispensable to the fashion, outfits and accessories of contemporary men and women.

This essay is divided into two sections. It first investigates the status and functions of political objects within visual representations, from current affairs images to works of art, in the belief that visualisation is not only fundamental

3. Giuseppe Augusto Cesana, *Ricordi di un giornalista*, vol. I, Milan, G. Prato, 1890, p. 179. On accessories and decorative objects made to commemorate Pio IX, see Ignazio Veca, "Oggetti animati. Materialità, circolazione e usi della figura di Pio IX (1846-1849)", *Il Risorgimento*, 1 (2017), pp. 63-97.

4. On material culture and historical studies, see "Storia e cultura materiale: recenti traiettorie di ricerca. Interventi di Fabio Dei, Giorgio Riello, Beverly Lemire, Manuel Charpy, Leora Auslander", ed. by Alessio Petrizzo and Carlotta Sorba, in *Contemporanea*, 3 (2016), pp. 439-482.

5. *Il Risorgimento*, 20 March 1848.

6. On Vincenzo Monti's snuffbox, see Mario Praz, *Gusto neoclassico*, Milan, Rizzoli, 2003 (1940), p. 253.

7. See the cartoon: Casimiro Teja, "A cosa servono i grandi uomini", *Pasquino*, 29 December 1861, discussed in Sandro Morachioli, "La pittura e le cose. Gli Induno e l'‘oggettistica' patriottica", in *Lo spettacolo della politica*, ed. by Marco Manfredi and Emanuela Minuto, Rome, Viella, 2018, pp. 39-66.

evidence of the uses of objects and the symbolic weight attributed to them, but also represents an early, unique form of mediation, endowed with its own language and specific conventions. Starting from the particular types of objects recurring in genre painting, such as busts and plaster statuettes, the essay will then attempt to delve into the dynamics of sale, production and perception of small-size sculpture, focusing on the figurine makers from Lucca and their relationship with politics.

2. *Illustrated, painted and carved objects*

In the visual chronicles of revolutionary events, patriotic objects linked to political mobilisation practices above all caught the attention of painters and designers. Hats, rosettes, brooches, flags, medals became fundamental vehicles of visual connotation and narration. They identified and talked about ongoing events. They functioned as present-day time machines, precisely dating the "here and now". The accessories of a bearded Lombard soldier evoked by an anti-patriotic satirical cartoon testify to the importance and spread of signs of national-patriotic identification even in the perception of political opponents.[8] The soldier's feathered hat looks crushed; instead of a rifle or a sword, the man is holding a rather dandy walking stick; around his neck he wears an oversized medallion, on which the words "I am a Lombard – run away" are clearly visible and are arranged around the sketch of two fleeing legs. The medallion not only accused Lombard patriots of cowardice, but also highlighted the fashion-conscious and swashbuckling aspects of his portrait.

Furthermore, patriotic objects sometimes changed their sign and, from accessories of identification and mobilisation, were transformed into powerful metaphors of revolutionary processes. In a full-page cartoon from the most important reactionary, illustrated publication of the *Risorgimento*, *La Grande Riunione*, the anonymous designer showed Cassandrino looking satisfied with an *Effetto del Sole di Luglio 1849*.[9] Cassandrino was a character from puppet theatre whose name had been used for a Roman clerical periodical and he thus, in the cartoon, symbolised and personified reactionary positions. In the aftermath of the fall of the Roman Republic, the entire Republican material culture was dissolving in the waters of the Tiber, carried away by the current. The metaphorical association between political solidity and material consistency allowed objects, in their ephemeral nature, to reflect the very precariousness of revolutionary politics, according to a satirical strategy already adopted in French counter-revolutionary culture.[10] This also

8. See "Costumi del primo secolo dell'ultima Repubblica Romana", in *Grande riunione tenuta nella sala dell'ex circolo popolare in Roma*, Rome, Tipografia Paterno, 1849, p. 195 (https://reader.digitale-sammlungen.de/de/fs1/object/display/bsb10941269_00201.html).

9. See "Effetto del sole al luglio 1849. Come si squagliano!!", in *Grande riunione tenuta nella sala dell'ex circolo popolare in Roma*, Rome, Tipografia Paterno, 1849, p. 73 (https://reader.digitale-sammlungen.de/de/fs1/object/display/bsb10941269_00079.html).

10. The idea was taken from a counter-revolutionary print produced in Paris in 1792, translated and republished in Northern Italy in 1799 (*Statua della democrazia composta*

applied to an iconographic theme recurring in publications around 1848, which insisted on the fragility and rapid wearing of plaster statuettes as tangible symbols of the provisional nature of political "fashions".[11]

When patriotic objects reappeared in a more strictly artistic field, they were imbued with emotion. If the firm patriotic gesture of the *Cospiratrice* (*The Female Conspirator*) by Andrea Appiani the Younger (Museum of the *Risorgimento*, Milan) is concentrated in the strong grip of a tri-coloured object,[12] Pietro Magni's *Leggitrice* (*The Reading Girl*) (Washington, National Gallery of Art, 1856-1861), offers a delicate blend of sensuality and political allegory, complete with a touch of *Risorgimento* knick-knacks (Fig. 3). The sculpture, presented at the national exhibition in Florence in 1861, in fact shows a young woman intent on reading, on whose naked breast hangs a (marble) medal with the portrait of Garibaldi (Fig. 3b).[13] Foreign observers praised the extraordinary intensity of the girl's facial expression but, perhaps because they were less emotionally involved in the allusions to the *Risorgimento*, considered the additional object inserts a mere pretext to attract the public.[14] Criticism aside, through the militant use of elements of contemporary patriotic culture, Magni's sculpture entertained a close dialogue with painting. During the 1850s, in particular, patriotic objects had triggered intense interactions between the ephemeral field of commercial production and exhibition art. In the mid-19th century, Italian genre painting initiated a process of alignment with the European context by attributing new (moral, social and patriotic) meanings to painting of Flemish tradition, which until then was mostly unengaged or confined to comical themes.[15] In the Italian context, the contribution

d'immondezze). See Christian-Marc Bosséno, "La guerre des estampes. Circulation des images et des thèmes iconographiques dans l'Italie des années 1789-1799", *Melanges de l'Ecole française de Rome. Italie et Méditerranée*, 102/2 (1990), pp. 367-400: 393. On material metaphors in revolutionary culture, see Richard Taws, *The Politics of the Provisional: Art and Ephemera in Revolutionary France*, University Park (PA), Pennsylvania State University Press, 2013.

11. See the two cartoons published in the Florence satirical paper *Il Lampione* in 1848: "Un regalo alla Sicilia" (14 October 1848) and "Generi passati di moda" (18 November 1848).

12. The painting was presented as *Giovane italiana emigrata (che tiene stretti sul cuore i colori nazionali)* ("An Italian Migrant Girl (Holding Her National Colours Close to Her Heart)") to the 1855 Paris Universal Exhibition.

13. There are several versions of this work. The one exhibited in Florence in 1861 (now held at the National Gallery in Washington) featured two sheets from Niccolini's *Arnaldo da Brescia* on the book, and the Garibaldi medal. Both details are missing from the version held at the G.A.M. in Milan, a copy exhibited at the Brera in 1864. See the presentation by Francesco Tedeschi in *100 anni: scultura a Milano, 1815-1915*, Exhibition Catalogue, ed. by Omar Cucciniello, Alessandro Oldani and Paola Zatti, Milan, Officina Libraria, 2017, pp. 132-133.

14. John Stewart, "The Exhibition at Florence", *Art-Journal*, 13 (1861), p. 341. See Albert Boime, *The Art of the Macchia and the Risorgimento: Representing Culture and Nationalism in Nineteenth-Century Italy*, Chicago, University of Chicago Press, 1993, p. 178.

15. On the emancipation of genre painting in Europe in the early 19th century, especially in the German context, see Sophie Kruijssen, "The Middle Classes and Contemporaries as *dramatis personae*: David Wilkie and the Emancipation of Genre Scenes in Europe", *Simiolus: Netherlands Quarterly for the History of Art*, 37/3-4 (2013-2014), pp. 249-266. On Domenico Induno, see Silvestra Bietoletti, *Domenico Induno*, Soncino, Edizioni dei Soncino, 1992, pp. 12-16.

made by Milanese brothers Domenico and Gerolamo Induno was fundamental.[16] Domenico, a pupil of Luigi Sabatelli and Francesco Hayez, first took the "path of the modern genre painting".[17] In the 1850s, Domenico (shortly after followed by his brother Gerolamo) turned towards a style of painting aimed, in line with the wishes of critic Carlo Tenca, at "questioning the contemporary life" of the people and "exploring the social conditions of our time",[18] specialising in the creation of scenes set in working-class interiors. During the Austrian occupation, these scenes were anything but free of political implications;[19] within them, the object details are elements of visual narration, fundamental to the composition and reading of the image, according to a narrative strategy decisively foreshadowed by William Hogarth. Italian genre paintings of the 1850s and 1860s overflow with painted political objects: prints, photographs and statuettes that connect the domestic interiors, populated by women, children and the elderly, with the external spaces of the mobilisations and battles of the *Risorgimento*, creating a circularity between inside and outside, the public and private elements of the national-patriotic struggle.[20]

The first painting in the new genre was Domenico Induno's *La Questua* ("Begging for Alms"). The painting – formerly in the Crivelli collection, known only as a reproduction (Fig. 4) – was exhibited in 1850, at the reopening of the *Pinacoteca di Brera* after its forced closure of 1848-1849. It shows two Milanese ladies visiting the home of an antique dealer whilst raising funds (for a patriotic rally). The house overflows with the most disparate merchandise, but one object has special prominence, thanks to its compositional centrality and a clear section of light in contrast with the otherwise gloomy interior: a miniature reproduction of Alessandro Puttinati's statue of Neapolitan revolutionary *Masaniello* (Museum of the *Risorgimento*, Milan). *La Questua* is in fact the first Italian painting in which a plaster statuette with political significance appears: Puttinati's statue had caused a sensation at the 1846 Brera exhibition for its explicit patriotic allusions and for the new, explosive sense of grandeur reserved for a working-class (historical) subject.[21]

16. For a discussion on the role of objects and "accessories" in the genre painting of the Induno brothers, see Morachioli, *La pittura e le cose*, and its bibliography.

17. Enrico Somaré, *Storia dei pittori italiani dell'Ottocento*, vol. I, Milan, Edizioni dell'Esame, 1928, p. 168.

18. Carlo Tenca, "Esposizione di Belle Arti nel Palazzo di Brera. III", *Il Crepuscolo*, 1/33, 22 September 1850, now in Carlo Tenca, *Scritti d'arte*, Bologna, CLUEB, 1998, p. 199.

19. On the reception of "social" genre painting in the 1850s, see Sandro Morachioli, *L'Italia alla rovescia. Ricerche sulla caricatura giornalistica tra il 1848 e l'Unità*, Pisa, Edizioni della Normale, 2013, pp. 284-294.

20. See *Intorno agli Induno: pittura e scultura tra genere e storia nel Canton Ticino*, Exhibition Catalogue, ed. by Mariangela Agliati Ruggia and Sergio Rebora, Milan, Skira, 2002, pp. 158-159.

21. The commentary on Puttinati's work for the 1846 *Gemme d'arti italiane* was censored and the publication of the engraving of the work forbidden. See Barbara Cinelli's contribution in *Il Veneto e l'Austria. Vita e cultura artistica nelle città Venete*, ed. by Sergio Marinelli, Giuseppe Mazzariol and Fernando Mazzocca, Milan, Electa, 1989, pp. 219-220. See also the presentation of the work by Niccolò D'Agati in *100 anni*, pp. 172-173.

According to Raffaele Sonzogno, journalist and personal friend of Domenico's, the first version of the painting dated back to 1848 and the statuette depicted by Induno was not Masaniello, but Pius IX.[22] According to Sonzogno, replacing the Pope with the Neapolitan revolutionary in the version presented to the Brera was a consequence of the rapid upheaval of the political scene: from the Pope's turnaround to the failure of the 1848 uprisings.

In the 1850s, Domenico Induno's style had a strong impact on critics, artists and the public, thanks also to multiple exhibitions which started a figurative shared language where the realistic representation of objects (political and otherwise) was, to say the least, insistent. Beyond the Lombardy-Veneto region, for example, a pro-Savoy painting such as Gaetano Ferri's *Il lutto del Piemonte* ("Piedmont's Bereavement"), exhibited in Paris in 1855, can be said to have been influenced by Induno.[23] In the painting, which is reminiscent of Caravaggio's style, a priest brings the news of Charles Albert of Savoy's death to the humble home of a Piedmontese soldier wounded during the first war of independence; a small bust of Victor Emanuel II placed on the mantelpiece is juxtaposed, as a sign of the dynastic and patriotic continuity of the Savoy family, to a flyer bearing the news of Charles Albert's death and his engraved portrait.

Induno's influence on Veronese *macchiaiolo* Vincenzo Cabianca is also absolutely clear in the latter's 1856 painting *Veterano che racconta le sue vittorie* ("A Veteran Telling of His Victories", Trieste, Revoltella Museum), where Napoleonic objects act as the narrative background to the stories of the elderly soldier.[24] Far from being merely anecdotal, the Napoleonic objects in the painting have the expressly functional purpose of making precise national-patriotic references, certainly not appreciated by the Austrian regime, which feared the unitary potential of the Napoleonic myth.[25]

The few examples above show how chamber sculpture was one of the most recurring and patriotically significant political objects in genre painting, used by painters to frame (and, if necessary, update) the scene in political terms. At this

22. Raffaele Sonzogno, "Domenico e Girolamo Induno. Studio postumo artistico e biografico", *Rivista europea*, 10/2, (1878), pp. 293-326: 300.

23. Gaetano Ferri's painting is now kept in the Palazzo Reale in Turin. See Piergiorgio Dragone, *Pittori dell'Ottocento in Piemonte: arte e cultura figurativa 1830-1865*, Turin, Banca CRT, 2001, p. 203.

24. See *Cabianca e la civiltà dei Macchiaioli*, Exhibition Catalogue, ed. by Francesca Dini, Florence, Pagliai Polistampa, 2007, p. 80.

25. In fact, in the Lombardy-Veneto region, the year after the painting was shown it was expressly forbidden to display on one's chest the Saint Helena medal, as established by Napoleon III on 12 July 1857. See Arianna Arisi Rota, "Tra desiderio e nostalgia. Declinazioni visive del culto napoleonico nell'Italia della Restaurazione", *Mélanges de l'Ecole Française de Rome*, 130/1 (2018), pp. 17-29: 22-23. It was not by chance that the first version of Domenico Induno's most famous painting about the *Risorgimento*, *Bollettino di Villafranca* – a visual interpretation of the disappointment with the armistice between France and Austria – featured in the foreground "an old man decorated with the Saint Helena medal" who "looks with tears in his eyes at the medal of the emperor who never stopped halfway through victories". (See Carlo Romussi, "Domenico Induno", *Il Raffaello*, 20-30 November and 10 December 1879, X, pp. 32-34).

juncture, it should be noted that, in most cases, these sculptures really existed, playing an important role in the universe of the *Risorgimento* art trade.

3. *The work of figurines: figurine makers and politics*

Let us return to *Masaniello*. The miniature of the statue in *La Questua* was not Domenico Induno's invention; sculptor Alessandro Puttinati had himself put some on the market, "both in scagliola and in bronze", in the wake of the Brera success of 1846 (Fig. 5).[26] Puttinati, moreover, had been one of the first 19th-century Italian sculptors to explore the serial potential of the small format. Between 1833 and 1838 he had exhibited at the Brera a series of full-relief plaster statuettes with portraits of illustrious men in contemporary clothes, whose modest and anti-rhetorical poses were expressly geared to their domestic destination.[27] The outcome was an "assortment of geniuses in dressing gowns and slippers" – as Giuseppe Rovani wrote, going a bit too far[28] – which included artists, writers and intellectuals: from Gian Domenico Romagnosi to Massimo D'Azeglio, from Francesco Hayez to Johann Wolfgang von Goethe and Honoré de Balzac (the latter also reproduced in marble). On a stylistic level, this production was closely linked to the latest "romantic" developments in portraiture explored by the circle of Bertel Thorvaldsen (starting with his *Byron*), of whom Puttinati had been a student in Rome.[29] From a commercial point of view, Puttinati had probably been inspired by the growing success of small-format sculpture in other European countries: not only in France – where, in the wake of Dantan Jeune's caricature sculptures, there was an explosion of small-format "statue-mania" which led to the opening of specialised shops such as Susse and Barbadienne[30] – but also, and even earlier, in

26. The statuette was advertised in Michele Leoni, "Storia di Masaniello", *Il Mondo Illustrato*, 11 December 1847, note 1, p. 791.

27. On this production, see Sergio Marinelli, "I gessi di Alessandro Puttinati", *Verona illustrata*, 11 (1988), p. 57-62.

28. Giuseppe Rovani, *Storia delle lettere e delle arti in Italia*, vol. IV, Milan, 1858, p. 521. The fact that Puttinati was ahead of the game on the future interests for the private sector of Italian genre painting is shown by the critical recovery of his small-format production by Rovani who, in the 1850s, praised his ability to obtain at the same time "the applause of the people and the praise of the intelligent". Not surprisingly, Rovani was writing when, in the most advanced artistic sectors of Milan's artistic-literary culture, educated attention to "popular" arts was spreading, fostered by genre painting. See, on this, Alberto Milano, "Stampe popolari milanesi in un quadro di Gerolamo Induno", *Rassegna di Studi e Notizie*, 27 (2003), pp. 249-273.

29. See, for example, the case of *Il principe Giovanni Raimondo* by Pietro Tenerani, where a sketch shows the subject seated and wearing contemporary clothes. See Stefano Grandesso, *Pietro Tenerani (1789-1869)*, Milan, Silvana Editoriale, 2003, p. 104. On the early 19th-century debate on how to portray illustrious men, started by Pompeo Marchesi and Pelagio Palagi's project for the *Monumento ad Andrea Appiani* in Milan, see *Scritti d'arte dell'Ottocento*, ed. by Fernando Mazzocca, Milan-Naples, Ricciardi, 1998, pp. 621-626.

30. See Pierre Cadet, "La Maison Susse", *Gazette des beaux-arts*, 109 (1987), pp. 207-216; Pierre Cadet, "La petite statuaire en France au XIXe siècle à travers les catalogues de vente de la Maison Susse", *Gazette des beaux-arts*, 114 (1989), pp. 207-215.

England.[31] Not surprisingly, precisely in line with England, in 1832 liberal historian Giuseppe Pecchio had been discussing the complex and contradictory dynamics of widening artistic fruition, associating reproduction prints to small-format sculptures, given that "many prefer to convert the price of a beautiful painting into a dozen prints, or the value of a marble statue into about twenty bronze and plaster figurines".[32] Taking into account the rather sophisticated choice of subjects and their high degree of finishing, it seems reasonable to think of a rather restricted circulation of Puttinati's 1830s figurines, probably conceived of as an innovative "ornament for fireplaces and writing desks of the rich".[33] Things were different for the *Masaniello*, made a decade later, at the peak of popular participation in political life: the statuette must have circulated very widely if, as late as 1861, we find a copy in the agitated Neapolitan climate, when "*Camorra* members, Garibaldi's followers, Nationalists and students, as well as men from the medical college, carried in a procession the liberator's bust and a plaster statuette of Masaniello in the act of calling the people to rebellion [...]".[34]

A painting by Gerolamo Induno presented at the Brera in 1859, with the title *Il venditore di statue di gesso* ("The Seller of Plaster Statues"), even didactically demonstrates how small sculptures represented within genre paintings were frequently linked to the sales circuits of figurine makers, in the cheapest sector of the sculpture market (Fig. 6).[35] In a modest house, a young street vendor shows merchandise that, according to reviewers, is bound to be "well known" to the public:[36] on the floor, in the foreground, there is a bust of Dante, the most

31. For an example of English small-format statuettes featuring seated men, see the portrait of Richard Beadon by Lucius Gahagan (1823) (London, National Portrait Gallery). We should also remember that at the same time Bartolomeo Pinelli was making small-format terracotta sculptures, selling them cheaply in the commercial circuits of the Grand Tour. See Stefano Grandesso, "L'antico e i soggetti di genere nella scultura classicista a Roma: Pinelli, Thorvaldsen, Schadow e i 'pensionnaires' francesi", *Studi neoclassici*, 4 (2016), pp. 81-90: 82-83. On Dantan, see Philippe Sorel, "Les Dantan du Musée Carnavalet, portraits-charges sculptés de l'époque romantique", *Gazette des Beaux-Arts*, 128 (1986), pp. 1-38 and 87-102. See also Laurent Baridon, "Dantan le caricaturiste de la statuomanie", *Ridiculosa*, 13 (2006), pp. 127-143.

32. Giuseppe Pecchio, *Sino a qual punto le produzioni scientifiche e letterarie seguano le leggi economiche della produzione in generale*, Lugano 1832, pp. 55-56, now in *Scritti d'arte dell'Ottocento*, p. 478.

33. Raffaello Barbiera, *Il salotto della contessa Maffei*, Milan, Baldini e Castoldi, 1903, p. 63. A real fashion for domestic decorative statues would not spread widely among the middle-class in Italy until the 1850s: see Francesco Tedeschi, "La scultura della 'scuola di Milano'", in *Due secoli di scultura*, Milan, Fabbri, 1995, pp. 64-89.

34. Giacinto De' Sivo, *Storia delle due Sicilie dal 1847 al 1861*, vol. V, Viterbo, Sperandio Pompei, 1867, p. 67. Even before then, the statue had reappeared in *Frammenti della Scapigliatura Milanese* by Cletto Arrighi (see *Almanacco del Pungolo*, Milan, Vallardi, 1858, p. 68).

35. See F.d.F [Filippo de Filippi], "Pubblica mostra di belle arti in Milano", *Rivista contemporanea*, Sept.-Oct. 1859. See also *Dipinti di Domenico e di Gerolamo Induno ordinati in mostra retrospettiva dalla Galleria dell'Arte e dell'Esame nel Castello Sforzesco di Milano*, ed. by Enrico Somaré and Giorgio Nicodemi, Milan, Edizioni dell'Esame, 1933, n. 159.

36. Lodovico Gatta, "Il venditore di statue di gesso", *Gemme d'arti italiane*, 13 (1860), p. 21.

"national" of poets; in the young man's hand, a small bust of Garibaldi, which must have been very popular in Milan around 1860 (Fig. 7).

Also known as "stucco workers", "figurinists" or *lucchesi*, as they came mostly from the Lucca area, the figurine makers were organised in companies of varying numbers, in a hierarchy of masters – those in charge of forming the "good moulds", which were used to reproduce the plaster statuettes – and apprentices, who were responsible for the street vending.[37]

During the 19th century the migratory flow of figurine makers – attested since the end of the 17th century – intensified significantly. While companies of street vendors were scattered all over Europe and even in America,[38] in the European imagination the association between the itinerant statuettes trade and Italy became increasingly marked; in an English spelling book of the early 19th century, for example, the "I" of "Italian" is represented by a figurine maker accompanied by this iconic caption: "Fine Images the Italian sells, and likes the English pence".[39] At the peak of this association we can place a booklet for children published in Paris in 1845 by the Catholic publisher Plon with the title *Le marchand de statuettes*, within the collection *Les petits livres de M.le curé: bibliothèque du presbytère, de la famille et des écoles*.[40] It is a decidedly pathetic story with plenty of veiled political references: it tells the adventures of an Italian nobleman, the Duke of Ronzoni, who in 1820-1821 takes part in a conspiracy against the King of the Two Sicilies. When the conspiracy fails, hunted by the police, the Duke flees with his family but, when eventually trapped, is daringly saved by a passing figurine maker, who first hides him in his humble home, and then, thanks to his international contacts (with other figurine makers, of course), organises his escape to Paris before being arrested in his place. The Duke has no further news of his saviour until, twenty years later, he chances to meet his son, who had just arrived in Paris to sell figurines. To express his gratitude, the Duke welcomes him into his home, raising him like a son. The happy ending is sentimental and social at the same time: in addition to marrying the Duke's daughter, the young figurine maker redeems his humble origins by becoming a famous painter. This story shows how, in the mid-19th century, figurine makers became emblematic figures of a benevolent gaze on people and popular culture, the basis of a myth that would last until the early 20th century.[41]

37. See the statement by Abbot Jacopo Chelini (1759-1824) in his *Zibaldone lucchese*, reported in Paolo Tagliasacchi, *Coreglia Antelminelli patria del figurinaio*, Coreglia, Comune, 2008, pp. 50-51.

38. In 1809 as many as 167 passports were issued in Coreglia; 40 in Bagni di Lucca; 54 in Borgo a Mozzano; 23 in Pescaglia (unfortunately no records exist up to 1866). See Maria Lera, *Gipskatter: gatti di gesso*, Lucca, Maria Pacini Fazzi, 1986, pp. 51 ff.

39. See *Colporteurs: i venditori di stampe e libri e il loro pubblico*, ed. by Alberto Milano, Milan, Medusa, 2015, p. 39.

40. Tonin Castellan, *Le marchand de statuettes*, Paris, Mellier, 1845.

41. This myth would remain unaffected even in the second half of the 19th century, when the profession of figurine maker would be increasingly associated with child trafficking: see Paola A. Sensi-Isolani, "Italian Image Makers in France, England, and the United States", in *Italian Americans Celebrate Life, the Arts and Popular Culture: Selected Essays from the*

At this point, it must be said that Gerolamo Induno was not the first to devote a painting to one of the anonymous protagonists of the "popular" arts trade, but fits within an iconographic vein that had already emerged in modern French genre painting since the 1830s, and later spread to Europe.[42] In 1833 Parisian painter and draftsman Hyppolite Bellangé had exhibited at the Salon a painting entitled *Le marchand de plâtres ambulant* (Fig. 8) – made famous throughout Europe by an engraving by Alexandre-Jean-Louis Jazet – while, some time later, the Flemish painter Jean-Henri De Coene had emphasised the political-ritual uses of the plaster statuettes, painting a toast "à la santé de l'Ancien" by a group of former Napoleon soldiers (Rueil-Malmaison, chateaux de Malmaison et Bois-Préau). These paintings – which, in Bellangé's case, raised the status of the iconography of popular prints devoted to itinerant crafts[43] – evidenced the profound perspective shift of the figurine makers and, above all, of the memory of Napoleon, which occurred during the July Monarchy. Both showed the plaster miniature of Charles Emile Seurre's "petit caporal", a bronze sculpture, now at the Invalides, created in 1833 for the Colonne Vendome within Louis Philippe's attempt to appropriate the Bonapartist past (and also present in the painting by Cabianca mentioned above).[44]

In the 1820s, in fact, things were quite different; the figurine makers were often arrested for political activities. In 1822, in the Moselle region, some medallions with Bonaparte's effigy were seized from street vendor Jean Dominique Santino (which sounds like an appropriate name invented by the figurine maker himself); in Lyon, in 1825, Napoleon's busts and medallions produced by one Mr Paoli, who was immediately expelled from France, were reported. In 1826, in Strasbourg, portraits of Bonaparte were seized from peddler Lorenzo Cazani from Coreglia. In 1827 Dominich Dominique from Lucca was arrested for displaying Bonaparte's busts on the public road. In the same year, other plaster busts representing Napoleon were seized in Limoges from a group of Italian street vendors.[45] Even in the Kingdom of Sardinia during the Restoration, the figurine makers caused serious concern to those in charge of public order to the extent that, in a circular

22nd Annual Conference of the American Italian Historical Association, ed. by Paola A. Sensi-Isolani and Anthony J. Tamburri, New York, American Italian Historical Association, 1990.

42. The topic of street vendors of statuettes was also taken up in the 1840s, but without political implications, in *Biedermeier* painting (Peter Fendi) and in England, by Pre-Raphaelite James Collinson (*Italian Image: Boys at a Roadside Alehoure*, 1849). On figurine makers in England, see Ralph Mills, "'A chimney-piece in Plumtree-court, Holborn': Plaster of Paris 'Images' and Nineteenth-Century Working-Class Material Culture", in *Paraphernalia! Victorian Objects*, ed. by Helen Kingstone and Kate Lister, London, Routledge, 2018, pp. 99-121.

43. See Alberto Milano, "Büsten, Figurenverkäufer", in *Lexikon der Revolutions-Ikonographie in der europäischen Druckgraphik 1789-1889*, vol. I, ed. by Wolfgang Cilleßen, Rolf Reichardt and Moritz Miersch, Münster, Rhema, 2017, pp. 608-624.

44. See Boime, *Art in the Age of Counterrevolution*, pp. 308-310.

45. See Salvatore Carbone, *Fonti per la storia del Risorgimento negli archivi nazionali di Parigi: i rifugiati italiani 1815-1830*, Rome, Istituto Storico del Risorgimento Italiano, 1962, pp. 86-87.

dated 30 December 1846, Genoa's Director of Police seemed to worry more about the circulation of plaster statuettes than of satirical or obscene prints:

> More than once was the Royal Government made to feel the need to prevent, by legal and effective means, the marketing of illustrations, images and other similar objects contrary to good morals and especially the activity, which is more commonly practised by manufacturers or itinerant sellers of plaster statues, who are largely from Lucca [...], shrewd and cunning individuals, who change their address every so often, and are thus very difficult to keep track of [...].[46]

It would be misleading, however, to think of the figurine makers as militants of Napoleon's memory or, later, of the *Risorgimento* cause. Visual sources, in this sense, can be deceptive. To the "shrewd and cunning" individuals of the judicial sources, painters and designers juxtaposed, as we have seen, a markedly sympathetic image of street vendors, not surprisingly focussing on the "apprentices" rather than the masters.[47] The figurine maker who walked the streets of Napoleonic Milan with ancient statues and a bust of Napoleon by Antonio Canova is exemplary in this sense, strangely ending up resembling Bonaparte himself, as if the designer had wanted to imply some form of militancy on the young itinerant's part (Fig. 9).[48]

While not excluding that there might have been some cases of actual political involvement, we should bear in mind that the main objective of the figurine makers was to sell their items, responding very attentively to the public's demand. It is no coincidence in this sense that, when talking of the aforementioned painting by Bellangé, a reviewer sensitive to political history such as Auguste Jal stressed the attention paid to the relationship between goods and customers by the figurine maker, "who sells a virgin to a peasant woman, mother of small children who were brought up in the religious beliefs of the Norman villages; and a statuette of Napoleon to the blacksmith, an old soldier of the empire who has preserved his admiration, his ancient faith, and who perhaps still believes that Napoleon lives on the islands, as the common people say".[49] Bellangé's painting then revealed the considerable ability of the figurine makers to be right up to date: as early as 1833, they already had a miniature of Seurre's statue of Napoleon (the same one featuring in De Coene's nostalgic toast and in the aforementioned painting by Cabianca),

46. *Circolare dell'intendente Direttore di Polizia di Genova*, 30 December 1846, Archivio di Stato di Genova, Gabinetto della Prefettura, b. 19, f. 49-1126 (*Istruzioni sullo smercio di figure di immagini e di altri simili oggetti contrarii ai buoni costumi*). On censorship and material culture during the Restoration, see Enrico Francia, "Oggetti sediziosi. Censura e cultura materiale nell'Italia della Restaurazione", *Mélanges de l'Ecole Française de Rome*, 130/1 (2018), pp. 31-41.

47. An exception was a late picture (1887, private collection) by Gerolamo Induno showing an elderly figurine maker in his workshop.

48. On the serial production (in thousands of copies) of Napoleon's (marble) busts in the Carrara workshops, with related attribution issues, beginning with copies of Antoine-Denis Chaudet and Antonio Canova, see Gérard Hubert, *La sculpture dans l'Italie napolénienne*, Paris, de Boccard, 1964, pp. 342-358.

49. A. Jal. [Auguste Jal], *Les causeries du Louvre: salon de 1833*, Paris, C. Gosselin, 1833, pp. 398-399.

which was later very popular. These elements – versatility and a readiness to change the ranges on offer according to the occasion, taste and expectations of the public – emerge quite clearly even from verbal sources. The *Equipaggio di stampe e figure consegnate a Domenico Lino Tomei con ogni attrezzo per il mestiere* ("Full set of moulds and figures delivered to Domenico Lino Tomei with every tool of his trade"), dated 27 July 1817, shows it well. This is the shopping list of a figurine maker/master, drawn up in view of his departure from Tereglio.[50] Unfortunately, we do not know whom he bought the items from, but Tomei was probably one of the first figurine makers, "if not the very first", to go to America.[51] The inventoried items include, in addition to some tools, "moulds" (i.e., shapes intended for reproduction, including three hundred moulds for medals and medallions) and "figurines" (ready for sale). The way in which Tomei's purchases attempted to interpret the dominant neoclassic taste is not entirely obvious. Meanwhile, compared to the devotional imagery usually (and normally, with good reason) attributed to figurine makers, the consistent secularity of his range of products is surprising: it was entirely pagan, almost entirely made up of reproductions of ancient statues or more generic ancient-style sculptures (fauns, bacchantes, genies, vestals and floras), in line with what the market most requested (and, probably, in view of a context perceived as secular, such as that in America).[52] The ancient sculptures included several copies of works that had just been returned to Italy after Napoleon's depredations and had recently been mentioned in the headlines (including the "Venere de' Medici");[53] there were also plenty of concessions to the Empire style ("one Egyptian woman suitable for a lamp"; "two Egyptian women holding basins") and to works by great artists ("Canova's Bacchante with a female companion"; "two busts by Michelangelo") together with some moral items suitable for any occasion (busts of ancient philosophers). The list also included some "political" images, which, because of their small size, were also among the cheapest in the entire range of the figurine maker.[54] Compared to the great events of recent history, it could not have been more cross-party; winners and losers of the Napoleonic wars coexisted peacefully,

50. *Equipaggio di stampe e figure assegnate a Domenico Lino Tomei con ogni attrezzo per il mestiere*, in Archivio di Stato di Lucca, Legato Prof. Giannini, 38. On this, see Giovanni Giannini, "Memorie storiche di Tereglio", *Bollettino storico lucchese*, 3 (1931), pp. 115-143 (on figurine makers, an unpublished memoir by Adriano Giannini is mentioned: pp. 121-125).

51. Giannini, "Memorie storiche di Tereglio", p. 123

52. Some interesting coincidences between this inventory and the Carrara marble workshops should be investigated further: see Luisa Passeggia, "Arte, gusto e cultura materiale in Italia, Europa e Stati Uniti tra XVIII e XIX secolo", in *Carrara e il mercato della scultura*, Milan 2005-2007, vol. I, Milan, 2005, in part. pp. 62-77. See also Cinzia Maria Sicca, *The Lustrous Trade: Material Culture and the History of Sculpture in England and Italy, c. 1700 - c. 1860*, London, Leicester University Press, 2000.

53. On Napoleon's depredations and the return of works of art from France, see *L'arte contesa: nell'età di Napoleone, Pio VII e Canova*, Exhibition Catalogue, ed. by Roberto Balzani, Milan, Silvana Editoriale, 2009. See also *Firenze 1815: il ritorno di Venere: riflessioni sul recupero toscano delle opere d'arte trafugate da Napoleone*, ed. by Giulia Coco, Florence, Edifir, 2018.

54. Prices ranged from 20 *scudi* for a Bacchus or a Vestal (4 ft reproductions) to one *scudo* for the small bust of La Fayette.

revealing an almost informative desire on the part of the figurine maker: here were the statuettes and busts of Napoleon alongside those of "Valentone" (Wellington) and "Blucer" (the Prussian general Gebhard Leberecht von Blücher), while "the bust of Faietta" (La Fayette) should probably be understood as useful for the American market (rather than an homage to the Revolution).

One of the most interesting documents to reconstruct the history of the mentality of the early 19th-century figurine makers is a set of letters sent to Pasquale Matelli, from Fibialla dei Canonici in the Garfagnana valley, in the province of Lucca, who moved to Piedmont to work as a master figurine maker.[55] His numerous changes of address within a few years (in the Vercelli area, then in Saluzzo, Nizza Monferrato, Chieri and Casale Monferrato) did not necessarily have to do with politics, but with the fact that the workshops of the figurine makers from Lucca operated (usually without any kind of license) on the boundary between legal reproduction and the most brutal counterfeiting. In this regard, it is useful to quote a letter from Pietro Tenerani to his colleague Santo Varni: the sculptor from Carrara writes that he had made the sketch of a Madonna for a princess, "who gave it to the Nuns of the Sacred Heart. They had several copies made, which became popular and came into the hands of the figurine makers from Lucca, so that by dint of reproducing them they are barely recognisable from the first".[56] Tenerani was especially concerned about the loss of quality of the copy, but there is no shortage of evidence, especially in France, of complaints for counterfeiting against Italian figurine makers.[57]

Particularly significant are the letters of Pasquale Matelli's brother, Francesco, a street vendor of statuettes who between 1829 and 1845 operated between Piedmont and France, taking in Saluzzo, Susa, Chambery, Briançon, Grenoble, Nice, Marseille, Pau and Toulouse. Francesco initially moved with a "company", but was always ready to make new contacts and acquire new skills that could progress his work. In a letter dated September 1830, for example, he tells his brother that, having left Briançon, he went to Susa with a "load" of statuettes of Christ, managing to sell them in less than an hour, for twenty-five or thirty *soldi* each. On 28 November 1830 he was in Grénoble, where he had just moved, leaving his old company; he wrote to his brother that he had no intention of retracing his steps: "[…] I received a letter from Filippo's wife and one from Filippo and they call me back a lot and they would like me to be with them as I was before but I think we were selling a lot for priests and for churches and after this change very little is sold […]".[58] In the meantime, in fact, the long-term

55. These documents have been partly discussed in Lera, *Gipskatter*. A copy of the documents is kept in the National Diaries Archive in Pieve Santo Stefano (AR).

56. Letter from Pietro Tenerani to Santo Varni, 15 March 1845, *Il Propugnatore*, 7 (1874), pp. 123-124.

57. In France, for example, frequent accusations of counterfeiting works were made by their "urban" competitors, such as the Maison Susse. See, for example, a trial brought by a Susse agent against two Italian figurine makers who had reproduced a statue of Saint Theresa belonging exclusively to Susse. See *Jurisprudence de la Court Royal*, Dijon, 1847, pp. 227-229.

58. Letter by Francesco from Grenoble, 28 November 1830.

consequences of the political landslides that had led to the July Monarchy had reached the French countryside and Francesco was ready, starting up a partnership with Paolo Mariani from Vitiana, who "as a figurine maker works very well [...] and ... we are currently selling busts of [the] new king to all the mayors of departments [to] all those who want [them] [...]".[59] The transition from devotional sculpture to that celebrating the new regime (with customers even among local institutions), therefore, was very rapid. After all, the popularity of the new king would not last much longer: in a caricature by Charles Philipon (seized by the government) there appears a figurine maker (it might be Francesco himself) with a load of European kings (which nobody wants), including, just visible, the bust of King Louis Philippe.[60]

In conclusion, it should be noted that, in parallel with what was happening in genre painting, the iconography of the street vendor of statuettes enjoyed considerable fortune in European political graphics and, around 1848, penetrated deeply into the imagination of the *Risorgimento*. In addition to the aforementioned material metaphors, the effectiveness of the motif is due to its profound meanings for the identity of the newspaper and readers. On the title page of the collection of *Caricature pittoresche di diverse attitudini di varie figure* (*Picturesque Caricatures of Different Attitudes of Various Figures*), engraved by Arnold van Westerhout in Rome in 1687 (Fig. 10) – one of the first visual representations of a street vendor of figurines – the Flemish engraver was already presenting himself as a grotesque and bespectacled figurine.[61] In line with this, the use of the iconography of the street vendor of statuettes by the personifications of some 19th-century satirical newspapers (*Lo Spirito Folletto*, *La Strega*), aimed to create an intermediatic symbolic solidarity in the context of widely distributed images.[62] It was no coincidence that, in 1832, the aforementioned Bellangé had entitled one of his watercolours dedicated to a figurine maker: *Le Dieu du Peuple*.[63] Becoming part of his merchandise was a clear sign of popularity, but that was not all: the figurine maker himself was an image of the people; not surprisingly, some Italian political figures (including, on several occasions, Count Cavour himself) were represented as statuette sellers. The *Garibaldi chincagliere* (Garibaldi the Trinket-seller) designed by Adolfo Matarelli (Fig. 11), for example, should not be read as an accusation of speculation against Garibaldi. On the other hand, using this motif does not only underline the disproportion between the great man, placed on the level of Italy and Europe, and the members of the Rattazzi government; rather, the entire identification between "great men" and sellers of great men strongly alludes to the deep bond between Garibaldi and the Italian people, a migrant people of which the figurine maker is an emblematic image.

59. *Ibid.*

60. Charles Philipon, *Personne n'en veut plus pour deux sous? (Le ministère en plâtre)*, lithography, 1831.

61. See Milano, "Büsten, Figurenverkäufer", p. 608.

62. See for example: http://velasquez.sns.it/caricatura/schedaCaricatura.php?id=51.

63. See Jules Adeline, *Hippolyte Bellangé et son œuvre*, Paris, A. Quantin, 1880, p. 105.

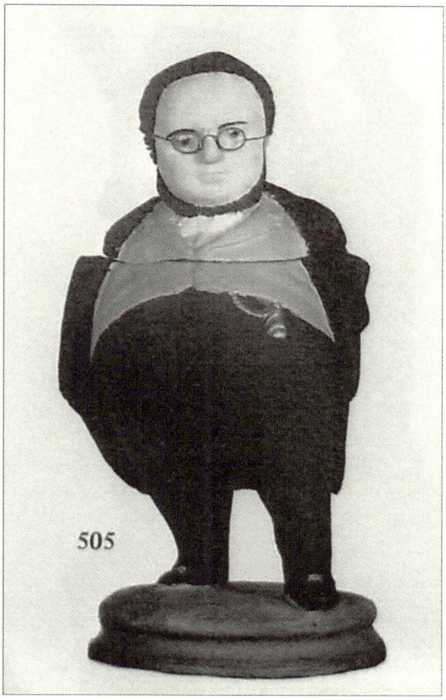

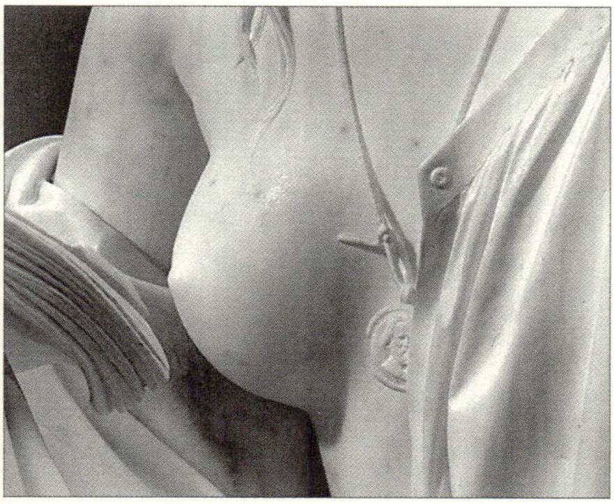

1. Francesco Redenti, "Attualità. Una speculazione curiosa", *Il Fischietto*, 12 Jan-uary 1854, lithography. Turin, Biblioteca Civica Centrale.

2. *Camillo Cavour*, coloured clay (height 32 cm), Istituto Mazziniano, Genoa.

3 a-b. Pietro Magni, *La leggitrice*, marble (height 122 cm), 1856-1861. Washington, National Gallery of Art.

4. Giuseppe Barni, [after Domenico Induno], "La questua", *Gemme d'arti italiane,* 1850, engraving.
5. Alessandro Puttinati, *Masaniello*, c. 1846, plaster (height 51 cm). Verona, Galleria d'Arte Moderna Achille Forti.

6. Domenico Gandini [after Gerolamo Induno], "Il venditore di statue di gesso", *Gemme d'arti italiane*, 1860, copper engraving.
7. *Le belle figurine*, Litografia Corbetta, 1860, lithography. Milano, Civica Raccolta delle Stampe Achille Bertarelli.
8. Joseph Louis Hyppolite Bellangé, *Le marchand de plâtres ambulant*, 1833, oil painting on canvas. Paris, Musée du Louvre.

9. Gaspare Cagnoni [after Gian Battista Bosio], engraving, *Costumi di Milano e suoi Circondari*, III-3, Milano 1807, tav. 18. Milan, Civica Raccolta delle Stampe Achille Bertarelli.
10. Arnold van Westerhout, *Caricature pittoresche di diverse attitudini di varie figure* (frontispiece), etching, 1687.
11. Mata [Adolfo Matarelli], "Garibaldi chincagliere", *Il Lampione*, 11 October 1862, lithography.

Alessio Petrizzo

Return to Order, and Material Culture: Missing Objects, Anti-Republican Narratives and Police Practices in Rome after 1849

1. *The political "temperature" of things*

Objects are powerful vectors of relationships and feelings, beliefs and narratives, ideologies and imagination. "The whole of Napoleon / Painted on a button", sings Italian singer-songwriter Vinicio Capossela,[1] condensing the social magic of things into a dazzling image: grandiose myths, powerful ideals and compelling epics keep the intensity of the bonds they evoke intact, even when they are scaled down to a miniature, a detail, an allusive symbol reproduced on trivial and everyday objects.

Research such as that by Emmanuel Fureix on political iconoclasm in 19th-century France has recently granted further substance and depth to the poetry and intuition of the Italian singer-songwriter. One of the many outcomes shown by Fureix's research has been the frequency and intensity with which, in the hectic months between the end of the First Empire and the start of the Restoration, settlings of scores and violence erupted at the mere sight of objects like Capossela's button. Rosettes, emblems and flowers, but also simple combinations of colours exhibited on the clothing of the militants of either the Napoleonic or the Bourbon camps, caused quarrels, assaults and fights.[2] We can also agree with Fureix that, beyond the heated political passions of private individuals, for a long time during that century, the repressive activity of the institutions themselves, directed against the liberal, radical and reactionary oppositions, took the form of a real "gaze police" – and not only in France, as Enrico Francia's recent studies have suggested in relation to the Italian *Risorgimento.*[3] Depending on the places, times and people involved – from governments to individual agents – the semiotics guiding the inspection of suspicious signs circulating in public spaces could be lucid and careful, exaggerated and paranoid or clumsy and coarse, but in

1. *Dove siamo rimasti a terra Nutless* (from the CD *Ovunque proteggi*, Atlantic/Warner Music, 2006).

2. Emmanuel Fureix, *L'oeil blessé. Politiques de l'iconoclasme après la Révolution française*, Ceyzérieu, Champ Vallon, 2019.

3. Enrico Francia, "Oggetti sediziosi. Censura e cultura materiale nell'Italia della Restaurazione", *Visualità e socializzazione politica nel lungo Ottocento italiano*, ed. by Alessio Petrizzo, *Mélanges de l'Ecole française de Rome*, 130/1 (2018), pp. 31-41.

each case it was for decades a core element in the work carried out by the European police to monitor and maintain public order. Observing and decoding any potentially seditious signs that appeared in public places or on the bodies of individuals was an activity that became part of police practices well before other disciplines, such as criminal anthropology, and other tools, such as mugshots, provided new theoretical frameworks, technologies and tangible clues on the bodies of criminals to observe, record and catalogue at the end of the century.[4]

In Rome, the focus of this article, if we look at the records made by the papal police during the Restoration and in particular in the 1830s and 1840s, after Gregory XVI's criminal codes were issued, we significantly find gathered under the same heading "mutinies", "weapons from abroad", "demonstrations", "sectarian signs (emblems, flags)" and "manuscripts". This sort of miscellany suggests the measure of danger associated, at least theoretically, with the circulation of political artefacts, assimilated with seditious writings, protest gatherings, insubordinations and weapons introduced illegally across the State borders.[5] The proliferation of political objects around 1848, favoured by the temporary freedom to manufacture, sell and exhibit them in public, certainly did not lessen this perception.[6] Once the revolutionary impetus died down, in the first few years of the so-called Second Restoration – the period discussed in this article – the set of objects that was briefly legitimated was largely banned again in most Italian States, as were the new signs devised by opponents to recognise each other and operate in hostile circumstances. In Rome, in the autumn of 1849, the pro-government press reported "anonymous, mysterious letters, notices posted up in the streets, death threats (written in coal)" at the hands of the Republicans, nightly chants, defamatory cries[7] and, consistent with these subversive acts – as in the police records from previous decades –, it also reported rumours regarding politicised artefacts. While the pontiff was slow to return to Rome, the losers apparently repeated "one of the most wicked lies", which had already circulated months back, namely that one of the first cannonballs that had fallen on the city

4. Laura Di Fiore, *Gli Invisibili. Polizia politica e agenti segreti nell'Ottocento borbonico*, Naples, Federico II University Press, 2018, p. 132-133.

5. See Monica Calzolari, "Il nuovo sistema informativo di polizia per la repressione dei delitti politici", in *Roma fra la Restaurazione e l'elezione di Pio IX. Amministrazione, economia, società e cultura*, ed. by Anna Lia Bonella, Augusto Pompeo and Manola Ida Venzo, Rome-Freiburg-Wien, Herder, 1997, pp. 79-98; *I regolamenti penali di Papa Gregorio XVI per lo Stato Pontificio (1832)*, ed. by Sergio Vinciguerra, Padua, CEDAM, 1998; Chiara Lucrezio Monticelli, "I circuiti informativi di polizia tra morale e politica dalla Restaurazione alla Repubblica Romana", in *Prescritto e proscritto: religione e società nell'Italia moderna (secc. XVI-XIX)*, ed. by Andrea Cicerchia, Guido Dall'Olio and Matteo Duni, Rome, Carocci, 2015.

6. Enrico Francia, "Oggetti patriottici. Una ricerca sulla cultura materiale del Risorgimento", *Culture visuali e forme di politicizzazione nel lungo '800 europeo*, ed. by Gian Luca Fruci and Alessio Petrizzo, *Passato e presente*, 100 (2017), pp. 37-44; Ignazio Veca, "Oggetti animati. Materialità, circolazione e usi della figura di Pio IX (1846-1849)", *Il Risorgimento*, 64/1 (2017), pp. 63-97; Costanza Bertolotti, Gian Luca Fruci, Alessio Petrizzo, *Icone politiche. Celebrità e nuovi media ai tempi del Risorgimento*, Mantua, PubliPaolini, 2018, pp. 24-61.

7. *L'Osservatore romano*, 5 October 1849 (article titled "Le vendette dei repubblicani").

was engraved with the words *Gift of Pius IX to the Romans.*[8] On the winners' part, from that moment and for years to come, the rumours, spread or allowed to spread by the police and reported in the news and in political trials, rather frequently listed (alleged) consignments, arrivals or discoveries of political objects: ties with sectarian colours or emblems, tri-coloured flags decorated with skulls, consignments of knives and daggers engraved with "Death to the Tyrants" or green hats in the style popular among "the demagogues".[9] Until at least the mid-1850s, this imagined arsenal of seditious objects was used by the restored authorities as a system of material icons of fear, in order to crush the memory of the Republic using its most controversial episodes, keeping alive the ghost of an organised and dangerous sect in order to justify the repressive policies in place.

And yet, alongside these kinds of undoubtedly "hot" political objects – sought, banished, fantasised – from the early days following the overthrow of the Republic, in early July 1849 a very different series of artefacts, around which a different police gaze was focussed, largely contributed to reiterating the republic's counter-revolutionary paradigm as a time of personal and collective insecurity, injustice, robbery and violence.[10]

These objects did not draw their political charge from the presence of explicit messages, yet they gravitated towards the same symbolic horizon outlined so far and helped define and strengthen the contents of the anti-republican discourse that would soon emerge in Catholic-reactionary intellectual or literary production. There were no shapes, colours, inscriptions or images inspired by political languages, celebrities or events, similar to the millions produced by the hand or for the use of militants and followers of many causes, in the age of cross-Atlantic revolutions.[11] Or rather, there were some that were not by chance caught up in the cogs of police investigations. However, they were objects of a completely different kind, indicative of another type of relationship between material and political cultures, more oblique than the production, circulation, use of or hunt for explicitly political things, but no less effective in soliciting interests and emotions, promoting belonging and directing memories.[12]

In fact, even objects totally or partially devoid of any explicit connotation – in short, buttons without Napoleon – can be powerful vectors of political

8. *Ibid.* (article titled "Varietà. Storia contemporanea", printed entirely in bold).

9. Nicola Roncalli, *Cronaca di Roma*, vol. III, *1852-1858*, ed. by Domenico Maria Bruni, Rome, Istituto per la storia del Risorgimento italiano, 2006, p. 101 (December 1852) and p. 138 (May 1853).

10. David Armando, Massimo Cattaneo, "La Repubblica romana del 1798-99 nella memoria dell'Ottocento", in *La democrazia alla prova della spada. Esperienza e memoria del 1799 in Europa*, ed. by Antonino De Francesco, Milan, Guerini, 2003, p. 277-329.

11. Leora Auslander, *Cultural Revolutions: The Politics of Everyday Life in Britain, North America and France*, Berkeley-Los Angeles, University of California Press, 2009. See also "Storia e cultura materiale: recenti traiettorie di ricerca. Interventi di Fabio Dei, Giorgio Riello, Beverly Lemire, Manuel Charpy, Leora Auslander", ed. by Alessio Petrizzo and Carlotta Sorba, in *Contemporanea*, 3 (2016), pp. 437-480.

12. *Objects of War: The Material Culture of Conflict and Displacement*, ed. by Leora Auslander and Tara Zahra, Ithaca (NY), Cornell University Press, 2018.

relationships and feelings, beliefs and narratives, ideologies and imagination. The political temperature of things is not measured only by their appearance or material value: objects that usually blend in with the backdrop and routine of everyday life can all of a sudden become "hot".

> The undersigned, Teresa De Rosa reports that in May 1849 last, the few objects she possessed both silver and copper and her linen (of which she appends a list herewith) were requisitioned, leaving the reporter's home almost completely stripped. The consequences were terrible: besides her spouse, who was already lying ill, both the reporter and her two miserable daughters became seriously ill due to the fright suffered. Such illness worsened when a gang of Garibaldi's followers came looking for the priest Domenico Viti, the reporter's brother, whose life they wanted to take at all costs and who could barely save himself by hiding in a basement.
> The poor reporter, having heard that there is a Commission appointed for the recovery of requisitioned objects, appeals to it, begging the Supreme goodness of the Most Excellent Gentlemen who sit on it to allow the poor reporter to recover as many of the objects as it is possible to find. Otherwise, she begs the excellent Heart of their Excellences to grant some help to her poor, desperate family that suffered so much under the Republican Government; together with her daughters, she will not fail to pray to God for their long and prosperous Preservation.[13]

What objects was this woman looking for, in whose words the age-old repertoires of supplication are joined by the lexis and dynamics of modern politics?[14] The list – one of the most recurrent discursive forms to pin down objects that have lost their function, according to Francesco Orlando[15] – soon follows: five pieces of cutlery, two holy-water vessels and a silver crucifix, a clock, a mattress, four pillows, thirteen sheets, eighteen towels, nine shirts, three wooden tables, two copper pots. The circumstances of the removal first, and the regime change later, gave this modest but not insignificant household property an unexpected political potential, which the sister of a priest who had escaped murder by some of Garibaldi's troops did not hesitate to use with the restored authorities, not only by way of compensation but as a deliberate and explicit channel to form a relationship.

13. Archivio di Stato di Roma (henceforth ASR), *Direzione generale di polizia* (henceforth *DGP*), *Commissione delle recupere* (henceforth *CR*), b. 10, n. 1738. The collection *Commissione delle recupere* is part of the collection *Direzione generale di polizia*, currently being re-classified. Ten envelopes are at present numbered historically from 1 to 10 and three have a modern classification in pencil: *Recupere fatte bb. 1-3, bb. 5-6-7, bb. 8-9.* I will use these classifications: the box number followed by the position number of each matter, which identifies the file containing the documents referred to or cited. I am grateful to the archive staff for facilitating my consultation of this material.

14. Yves-Marie Bercé, *La dernière chance. Histoire des suppliques*, Paris, Perrin, 2014; "Suppliques. Lois et cas dans la normativité de l'époque moderne", ed. by Simona Cerutti and Massimo Vallerani, in *L'Atelier du Centre de recherches historiques*, EHESS, 13 (2015), pp. 5-17; Marco Meriggi, "Contro la costituzione. La mobilitazione legittimista nel Mezzogiorno post-quarantottesco", *Le carte e la storia*, 25/2 (2019), pp. 7-18, and Marco Meriggi, *La nazione populista. Il Mezzogiorno e i Borboni dal 1848 all'Unità*, Bologna, il Mulino, 2021.

15. Francesco Orlando, *Obsolete Objects in the Literary Imagination: Ruins, Relics, Rubbish, Uninhabited Places, and Hidden Treasures*, New Haven-London, Yale University Press, 2006.

As we shall see, everyday objects that, following the Republic's requisition orders or voluntarily surrendered under collective pressure in the climactic stages of the defence, were taken from their respective owners and destined to public uses very different from their original or private purposes, became, in the days following the fall of the Republic, very tangible reflections of the past political upheaval and, at the same time, instruments of its possible overcoming. Mattresses, sheets, shirts, offcuts of material sent to military hospitals; timber, poles, railings, nails and work tools of all kinds destined to build barricades and fortifications; bells, sacred furnishings, silver or copper objects removed to be melted in order to make weapons or coins; objects that were stolen or destroyed in bursts of iconoclasm by sympathisers or by violent or dishonest republican agents, became the vehicle of a renewed, reciprocal positioning between the restored authorities and their subjects. At the same time, they provided the police investigating their fate with an opportunity for a vast, multi-faceted and often informal investigation of the five months of republican government, its methods and its past and present supporters. The outcomes of this investigation preceded and were often useful in instructing the political processes held shortly thereafter.

Not surprisingly, after her report, Teresa Viti De Rosa was soon summoned.

2. *The Recoveries Commission*

On 18 November 1849 Teresa climbed the stairs of the Government Palace (*Palazzo Madama*, now the seat of the Senate of the Italian Republic) and took a seat in the second-floor office where the commission to which she had addressed her request was located: the Commission – to give it its full name – for the Recovery and Return of Items, Furniture and Furnishings Requisitioned by the Abolished Government, more often abbreviated as the Recoveries Commission. Sometime later, the woman entered the premises of the former hospital of Saint Francis of Paola and there, among the furnishings and objects left in the convent after the closure of the war hospital that had been created there, she recognised her copper objects and linen and – whether this was really so or represented a tacit compensation for the information that she had been able to provide – regained possession of at least part of her lost belongings.

Teresa's case was certainly not unique. The Commission had been operational – in fact, had been very active – since the previous July, and by November hundreds of people had made similar claims. A few days before Teresa had addressed her request, the Commission had the 11th out of 17 notices published between August 1849 and July 1850 in up to 300 copies posted around the city. This brought to the public's attention the returns made and the summary descriptions of the goods found and in its possession, all scrupulously ordered and numbered. Official or aligned channels such as the *Giornale di Roma* or the *Osservatore Romano* systematically reported on these notices, almost always on their front pages, either including the long lists in full or merely reporting the publication of yet another notice, inviting all concerned to go to the places where public notices were usually posted for detailed information, in an inter-media circle that ran from modern printed paper to the traditional format of the notice. The *Eleventh Notice* of 9 November, in fact, contained 152 reports: from "1819. An iron altar cross. 1820. A painting on canvas representing the Virgin Mary and St Anthony. 1821. Two carriage wheel bands. 1822. A four-wheeled cart (*Returned to the agent of the Austrian Embassy*). 1823. 11 cart loads of roof tiles and 5 of roof slates (*Returned to their owner Mr Bresiri*)" and to "1970. Four pieces of lace used for long and short surplices", even including "a bay mare approximately 8 years old branded on its right thigh with the letters C.*R. (*Returned to its owner Mr Ferdinando Rossi*)", "two bunches of artificial flowers of different colours (*Returned to Mr Pietro Luccarini for the Lateran Archpriesthood*)" or "a black felt coat, a short cape in clerical cloth, two pairs of red breeches, a pair of shoes, four shirts, three coloured handkerchiefs, a hat, a satin bag, and other iron objects, a small broom and comb (*All returned to their owner Pietro Danesi*)".[16] Giuseppe Spada, who well recalled those "great lists" posted around the city in his *Storia della rivoluzione di Roma* (*History of the Rome Revolution*), having personally kept them all, pointed out that they "included no fewer than 2,954 items".[17] Work was intense especially in the first few months after the fall of the Republic: a time of transition, settling and a spasmodic gathering of information that represented one of the earliest, most meticulous and overt (and therefore sometimes also controversial) measures of the return to order, during the long-awaited return of the sovereign.

In truth, the delicate issue was not ignored by the Republican government either: it intervened several times to inform the public, and discipline its agents, on the correct requisitioning procedures[18] and set up appropriate offices. The Commission for the Preservation and Distribution of Requisitioned Objects and Premises, led by deputy Orazio Antinori, was charged with keeping watch over "the abuses by self-appointed requisitioners, which marr the sacred name of the Republic and of freedom with undignified acts". It was joined by a special small commission invested with full powers. The former met in the Government Palace (where soon afterwards the Recoveries Commission would also be located), the latter in the Montecitorio Palace. There was also a Military Commission for the Repression of Attacks to the Property of Others.[19] On 28 May 1849 all citizens had been invited to present within two weeks all the evidence about the requisitions they had suffered, and the first returns of the ones judged illegal had taken place

16. Archivio del Museo Centrale del Risorgimento, Rome (henceforth MCRR), *Bandi* 88/42. The complete series of notices can be reconstructed using the *Bandi* collections in the MCRR and in the library of the ASR. The notice of publication is in *Giornale di Roma*, 13 November 1849.

17. Giuseppe Spada, *Storia della rivoluzione di Roma e della restaurazione del governo pontificio dal 1 giugno 1846 al 15 luglio 1849*, vol. III, Florence, Pellas, 1869, p. 623. Spada incorrectly mentions 16 notices, having misinterpreted the title of the last one, dated 12 July 1850.

18. See the notices *Romani!* (both dated 4 May 1849), one by war minister Giuseppe Avezzana and the other by the triumvirs, in *Bollettino delle leggi, proclami, circolari, regolamenti ed altre disposizioni della Repubblica romana*, Rome, Tipografia Nazionale, 1849, nos 312 and 313.

19. *Bollettino delle leggi*, nos 337 and (for the quote) 354.

as early as June, even though the need to defend the city had later caused them to be suspended.[20] Consequently, immediately after taking the city, the urgency also arose for its French occupiers.

In the same days when – as usual in changes of regime – a decree by General Nicolas Charles Victor Oudinot (8 July) ordered the removal of the Republic's eagles, tri-coloured flags and Phrygian caps, thus beginning the settling down of symbols of power in the public space,[21] their gaze was directed elsewhere, too. They were concerned with putting order in the disrupted premises and possessions of churches and religious bodies, as well as in the private sphere of many citizens affected by the requisitions, occupations or demolitions ordered by the Republic in the previous months, by the final stages of the siege and by the unrest that followed. The then police prefect, French Lieutenant Colonel François Chapuis, issued two ordinances that (re)started the returns process. The first, as early as 8 July, announced that the "sacred receptacles, church furnishings and bells removed from the religious establishments of Rome" still in the public storerooms – so, never melted down – were available to be returned. The second one, on the following day, ordered that: "the horses, carriages and other objects requisitioned by the past government, and currently in the hands of inhabitants and soldiers, must be returned to their owners" and anyone who did not hand them back within three days would be liable to prosecution for aggravated theft.[22]

These ordinances probably responded to the pressure to protect the wealth of the church and reverse the material damage suffered by many religious bodies and personally brought to bear by many cardinals, diplomatic representatives and aristocratic families. Together with the problem of the bells, urgent because it affected many churches in Rome,[23] some cases were immediately pressing. The College of Pontifical Masters of Ceremonies, for example, reported the disappearance from the Quirinale Palace of the great chalice and silver pyx used in the conclave to store the ballots in a pontiff's election: "After the removal of the Republican Government the door was found breached, and the objects themselves stolen".[24] Cardinal Mario Mattei reported the theft "of all my furniture, furnishings, books, paintings, papers […], chasubles, lace, clothing" and of objects from the estate of Pope Gregory XVI, of whom he was executor.[25] The Minister of the Kingdom of the Two Sicilies, Count Ludolf, pressed for the return of the goods

20. Some ledgers of the Republican Commission have ended up among the first files in the collection; see ASR, *DGP*, *CR*, b. *Recupere fatte 1-3*, nos 2, 3 and 6.

21. The text is in *Il Costituzionale romano*, 9 July 1849 and the notice is in ASR, *DGP*, *CR*, b. 9, n. 1513.

22. *Ibid.* (for the texts and notices of both).

23. Many of the documents from the Recoveries Commission contain requests for the return of requisitioned bells: for those which could not be found, at the beginning of October 1849 a refund in metal was arranged; ASR, *DGP*, *CR*, b. 7, folder *Campane*; MCRR, *Bandi* 88/18. See Daniele Arru, *La legislazione della Repubblica romana del 1849 in materia ecclesiastica*, Milan, Giuffrè, 2012, pp. 133-135, and Jacopo De Santis, *Tra altari e barricate. La vita religiosa a Roma durante la Repubblica romana del 1849*, Florence, Firenze University Press, 2020.

24. ASR, *DGP*, *CR*, b. 2, n. 227.

25. *Ibid.*, b. 1, n. 48.

and documents left in his rooms in Palazzo Farnese, occupied by the republican Barricades Commission.[26] A substantial matter then concerned the dozens of weapons requisitioned from the former King of Portugal, the exiled Don Miguel, several of which were precious.[27] There were many such urgent cases, and they were often given a priority, which also ran through traditional informal channels. But the two police ordinances mentioned resulted in putting people, things and words feverishly into motion even beyond the institutional, social and political circuits closest to the throne of the pope-king.

An initial commission, composed of two French and one Italian military servicemen, began to collect complaints relating to horses and carriages in an inn in Piazza del Popolo.[28] The district authorities carried out inspections and drew up lists, and the municipal authorities also started an inventory of the goods amassed in the warehouses and deposits they were responsible for.[29] Whatever was too damaged was piled up in the courtyard of the Campidoglio Palace, where between grates and balcony railings, furniture and carriages in pieces, fragments of statues and pieces of painted canvases also emerged. To those French who supported the mission of restoring the papacy, such spectacles did not just seem a "sad museum" but confirmed that "what was called the awakening of the Italian nation" was in reality nothing but great plunder.[30]

In Castel Sant'Angelo there were the surviving elements of the cardinals' carriages, requisitioned ahead of the clashes of 30 April and then again in May and, from 10 July, *chargés d'affaires*, house masters, servants and coachmen of various cardinals had been granted access permits. And while chroniclers reported that "priests, friars and some prelates begin to be seen walking around Rome",[31] the representatives of many religious institutions came forward, asking to return to the places whence they had been evicted, to regain possession of, or at least be compensated for, the bells and other goods of which they had been stripped. Made almost always in Italian and rarely in French, often accompanied by copies of the receipts regularly issued by the Republican agents in charge of the requisitions, in those days such requests took different paths and were addressed either directly to Oudinot, or to the Governor of Rome, General Louis de Rostolan, or to Chapuis or to other police departments, or to Rome's commander in chief, General Sauvan, or even to the new Provisional Municipal Commission.

In order to coordinate these separate and partial initiatives and routes, and make the action more effective in a context where, day after day, in different offices, cases and requests multiplied, on 19 July, a few days after the formal

26. *Ibid.*, b. 7, n. 909.

27. *Ibid.*, b. *Recupere fatte 1-3*, n. 375.

28. *Il Costituzionale romano*, 11 July 1849.

29. ASR, *DGP*, *CR*, b. *Recupere fatte 1-3*, n. 374 and b. 4, n. 604.

30. *Rome en 1848-1849-1850. Correspondance d'un officier français de l'armée expéditionnaire d'Italie, publiée par l'abbé T. Boulangé*, vol. I, Limoges, Barbou, 1851, p. 295.

31. Nicola Roncalli, *Cronaca di Roma 1844-1870*, vol. II, *1848-1851*, ed. by Anna Franca Tempestoso and Maria Luisa Trebiliani, Rome, Istituto per la storia del Risorgimento italiano, 1997, p. 200.

and solemn restoration of temporal power, the creation of an *ad hoc* commission was finally announced. Led by the new police prefect Le Rouxeau as its president, the Recoveries Commission was made up of five men closely linked to the aristocracy, the curia and the pontifical administration: Prince Girolamo Odescalchi (brother of the Pietro already appointed by Pius IX to the State Council in 1847, to the Senate in the constitutional period, a few days before placed at the helm of the Provisional Municipal Commission and also president of the Monti district);[32] Cavalier Ferdinando De Cinque, a Roman patrician, between the 1830s and 1850s on several occasions appointed as one of Rome's *Conservatori*; lawyers Pietro Bertini (first judge of the Criminal Court in Rome, in August also called to be part of the Commission for the Direction of Political Trials, of which he later became president) and Francesco Tomassetti (also shortly afterwards secretary of the Central Commission for Censorship and brother of the secretary of the Council Congregation, Monsignor Luigi Tomassetti); and Domenico Farina as secretary.[33]

The commission had the power not only to manage the goods found in public storerooms and former military hospitals but also – as suggested by the tangled events just cited about other crucial organs of the restoration that was about to begin – to order investigations and searches, to interrogate witnesses or suspicious individuals in order to track down the requested goods that were still elusive and to identify those responsible for any theft, handling of stolen goods or violence brought to its knowledge by the complainants. Like the police chiefs, with whom it worked in close contact, it resided in the Government Palace, where three days a week it received supplications, petitions, complaints, detailed lists of objects missing or found, police reports and indications of places and people to check. There it also summoned those it wished to hear, whenever it did not have to go and interrogate people already under arrest. Not only that: the courtyard of Palazzo Madama also became a storeroom for bulky goods – military vehicles, wagons and horses – which were delivered to the commission and could not immediately be stored in other warehouses. For months the Government Palace, no less than other public storerooms, resembled a market where all those who had, or claimed they had, suffered damage by the Republic wound up from all over the city and the countryside to review the goods available for complaints, on which to assert (or claim) property rights.[34]

32. Marco Bocci, *Il municipio di Roma tra riforma e rivoluzione (1847-1851)*, Rome, Istituto nazionale di studi romani, 1995, pp. 107 ff.

33. For information on these figures, see the report by Tocqueville's envoy in Rome, in *Rome et les Etats Pontificaux sous l'occupation étrangère: lettres du colonel Callier (juillet 1849-mars 1850)*, ed. by Abraham B. Duff and Maurice Degros, Paris, Imprimérie Nationale, 1950, pp. 104, 107, 112; *Almanacco romano ossia Raccolta dei primari dignitari e funzionari della Corte romana*, Rome, Chiassi, 1855; Carla Lodolini Tupputi, "La commissione direttrice dei processi. Ricerche sulla Restaurazione pontificia del 1849", *Rassegna storica del Risorgimento*, 111 (2004), pp. 369-416.

34. For some of the many examples, see ASR, *DGP*, *CR*, b. 3, n. 342; b. 7, n. 1076; and b. 9, n. 1627.

This gaze police, which was quickly set up to protect the victims of the Republic – and therefore eminently political even if called to scrutinise, measure and compare objects and descriptions of objects which formed an unusual bazaar – was no less meticulous than that directed at explicitly political objects, with which, however, it continued to coexist. Whenever tricoloured rosettes, "a brass eagle symbol of the republic",[35] "two uniforms of scarlet cloth in the *Garibaldese* style", "a three-coloured merino sash, another similar silk one with a gold fringe" (both found in August in a noblewoman's house, cousin of Orazio Antinori, where they had gone in search of stolen silver),[36] civil-guard uniforms, jackets or coats of the 1848 Roman Legion, sometimes with medals from the battle of Vicenza and the Republic, and perhaps accompanied by a bundle of obscene prints[37] were found during the commission's investigations,[38] they were requisitioned and gave rise to further investigations.

Above all, this initiative was immediately conceived, in no uncertain terms, as urgent and rigorous. The circular sent three days after the creation of the commission to the police officers at the city gates, with the order to keep it posted in their respective offices, leaves no doubt about it:

> The Police Officers assigned to the City Gates are reminded of their obligation to watch for the discovery of objects [violently requisitioned by the deposed Government]; warning, that if their removal were to occur due to their negligence or complicity, they will be dismissed from employment, without prejudice of the crimes, which they would commit depending on cases and circumstances.[39]

Very severe penalties were therefore envisaged for the officers themselves. After all, post-Republican Rome appeared and remained a disturbing space for a long time and not only for the visible traces of the war, due to the cannonballs that had fallen even on churches and historic buildings or to the measures ordered for its defence: trees had been cut down to block access to the streets, country houses had been demolished in the suburban vineyards, many inhabitants had been moved from the areas most exposed to cannon fire to private properties or requisitioned convents. Even on a social and political level, the city appeared to be a scrambled, fluid, porous and treacherous space, despite the curfew, the order to hand over any weapons and the ban on wearing uniforms. Moreover, as alleged Republicans had not yet left the city, there were fears that rivers of precious stolen goods might take the road to the provinces or be moved beyond the state borders altogether: the press had already reported that in the countryside "individuals who had left Rome were selling at not inconsiderable price pieces of silverware broken and rendered useless".[40] In other words, there was a need to act quickly.

35. *Ibid.*, b. *Recupere fatte bb. 5-6-7*, n. 515.
36. *Ibid.*, n. 516.
37. ASR, *DGP*, *CR*, b. 8, n. 1421/1468. See also *ibid.*, n. 1491.
38. *Ibid.*, b. 7, n. 1106.
39. Biblioteca di storia moderna e contemporanea, Rome, Bandi a. 203/66.
40. *Il Costituzionale romano*, 13 July 1849.

3. *Maps of suspicion, denunciations and declarations of faith*

In response to the first French ordinances (but often many weeks later), sometimes those who found themselves in possession of goods that had suddenly become compromising, even as the mere consequence of a careless purchase, preferred to present themselves spontaneously. This was the case (one of many) with a bookseller who claimed he had bought from "a soldier" some volumes taken from the library of a religious institute with the sole purpose of saving them and returning them in due course; or the owner of a horse purchased from "a captain of Garibaldi's Legion named Lorenzo Minuti", who did not issue a receipt.[41] Or with a landowner who in October reported a saddler employed by a coachman in Piazza San Silvestro for selling him the gold decorations of cardinals' carriages and the bows from their servants' liveries (both occasionally torn off by "mobs of people" as aristocratic symbols from the day following the proclamation of the Republic the previous February).[42]

But the – presumed and often suspected – goodwill of the Romans was not enough. The Recoveries Commission drew up inventories of the goods stored in public warehouses, contacted the *Monte di pietà* where part of the disappeared objects may have been pawned and drew up inventories of the objects left in the convents requisitioned for military purposes by the Republic (and in several cases now occupied by the French troops). Above all, immediately and for months, it also made use of the daily work of police officers, papal *carabinieri* and district presidents, who collected the outcomes of investigations and informants' reports on the ground. Since 16 July "some Roman citizens who love order and public peace, and tired of having suffered up to now the yoke of the past violent government of murderers" anonymously supplied Rostolan with the address of the hiding places of "many copper, metal and other objects considered to belong to the Holy Apostolic Palaces", returning the following day to reveal the existence of a warehouse in San Giovanni dei Fiorentini where other stolen goods might be "and even – they believed – the Pope's superb white mule".[43]

An extensive map of suspicion thus took shape and fed on itself: inspections, searches, denunciations and interrogations did not only return sought-after goods or unexpected objects – from velvet waistcoats made with the upholstery of cardinals' carriages dyed a different colour, to the dirty clothes belonging to the famous legion led by Luciano Manara[44] – but also new addresses and new names, which the commission could check. So, for instance, the houses of those who had coordinated the occupation of convents and the construction of barricades and of a lawyer from the "liberal party" were searched,[45] as well as hatter Ilario Iovarra's, "who in the former Republic served in the Legions as a soldier"[46] or the property

41. ASR, *DGP*, *CR*, b. 2, n. 345 and n. 346 respectively.
42. *Ibid.*, b. 6, n. 994; Roncalli, *Cronaca di Roma*, vol. II, p. 85.
43. ASR, *DGP*, *CR*, b. *Recupere fatte bb. 5-6-7*, n. 530.
44. *Ibid.*, b. 3, nos 425 and 430 respectively.
45. *Ibid.*, b. 6, n. 908.
46. *Ibid.*, b. 5, n. 796.

of a country merchant to whom Garibaldi himself had allegedly left dozens of horses.[47] Searches were also carried out in well-known Republicans' meeting places, such as a tavern in Piazza di Spagna[48] and various premises occupied by various Republican military corps where hidden or abandoned weapons, barrels of gunpowder and cartridges,[49] flammable, corrosive and explosive liquids[50] or the usual objects of illicit origin might be and were often found. For example, five journeys were needed to take to the commission's warehouses all the furniture, rugs, desks, coat stands, two wicker trunks of books and papers, the wheels of cardinals' carriages and timber used as "mobile barricades for infernal machines" discovered during a search of the premises of the dissolved club of the Sappers of the military engineering corps.[51]

The addresses of entire suspect families were noted. On "the second floor of 105, via delle Quattro Fontane" lived the Manzi brothers, 19-year-old twins Pietro and Giovanni, a printer and a colourist, and Filippo, 18, a mosaic artist, former members of the mobilised civic guard believed to be responsible for thefts from the "foremost houses in Rome"; their father Antonio, a clerk, was allegedly hiding a Greek man without papers, a former Republican fighter.[52]

"This morning a secret informer assured that in the house inhabited by Vincenzo Fabiani on the second floor of n. 12, Vicolo del Pavone, several objects were kept hidden, stolen at the time of the former anarchy (in which Fabiani also greatly distinguished himself)". A search confirmed the suspicions about the individual, who was in possession of various altar decorations, prints of the Barricades Commission, bayonet holsters of the civic guard and the regular army, the handle in red embroidered satin from a cardinal's carriage, as well as various decorations from French uniforms.[53] But addresses without any apparent connection to the political past of those who lived there were also gathered, and notes recorded in detail the location of flats, rooms, stairways, entrance halls, attics, cellars, hidden trap doors, warehouses too far away and fortunes too flaunted: "Trajan's Column. A coffee brewer named Baldassarre. Inside the shop, near the counter, there is a hidden door leading to the cellar"; "34, Via Alessandrina. A closed scrap-metal dealer. The woman who owns it lives on the top floor"; "Suburra. A barber shop named Benedetto has a small door leading to Via Urbana"; "Gregorio, the carter at the slope leading to Santa Maria Maggiore, before the Republic was destitute but now owns carts and horses".[54] In the autumn, systematic investigations on reports such as these spread to the countryside and the provinces. Up until then,

47. *Ibid.*, b. *Recupere fatte bb. 1-3*, n. 377.
48. *Ibid.*, b. 7, n. 1075.
49. In this respect, a report to the commission of mid-August 1849 about some "unknown individuals", in relation to the bridge builders who occupied Sant'Andrea della Valle, has not been found; *ibid.*, b. 4, n. 483 and b. *Recupere fatte bb. 5-6-7*, n. 505.
50. *Ibid.*, b. 4, n. 562.
51. *Ibid.*, b. *Recupere fatte 1-3*, n. 446
52. *Ibid.*, b. 9, n. 1582.
53. *Ibid.*, b. 4, n. 564.
54. From a list with no date or any other information; *ibid.*, b. *Recupere fatte bb. 8-9*, n. 880.

mostly reports relating to horses (very many), carriages, ordinary or precious metal objects requisitioned in the past and directed to the capital, but also news of coffers abandoned by Garibaldi's troops fleeing from Rome, were published on the front pages.[55] Odescalchi then reminded the government authorities of the outer districts to address this activity: "It has come to the knowledge of this Commission [...] that very many of the valuable objects [...] belonging to Churches, Pious Places and to private individuals were taken by Garibaldi's Gang and other soldiers of similar mettle to the various towns of the Papal States, where he had plenty of followers [...]". He invited them to check "the homes of those who have shown shameful participation in the former anarchy disguised under the name of liberty", but the investigations did not yield positive results.[56]

Intertwined with a conscious use of disclosure and denunciation, in those who presented the bill for the damages of the Republic to the restored authorities without being immediately recognisable, there was the need to declare their loyalty as subjects, in the past and for the future. There were those who waited months before asking for the return of the weapons that they had spontaneously handed over in compliance with the order following "the entry of the generous French troops" and, as evidence of the loyalty of a lifetime, even boasted about the service provided in the first Restoration, in the civic guard reorganised after the return of Pius VII to the Church States in 1814.[57] Others went beyond self-certification. Vincenzo Magni, who searched for his hunting rifles, stolen by order of "General Caribaldi, and Sterbini", attached to his request the certification of political faith by the Frosinone police deputy and by the parish priest of Patrica, who assured that Magni "for many years served the Pontifical Government as Commander of Centurions for the eradication of the so-called brigands, later he always remained faithful to the legitimate Government and in the recent times of anarchy he showed himself a *staunch* defender of the Pope's rights, talking about it without fear and showing it beyond doubt, so that he was subject to persecution and marked out as a so-called reactionary".[58] The prior of the Municipality of Zagarolo (as well as the parish priest in this case, too), certified the "irreproachable political and moral conduct" of Vincenzo Fittozzi, also interested in finding his own hunting rifle, the only means of support for his family.[59] Two officers of the papal gendarmerie also finally recognised their stolen rifles in the weapons warehouse in Palazzo Borghese. In their requests to be allowed to collect them, one made sure he specified that the theft had occurred while he had "retired to the countryside so as not to mix with the sectarian supporters", the other that it happened while the past regime had imprisoned him.[60] In fact, many claimed they had suffered harassment and persecution, and several even detention, for their political opinions. They gave assurances they had succumbed to voluntary

55. *Giornale di Roma*, 28 September 1849.
56. ASR, *DGP*, *CR*, b. 9, n. 1517.
57. *Ibid.*, b. 6, n. 962.
58. *Ibid.*, b. 4, n. 491.
59. *Ibid.*, b. 5, n. 802.
60. *Ibid.*, b. 6, n. 934 and n. 935.

surrender only for fear of "some injury, and revenge".[61] A porter from Piazza di Pietra claimed that he had "never meddled in the affairs of the Republican government" and that he had "only worked on the barricades when compelled to do so by force".[62] Antonio Leonardi, an inspector who remained in service in the Campitelli and Sant'Angelo districts "at the time when this city was shrouded in anarchy and disorder and justice was the only whim of the Deputies and People's Leaders", justified having done so just to feed his seven children, but had carefully monitored what was happening: and in fact now he could redeem himself with plentiful information on one of the cases the commission was most concerned about: the dispersion of Cardinal Giacomo Antonelli's assets and precious collections.[63] Moreover, even two of the five members of the Republican Protection and Awarding Commission, Giovan Paolo Muti and Alessandro Malvezzi, to safeguard their reputation "following the many very serious charges that are being made every day", as early as July distanced themselves in the press from the abuses that the commission had allegedly committed. In a letter sent to the papers, they declared they were unconnected to the notorious harassment by some of its well-known agents, and indeed stated that they had resigned following certain episodes, such as the violent dispossession and imprisonment of the goldsmith Domenico Masotti, which several months later still continued to be given room in the pro-government newspapers.[64] "When our capital was exposed to violence of all sorts due to the revolutionary government, each citizen tried to protect his property as much as possible", was the beginning of the complaint of another gendarmerie officer, Giuseppe Ruggeri: as many others did, as early as the previous spring, when on the walls of the city the notices signed by the triumvirs began to be defaced and anonymous writings and graffiti warned that "their steps le(a)d to looting",[65] Ruggeri hid his silverware for safekeeping in the basement of a country building he had rented from the Orsini princes outside Porta San Pancrazio. But in May the "iniquitous Garibaldi's hordes" occupied, devastated and stripped the building. "As was certain in the anarchy in which things were", the complaints made in this regard to the Republican commission proved to be useless. But now, at last, "from the searches that our excellent and provident government has arranged in the abodes of the Israelites, the speaker understood that many stolen objects are being found" and could thus forward to the commission the detailed note of the objects he hoped might be returned to him.[66]

Ruggeri wrote to the commission following a vast operation that from the night of 24 October 1849 saw a detachment of the French army and papal gendarmerie surround the ghetto, while the police and the *carabinieri*, inside and for two whole days, from the dawn of the 25th to the evening of the 26th, subjected

61. *Ibid.*, b. 7, n. 1089.
62. *Ibid.*, b. 8, n. 1437/1451.
63. *Ibid.*, b. 9, n. 1483.
64. *Giornale di Roma*, 21 July 1849; *L'Osservatore romano*, 19 October 1849.
65. Roncalli, *Cronaca di Roma*, vol. II, pp. 105-106.
66. ASR, *DGP*, *CR*, b. 6, n. 1074.

dozens of houses, shops and warehouses of Jews to sweeping searches.[67] Until then, there had been no lack of investigations and searches aimed at individual Jewish shopkeepers,[68] but such an operation, the expression of institutionalised anti-Judaism that many no longer believed possible under Pius IX,[69] aroused the immediate disapproval of the Prussian, Swiss and British consular representations and exacerbated tensions within the French side.[70] The Roman press was authorised to print only an anodyne paragraph confirming that "the effect had been achieved", but the news rebounded in the liberal and radical Tuscan, Genoese and Turin newspapers and raised criticism and debate from Paris to Hamburg, from London to the many British, Scottish and Irish newspapers, where great space was given to the denunciation of the unprecedented persecution of the Roman Jews. The news was accompanied by emotionally touching anecdotes, typical of the lexis of international humanitarianism, of doctors prevented from entering the ghetto to assist the dying or of (three) women giving birth but left with no assistance.[71] In a pamphlet sold just two weeks later in Piedmont for the benefit of Italian emigrés, the Commission official who supervised the searches in the ghetto was attributed "this infernal sentence: *If we cannot find two tapestries missing from the Doria house, we will turn the Ghetto upside down, we will incite the people against you, we will massacre you…!!*".[72]

Despite the predictably more controversial aspects, which actually contributed to spreading the black legend of the Roman reaction in European public opinion, the police operation was organised and conducted with unprecedented firmness, because in the map of suspicion that took shape over the previous months, the ghetto was the place in Rome where the mindset of the partisans of law and order most imagined were hiding heaps of the goods that were being

67. *Ibid.*, b. 6, n. 1073 (with long reports and exchanges of letters on this matter). On the operation, see Elvira Grantaliano, *Gli ebrei di Roma tra repressione e integrazione: "letture" dalla serie "Ebrei e scismatici" dell'archivio della Segreteria di Stato-Ministero dell'interno e dai documenti della polizia pontificia, presso l'Archivio di stato di Roma*, in *Judei de Urbe. Roma e i suoi ebrei: una storia secolare*, ed. by Marina Caffiero and Anna Esposito, Rome, Ministero per i beni e le attività culturali-Direzione generale per gli archivi, 2011, pp. 108-113 and 120-127, and Giancarlo Spizzichino, "Pio IX e l'Università degli ebrei di Roma: speranze e delusioni (1846-1850)", in *Ebrei a Roma fra Risorgimento ed emancipazione (1814-1914)*, ed. by Claudio Procaccia, Rome, Gangemi, 2014, pp. 329-332.

68. ASR, *DGP*, *CR*, b. 4, n. 637 (in this case, the investigations are dated to the beginning of August 1849).

69. Ignazio Veca, "La strana emancipazione. Pio IX e gli ebrei nel lungo Quarantotto", *Contemporanea*, 1 (2014), pp. 3-30.

70. *Rome et les Etats Pontificaux*, pp. 76-77; Spizzichino, "Pio IX e l'Università degli ebrei di Roma". See also David I. Kertzer, "The Lost Cause: Failed French Ultimata and the Restoration of Papal Rule in Rome in 1849", *Journal of Modern Italian Studies*, 5 (2017), pp. 555-570.

71. For example, see *Giornale di Roma*, 27 October 1849; *Journal des Débats*, 10, 13, 29 November 1849; *Times*, 12 November 1849. On the rhetoric of the international humanitarian discourse, see Lynn Hunt, *Inventing Human Rights: A History*, New York, W.W. Norton & Company Press, 2007.

72. Leone Carpi, *Blocco dei francesi al ghetto di Roma nell'anno di grazia 1849 e secondo della loro repubblica*, Turin, Stamperia sociale degli artisti tipografi, 1849, pp. 13-14.

sought ("treasures", said Luigi Carlo Farini).[73] "As everyone knows"[74] – this phrase became ubiquitous, with other variations: "as it was well known that",[75] "it was already known that",[76] "the universal vote in Rome show(s) that"[77] – scrap merchants eager to do business were alleged to have purchased, in large quantities and cheaply, items of illicit origin from customers no less eager to get rid of the stolen goods quickly. And, not infrequently, those who were found in possession of objects of suspect provenance said in their defence that they had purchased them from Jewish shopkeepers. There was also a rumour that the most precious fruits in the handling of the stolen goods, the silver looted from Apostolic Palaces, sacred buildings and private individuals – churchmen, aristocrats and bourgeoisie – may have been dispersed among the Jews in the other cities of the state, or secured and even already smelted beyond the borders. In particular in Livorno: a port city with a strong Jewish presence and, not surprisingly, with the most recent radical past.

In fact, in addition to the age-old prejudice that the "strange emancipation" of 1848 had certainly not been eradicated,[78] and the suspicion that the Roman Jews, out of greed and interest, had easy game in hiding goods of all kinds in their warehouses, another persuasion now weighed against them: that they were among the staunchest supporters of the Republic.[79] The official report of police operation in the ghetto, which many foreign newspapers published in full, not surprisingly recalled the presence of Roman Jews "in the front ranks of the demagogues, in the municipal government, in the clubs, and in other sectarian assemblies".[80] Consistently with these practices, they were therefore accused of conniving with even the most corrupt agents or the most plebeian and criminal members of that regime. In the months following the searches in the ghetto, which meant for some preventive detention of various lengths, for many the exhausting production

73. Luigi Carlo Farini, *Lo Stato romano dall'anno 1815 al 1850*, vol. IV, Florence, Le Monnier, 1853, p. 260, where the liberal Catholic insists a great deal upon the links between prejudice and police revenge as the origin of the operation.

74. ASR, *DGP*, *CR*, b. 9, n. 1491. Said by an innkeeper found with military clothes to justify himself.

75. *Giornale di Roma*, 27 October 1849.

76. Roncalli, *Cronaca di Roma*, vol. II, p. 236.

77. On the draft of the commission's final report on the searches, dated 30 October 1849, in ASR, *DGP*, *CR*, b. 6, n. 1073 (which also states that the commission had proposed the action in September but the Prefect of the police and the Governor of Rome, both French, only agreed two months later).

78. Veca, "La strana emancipazione". See also Marina Caffiero, *Storia degli ebrei nell'Italia moderna. Dal Rinascimento alla Restaurazione*, Rome, Carocci, 2014, and Sandro Morachioli, "Forme del pregiudizio. Per una storia visiva dell'antiebraismo nel Risorgimento", *Visual History*, 2 (2016), pp. 77-103 (esp. pp. 80-91).

79. Luana Montesi, "La partecipazione alternativa: donne, ebrei, circoli", in *La primavera della nazione. La Repubblica romana del 1849*, ed. by Marco Severini, Ancona, affinità elettive, 2006, pp. 226-236. See also Giovanni Miccoli, "Santa Sede, questione ebraica e antisemitismo", in *Storia d'Italia. Annali 11. Gli ebrei in Italia*, ed. by Corrado Vivanti, vol. II, *Dall'emancipazione a oggi*, Turin, Einaudi, 1997, pp. 1380-1401.

80. *Evening Mail*, 12 November 1849.

of evidence (purchase registers, sworn witness statements) and for the Jewish representative bodies repeated protests and continuous searches for mediations, the goods removed on 25 and 26 October must have been in large part returned. Thanks to the French mediation, for example, the Jewish Deputation obtained that those still in possession of the commission in January 1850 but not verified be not included in the commission's *Fourteenth Notice* then being prepared, as had been previously reported instead.[81] But in any case, in addition to the criss-cross effect of ancient prejudice, widespread maps of suspicion and the content of often biased reports, the Jews – by now pro-Republicans themselves – fell into a wider criminalisation mechanism, which in the police practices of the Recoveries Commission ended up targeting not only the usual victims of religious prejudice, but in general the protagonists of the politicisation and democratisation processes culminating in the five months of the Republic.

4. *"A Government of Murderers and Thieves"*

In the aftermath of 3 July 1849, institutional communications offered a new political framework to those who intended to claim their assets: if for months the extent to which the pontifical government intended to preserve Pius IX's liberal and constitutional politics prior to the insurrection of November 1848 remained controversial, the frontal attack on the Republic, which had fallen under the French bombs, was without appeal and without misunderstandings.[82] The aforementioned Oudinot's ordinance of 8 July had already defined the Republican emblems as "insignia of terror and anarchy". As soon as the papal government was restored, censorship was reorganised and the newspapers came out again, the denunciation of the "party whose purpose is thieving and destruction, which, born in blood, does not found its empire but on blood"[83] became a daily refrain and these issues appeared increasingly useful, if not necessary, when engaging in dialogue with institutions. Those who turned to the Recoveries Commission, even from subaltern groups, showed full awareness of these processes and knowledge of how to use the necessary rhetoric in the spaces that the promise of restitution had opened. "Since those in the fallen government became despotic masters of properties and particular objects", Rosa Ricciani pleaded, "they even snatched from the hands" of a poor widow, a landlady like her, her only source of sustenance: two mattresses and a straw pallet, which she was now looking for.[84] Formulas like

81. ASR, *DGP*, *CR*, b. *Recupere fatte 8-9*, nos 1404 and 1422. For the returns procedures, see *ibid.*, b. 7, nos 1106 and 1107 and, for a practice which continued until May 1850, b. 8, n. 1102/1162/1464.

82. Alberto M. Ghisalberti, *Roma da Mazzini a Pio IX. Ricerche sulla restaurazione papale del 1849-1850*, Milan, Giuffrè, 1958; Giacomo Martina, *Pio IX (1846-1850)*, Rome, Università Gregoriana, 1974, pp. 330-422; Carla Lodolini Tupputi, "Sulla tacita soppressione dello Statuto di Pio IX", *Rassegna storica del Risorgimento*, 114 (2007), pp. 323-344.

83. *L'Osservatore romano*, 5 October 1849 (*Le vendette dei repubblicani*).

84. ASR, *DGP*, *CR*, b. *Recupere fatte bb. 1-3*, n. 254.

this, which followed the now dominant phraseology in public and overall labelled the "extinct government (really anarchical and terroristic)",[85] were very frequent and above all had the function of highlighting the distance of the authors of the requests from the recent past and of showing their promise of loyalty. In July 1850, shortly before its dissolution, the Recoveries Commission itself claimed to Domenico Savelli, Minister of the Interior and Police, during a prolonged dispute with the Ministry of Finance regarding the ownership of unreturned assets and the chances of making use of it for compensation, to be one of the first organs of the restoration to have "justified with fact that the Government of the self-styled Roman Republic was a Government of Murderers and Thieves", that is to say, it embodied "anarchy, communism, socialism, assassinations directed by its chief-thief Mazzini and his acolytes"; and for this reason, "the Sectarians, Liberals and Republicans declared war on it".[86] Interestingly, what provided the substance to this anti-Republican indictment focused on the attack on property was in fact, after July 1849, a choir of voices: they belonged to the willing people who had been damaged by the Republic or who presented themselves as such, with their wealth of biased and politically skilled stories, repetitive narratives in terms of plots and protagonists built around the anthropologically and materially dense, and even fabulous, core of their lost objects, neat in assigning roles to victims and oppressors. These stories of things, of injustices, threats and abuses, short, dark and violent fables, accompanied the sometimes endless lists of objects – a ubiquitous form in which the owners strove to arrange their lost world – or the equally frequent verbal descriptions of the lost and sought-after assets – another unprecedented and tiring exercise in *ekphrasis* of the ordinary – to provide the intellectual and institutional architects of the second restoration with the innumerable pieces needed to compose the moral and political puzzle of the Republic as a regime of institutionalised thievery.[87] This image would be central to the legal condemnation of Republican leaders as well, as Catherine Brice recently pointed out with respect to Mazzini and Carlo Armellini and as also confirmed by the judicial case of Alessandro Calandrelli, Deputy, Minister and Member of the Second Triumvirate in the last days of the Republic's life – as well as President of the Republican Commission dealing with illegal requisitions – who was arrested in the autumn of 1849 and sentenced in 1851 for theft.[88]

85. *Ibid.*, b. 1, n. 78.

86. *Ibid.*, b. 10, n. 1850-1718/1729/1733bis/1821bis.

87. A choral version, and in some cases certainly from below, of the melodramatic style which not only characterised fictional narratives, but this time to a large extent also political discourse, and whose links with the repertoires of popular culture deserve further investigation; see Carlotta Sorba, *Politics and Sentiments in Risorgimento Italy: Melodrama and the Nation*, Cham, Palgrave Macmillan, 2021.

88. Catherine Brice, "Entre délit politique, sacrilège et droit commun. L'iconoclasme révolutionnaire en procès (Rome, 1849-1850)", in *Iconoclasme et révolutions de 1879 à nos jours*, ed. by Emmanuel Fureix, Ceyzérieu, Champ Vallon, 2014, pp. 179-193; Catherine Brice, "L'affaire de la Mano Regia de Carlo Armellini (1849-1851)", in *Propriété et politique: exil, séquestres, confiscations dans l'Italie du XIXe siècle*, ed. by Catherine Brice, *Mélanges de l'Ecole française de Rome*, 129/2 (2017), at https://doi.org/10.4000/mefrim.3284; Giuseppe

In those stories the entire institutional space of the Republic was populated by grabbers, profiteers and thieves. The agents of the commissions in charge of the requisitions, in particular that of the barricades, directed by Enrico Cernuschi, and that for gold and silver directed by Orazio Antinori and suspected of not having deposited all that had been requisitioned in the Mint as it was supposed to, had acted "beyond their power" and "with threats";[89] they had refused to leave regular receipts and, "armed like brigands", had threatened the unfortunates on duty to "[send] their souls to the Devil";[90] they had travelled together with "infamous emissaries" of popular clubs like the *Circolo Popolare* and had acted as a "gang of killers ready to take away the life" of those who tried to oppose the looting and devastation.[91] Two of the most notorious, in this regard, were former sculptor Angelo Bezzi who became a police commissioner, very close to Mazzini himself, and Agostino Borghi, from Modena, already suspected of being involved in many political troubles, the recent owner of a bullet factory in Rome and Antinori's collaborator, whose crime-novel misdemeanours at the head of his "gang of ruffians" were reported in newspapers like episodes of a penny dreadful.[92]

Describing in such terms the action of institutions like the Barricades Commission was equivalent to attacking and delegitimising one of the foremost symbols of 1848's popular and national sovereignty in Europe, the barricades and urban defences.[93] However, the Republic was on the whole a time when deputies and ministers ordered thefts – the agent of Cardinal Castracane accused deputy Giulio Govoni, a member of the Protection and Awarding Commission, of having stolen silverware and furniture from the prelate[94] – and they went round accompanied by thugs – "A companion of the notorious Calandrelli was one Vito Enea, always at his side armed with an arquebus".[95] There were also countless abuses attributed to commissioners of public security and, in particular, to members of the civic guard reorganised by the Republic (and dissolved by Oudinot as early as 6 July 1849): priests were beaten up, had their homes expropriated, were imprisoned ("*Shut up there, you bust my balls, now we are in charge*. Nice talk from a Commissioner and Secretary, who

Monsagrati, "Un episodio della seconda Restaurazione pontificia: il caso Calandrelli", *Rassegna storica del Risorgimento*, 4 (1972), pp. 531-562.

89. ASR, *DGP*, *CR*, b. 1, n. 37.

90. *Ibid.*, b. 4, n. 592.

91. *Ibid.*

92. *Giornale di Roma*, 11 October 1849.

93. Catherine Brice diminishes the symbolic value of the Roman barricades in "La Commission des barricades de la République romaine (1848-1849): une 'technologie politique'? Réflexion sur les contextes mouvants de l'innovation", *Diasporas*, 29 (2017), https://doi.org/10.4000/diasporas.791. On the other hand, Alessandro Capone stresses it in an unpublished paper presented at the workshop *Barricades: Methods, Styles, and Dynamics of Contention* (University of Warwick, 17 May 2019; I am grateful to the author for allowing me to see the text). See also Mark Traugott, *The Insurgent Barricade*, Berkeley-Los Angeles, University of California Press, 2010.

94. ASR, *DGP*, *CR*, b. 1, n. 40.

95. *Ibid.*, b. 8, n. 1467.

are supposed to be guardians of public order"),[96] silverware was stolen from sick eighty-year-olds surrounded by grandchildren and helpless servants, with a behaviour that was "almost furious, with threats to arrest everyone, to smash the house up, with shouts and such outlandish behaviour".[97] In general, the armed men of the Republic were often accused of taking advantage of a position of strength. The soldiers who after the first clashes on April 30 were in charge of the fortifications and demolitions around the city walls or the requisitions in the province – from the sappers of the engineering corps to the mobilised civic guard to Garibaldi's troops – were accused of thefts and looting (such as that in San Giovanni in Laterano).[98] Those who during field days such as 3 and 4 June to help the wounded scoured private houses and religious institutions behind the firing line in the pressing search for mattresses, sheets, shirts, rags for bandages also appeared "like murderers" to the prioress of an orphanage, forced to hand over 55 sheets upon receipt.[99]

Inevitably, many of the stories about the military concerned Giuseppe Garibaldi and his volunteers, who on the opposite political front had already been ascribed as martyrs to the epic cause of patriotic heroism, but who, to those who claimed damages from the Recoveries Commission, were only thieves, violent and impostors.[100] At that time a novelty in the political-military landscape, these appellations are illuminating. Whereas they were referred to in a neutral way as Garibaldi's troops, Garibaldi's followers or "*Garibaldesi*",[101] when a clearer distance was required, they became Garibaldi's "gangs of soldiers"[102] or "legionaries" – a term that refers to the actual name of the corps, Legion, but at the same time it brought negative echoes of the volunteers of the Roman Legion who, after the demobilisation of the summer of 1848, represented one of the most powerful levers of instability and political radicalisation in the Papal States.[103] To those who wanted to absolutely stress their alleged extortions, especially in the province, in the name of defence or during their flight in July 1849, with a very poignant stereotype in a state that had had wide experience of the phenomenon of banditry, they became "Garibaldi's gangs"[104] and he "the famous gang-leader Caribaldi".[105] In Anagni the case of self-styled "great and wealthy Neapolitan nobleman", as well as Bourbon general-in-chief, Giuseppe Caputo was reported. He obtained large credits in cattle from a breeder taking advantage – he suggested – of his political loyalty: but then he turned out to be a "fugitive, and with a criminal

96. *Ibid.*, b. 2, n. 173.

97. *Ibid.*, b. 2, n. 184.

98. *Ibid.*, b. 1, n. 94.

99. ASR, *DGP*, *CR*, b. 2, n. 232.

100. Lucy Riall, *Garibaldi: Invention of a Hero*, New Haven-London, Yale University Press, 2007. See also Silvia Cavicchioli, *Anita. Storia e mito di Anita Garibaldi*, Turin, Einaudi, 2017.

101. ASR, *DGP*, *CR*, b. 8, n. 888/1105/1195/1249/1309/1351/1442.

102. *Ibid.*, b. 3, n. 369.

103. *Ibid.*, b. 8, n. 1290.

104. *Ibid.*, b. *Recupere fatte 1-2-3*, n. 202.

105. *Ibid.*, b. 4, n. 583. See also Laura Di Fiore, "Da liberali a criminali. I patrioti del Risorgimento meridionale", *Storica*, 73 (2019), pp. 72, 75-76.

record and a very close friend of Caribaldi", on whose head hung a reward from the king of Naples.[106]

From the example of the volunteers (as from that of the Jews mentioned above), it is clear that the Republic's criminalisation device, built around requisitioned or robbed assets, did not just target the institutional space, but accused the entire arena of political participation. In particular, it focused on the marginal and subordinate actors of the process of social mobilisation, politicisation and democratisation of the previous months, which also had ambivalent roots in the liberal reforms and constitutional order desired by Pius IX.[107] On their actual use of violent practices and on the boundaries between politicisation and common crime, it would be desirable to finally pursue further research,[108] but in any case it can be noted that even before the advent of the Republic, the stereotype of the dangerous classes hovered over them.[109] In this regard, it is no coincidence that among the instigators and protagonists of theft and violence often cited to the Recoveries Commission were the *Capipopolo* (people's leaders), those formidable figures of semi-institutional mediators who emerged in the Roman districts in the years preceding 1848 and represented a link between the popular classes and politics, first liberal and then radical.[110] Those who were often caught acting on one or other scene of crime were: Giuseppe Volpari, *Capopopolo* of the Campitelli district;[111] Michele Lucatelli "fishmonger and *Capopopolo* of the Monti district";[112] the "*Capopopolo* Innocenzo Zappacuore" from the Pigna district;[113] and of course Angelo Brunetti, the "very well known" Ciceruacchio,[114] *Capopopolo* of the Campo Marzio district. He was accused – with his vast following of "plebeian" militants and family members active in the Roman radical and popular sociability, from his son Luigi (suspected of being the material executor of the murder of Pellegrino Rossi on 15 November 1848) to his brother Vincenzo – of a long sequence of undue appropriations during searches in private houses, churches and convents. These ranged from the Verstappen and Terziani vineyards outside San Giovanni's gates to the nunnery of Santa Lucia in Selci;[115] from the convent of San Pietro in Vincoli whence papal bulls and codices

106. ASR, *DGP*, *CR*, b. 2, n. 154.

107. Ignazio Veca, *Il mito di Pio IX. Storia di un papa liberale e nazionale*, Rome, Viella, 2018.

108. This topic has been largely left out even by the most recent general reconstructions, for example in Giuseppe Monsagrati, *Roma senza il papa. La Repubblica romana del 1849*, Rome-Bari, Laterza, 2014.

109. Alessio Petrizzo, "Épées, cocardes, tuniques et poignards: fraternité, violence et appartenences politiques en Italie durant la longue année 1848", in *Frères de sang, frères d'armes, frères ennemis. La fraternité en Italie (1820-1924)*, ed. by Catherine Brice, Rome, École française de Rome, 2017, pp. 73-98.

110. Salvatore Puglia, "Conflittualità, controllo, mediazione in un quartiere di Roma intorno al 1848", in *Subalterni in tempo di modernizzazione. Nove studi sulla società romana dell'Ottocento*, Fondazione Lelio e Lisli Basso-Issoco, *Annali*, 7 (1983-1984), pp. 225-244.

111. ASR, *DGP*, *CR*, b. 9, n. 1493.

112. Ibid., bb. *Recupere fatte bb. 5-6-7*, n. 786.

113. Ibid., b. 7, n. 960.

114. Ibid., b. 2, n. 143.

115. *Ibid.*

"of the greatest interest to history and science"[116] disappeared to the church of Santa Maria dei Miracoli in Piazza del Popolo, whence the pulpit and confessionals were taken;[117] from the Roman Seminary, emptied of its wine, tableware and other goods[118] to the homes of "supporters of His Holiness", stripped and sullied.[119] None of what was expected to be found, however, came from the search ordered by the Recoveries Commission in September 1849 of Ciceruacchio's house, when he and his children (including 13-year-old Lorenzo), who had escaped from Rome, had already been shot by the Austrians. His daughter Agnese[120] was called upon to vouch for the origin of harmless objects: a regularly registered blade, medals celebrating Pius IX, the sonnet dedicated to her father by an admirer and a printed prayer by the liberal preacher Gioacchino Ventura.

Ciceruacchio's wife, Anna Cimarra, also appears in the Recoveries Commission's documents, but only as a signatory (like her son Lorenzo) of vouchers for the purchase of bread distributed in late May, which some bakers must have presented to the Commission or some police investigation must have found.[121] In fact, Republican women rarely appeared in these complaints: but when they did, they were fully involved in the generalised attack on property.[122] For example, an undated confidential memo (but going back to autumn 1849), in the context of the investigations to find four precious allegorical statues, with wax masks and valuable clothes and decorations, made by the nuns of Sant'Urbano, revealed that they had been hidden by some women: the Giovannelli and Ramoneda sisters, neighbours in via Alessandrina, the "well-known music teacher Bolognetti née Aspri" and finally "the woman who was the Director at the Hospitals of Annunziatina and Sant'Urbano". The latter deserved an asterisk in the margin: "She is a relative of the well-known Father Gavazzi, and who knows how many other objects she might be hiding upon the aforementioned's commission!" This memo threw the suspicion of instigation to theft on another prominent political celebrity, as well as figure of scandal, at the time of the Republic, Barnabite Alessandro Gavazzi, radical preacher, military chaplain and one of the men responsible for the military hospitals. The other women mentioned in the memo were also involved in the military hospitals, and were ironically defined as "zealous leaders of the healing of the Martyrs of the Republic!!!" but actually described as thieves of works of art and sacred furnishings in the premises occupied to treat the wounded (with the assistance of "Captain Maceroni of the civic guard of the Monti district", who "was a joyful witness of the despoiling and participated in some depredations)".[123]

116. ASR, *DGP*, *CR*, b. 2, n. 149.

117. *Ibid.*, b. 2, n. 156.

118. *Ibid.*, bb. *Recupere fatte 1-2-3*, n. 246.

119. *Ibid.*, b. 4, n. 587.

120. *Ibid.*, b. 5, n. 841.

121. *Ibid.*, b. 5, still sealed, without number or any other information.

122. See Rosanna De Longis, "Tra sfera pubblica e difesa dell'onore. Donne nella Roma del 1849", *Roma moderna e contemporanea*, 1/3 (2001), pp. 263-283, and Montesi, "La partecipazione alternativa", pp. 206-226.

123. ASR, *DGP*, *CR*, b. 6, n. 1005.

Regardless of the veracity of accusations like these, clues to which one way or the other we occasionally find in the commission papers, it is interesting to note this real-time recording of stories that fit within a discourse still under formation and contributed, often even from subordinate and marginal positions, to criminalising the most famous and popular figures of the Roman Republic, the men who wore its many uniforms – the institutional figures in the tricoloured sashes, the civic guards, the military, the red shirts – the *Capipopolo*, the workers employed in fortifications and on the barricades, the women engaged in the public sphere. In this way, symbolic places in the Republican epic and in its defence were demolished one by one, be they the assembly elected by universal suffrage, or the battles, barricades and military hospitals. In the stories to (and prompted by) the Recoveries Commission, the space of collective experiences of the Republic was literally dismantled and returned to the private sphere in a myriad of individual requests. Meanwhile, the social aristocracies, religious institutions and diplomatic representations, presenting themselves as the designated victims of Republican thievery, once again asserted their rights as the only legitimate voices – and guarantors – of stability and order for the people of the Papal States.

5. *A laughing matter?*

In the medium term, the strategy of pontifical restoration did not work: what started then and ended with the taking of Rome by the army of the Kingdom of Italy on 20 September 1870 was a time of growing internal and international delegitimisation. But the policy of restitutions certainly cannot be blamed for this. On the contrary, at least during the brief period when order returned, this policy and its aggressive communication, which also gave rise to controversies within the pontifical administration itself, seem to be some of the measures which most impressed – and involved – the imagination of contemporaries,[124] despite the irony expressed by the defeated. "If this commission had not given rise to endless imprisonments, the meanness of its effect and its comic acts would be risible", early in 1851 ran from Lausanne the attack by the pro-Mazzini paper *L'Italia del popolo*, in presenting the pamphlet *Roma e gli Stati romani nel 1850* ("Rome and the Roman States in 1850"), which denounced the acts of the papal reaction, published anonymously at the end of December 1850 from a clandestine printing house in the city, in apparently 2,000 copies, provocatively sent even to the pontiff, the Secretary of State Cardinal Giacomo Antonelli and other personalities.[125] In the pages of this pamphlet, the Recoveries Commission was not forgotten, even if to make fun of it ("a Frenchman who knows no Italian presides over it, and it is

124. The pro-government press in the Kingdom of the Two Sicilies, for example, while Pius IX was still in Gaeta, promoted the action of the Recoveries Commission with the local public, as in fact did a long article on the first page of *L'Araldo* (Naples), on 25 October 1849 ("What the Republic took away, the principality is giving back").

125. "Roma e gli Stati romani nel 1850", in *L'Italia del popolo*, series II, n. 3 (January), Lausanne, Società Editrice l'Unione, 1851, p. 87. See Roncalli, *Cronaca di Roma*, vol. II, p. 308.

made up of Romans who know no French").[126] In fact, we can smile at the fact that the courtyard of the Government Palace for months resembled a market square, or that in three days at the beginning of April 1850, just before the return of Pius IX to the capital, an auction of the remaining goods in possession of the Commission and still unrecognised or claimed was organised. The goods were exhibited and auctioned in the same courtyard: "hardware, harnesses, wagons and carts" on the first day, "Copper and silverware" on the second, "Saltpetre, Timber, Furniture, and any other goods" on the third.[127] More generally, massive bureaucratic practices and inquiries were often set up around assets of very little value: there are more than 1,800 items listed by the heading Recoveries Commission at the Rome State Archives. But if "Liberals and Republicans declared war on it", as we have seen, certainly following the police operation in the ghetto, but also before or regardless of it, as shown by the cases of Calandrelli himself and of Leopoldo Spini – a figure of the first importance in Rome's political journalism and secretary of the executive of the Republic, who tried to defend himself in the press from the accusations addressed at him and denounced the searches that he or his family members had to suffer from the Commission[128] – perhaps this means that its work was not perceived at all as unimportant and that the attempt to reconstruct in real time and with tangible evidence the feelings of loyalty and political legitimacy and illegitimacy represented a real threat to the defeated Republicans.

On the one hand this was so for their followers and activists: as *L'Italia del popolo* mentioned, the investigations ordered by the Commission, with the help of willing citizens eager for material compensation, revenge or displays of loyalty, collected a wealth of information that proved valuable in subsequent political trials and purges. But, precisely for this participatory dimension and for its rapid and fruitful assimilation in the intellectual productions of the reaction – be they political pamphlets or treatises,[129] novels,[130]

126. *Roma e gli Stati romani nel 1850*, p. 87.

127. The *Notice* announcing the auction and other documents are in ASR, *DGP*, *CR*, b. 10, n. 1718/1729/1733bis/1821bis.

128. *L'Osservatore romano*, 17 October 1849 (Calandrelli's self-defence backfires) and 28 December 1849 (article titled "I ladri onorati", in reply to Spini's battle in Turin's *Concordia*).

129. Beyond the numerous references to thefts and requisitions, the passages about the mobilised civil guard in Gaetano Valeriani, *Storia della repubblica romana, tutta corredata di autentici documenti*, Rome, Ajani, 1850, are interesting. Here, the scenes and rhetoric that filled the requests to the Commission appear again: "There was no excess, no crime, no infamy that [this corps] did not commit. No theft, and often no murder took place, that was not in the presence of some mobilised Guard. The Convent and Church of *Santa Croce in Gerusalemme* were stripped by this Corps; by this Corps *S. Pietro a Montorio* and other places were ransacked. In terms of furniture, we can say the Vatican was destroyed. Four or five armed men would turn up at religious institutions or private homes and committed all kinds of vandalism" (vol. II, p. 234). See [B.M.D.S.], *Le ostilità della rivolta contro il cattolicesimo negli ultimi avvenimenti di Roma. Memoria storico-polemica*, Rome, Aurelj, 1850, pp. 138-140.

130. In Antonio Bresciani's novels, set in the days of the republic, first published in the early 1850s in the magazine *Civiltà cattolica* and repeatedly re-edited in book form, the full repertoire of the scenes we have seen is everywhere: thefts, devastation and looting of churches, sacred palaces and private homes; gold and silver items broken up and sold in the

memoires, even available abroad,[131] or dictionaries compiled by supporters of the restoration, under the heading *recupere* (recoveries)[132] – the stories of these lost objects still represented a threat to the Republicans also on the levels of the imagination and future memory: defeated, hunted down, imprisoned, exiled, they would for over twenty years be kept away from the future capital of Italy. In Rome, moreover, people were already focusing well beyond police practices on the hot topic of the Republican requisitions and thefts. Not only the shock of those experiences *per se* but the intensity of the Commission's work until the winter of 1850 and the spread of its notices, spotted "posted on street corners"[133] everywhere by many observers – in a sort of institutional compulsion to repeat – suggested that the topic of the day should also be appropriated by the revived language of visual satire. The political communication of 1848 had loyalised to this the large audience, now orphaned, of the discontinued *Don Pirlone*, an illustrated satirical newspaper, liberal at first and then radical, which until 2 July 1849 had thousands of compulsive readers of all political colours (as many as 1,200 were subscribers).[134] Now the field was free for an illustrated periodical from the opposite camp, which had already started publishing in the autumn: the *Grande riunione* (*Great Meeting*) was in the form of a long dialogue between various characters about the political events of recent years. It was printed by the same Paternò press as the governmental *Osservatore Romano*, and readers suspected there was a link between the two (which the editors denied, asking readers to forward the letters sent to them for the *Grande riunione* elsewhere).[135]

Well, the pages of this illustrated periodical include numerous cartoons that concern our topic. One such cartoon, ridiculing an article by Mazzini on the eve of his departure from Rome, depicts a large eagle ridden by a putto with lictors' rods and a Phrygian cap, both Republican emblems. The eagle is escaping from the city clutching in its beak and claws "silver, gold, precious items, valuables", while from its rear end banknotes, which are actually waste paper, are discharged (Fig. 1).[136]

ghetto; extortion and violence perpetrated by fleeing Garibaldi soldiers; even the portrayal of a personified Republic confessing these sins to Father Gavazzi and receiving absolution from him; *Della repubblica romana. Appendice all'Ebreo di Verona*, Milan, Tipografia Arcivescovile, 1855, pp. 129-132. See also Nicola Del Corno, "Letteratura e anti-Risorgimento. I romanzi di Antonio Bresciani", in *Letteratura e politica. Sulla contro-rivoluzione nell'Europa del XIX secolo*, ed. by Jordi Canal, *Memoria e ricerca*, 24 (2007), pp. 21-32.

131. Eugénie de la Rochère, *Rome. Souvenirs religieux, historiques, artistiques de l'expédition française en 1849 et 1850*, Tours, Mame, 1853, pp. 108-110, 164-166.

132. Gaetano Valeriani, *Vocabolario di voci e frasi erronee al tutto da fuggirsi nella lingua italiana*, Turin, Steffenone, Camandona e C., 1855, p. 734.

133. *Rome en 1848-1849-1850*, p. 294.

134. Ilaria Torelli, "Il '48 a Roma. *Il Don Pirlone* e la *Grande Riunione*", in *Un diluvio di giornali. Modelli di satira politica in Europa tra '48 e Novecento*, ed. by Antonello Negri and Marta Sironi, Milan, Skira, 2006, pp. 16-37.

135. *L'Osservatore romano*, 12 December 1849. See also Giulio Battelli, "L'Osservatore romano degli anni 1849-1852", *Strenna dei romanisti*, 63 (2002), pp. 17-30.

136. *Grande riunione tenuta nella sala dell'ex Circolo popolare in Roma*, vol. I, Rome, Paternò, 1849, p. 18.

Many other illustrations played on almost all types of objects that the Recoveries Commission had dealt with: carriages (Fig. 2), horses (Fig. 3), mattresses (Fig. 4), clothing, railings, confessionals, wine, houses. On those crime scenes, and in the frequent series of portraits of Republican types in the *Grande riunione*, the same protagonists of the stories of violent requisitions, thefts and threats that we have read are ubiquitous: from Ciceruacchio to the "Pirate of Monte Video" Garibaldi and his men "devoted to wine";[137] from the commoners to the civic guards; from the agents of the requisitions (as well as the President of the Barricades Commission, one of the most active in this sense, Enrico Cernuschi) to anonymous military dragoons or sappers; from deputies and triumvirs to Mazzini, all depicted as conjurers, modern alchemists or *tout court* thieves, amid countless violence and daggers, dressed in their tricoloured sashes and Phrygian caps.

This symbolic and narrative system of protest against Mazzini's Republic would remain current practice well beyond the circle of supporters of the pontifical restoration.[138] The police practices started as early as July 1849 and showed the extent to which not only the central objects in a political battle, but also those that are familiar and ordinary, those that have low emotional intensity, that populate the landscape of everyday life, can leverage imagination, a sense of belonging and legitimacy: "even broccoli" (Fig. 5).

137. *Grande riunione*, vol. II, p. 145.
138. Di Fiore, "Da liberali a criminali", p. 83.

1. *Grande riunione tenuta nella sala dell'ex Circolo popolare in Roma*, vol. I, Paternò, Rome, 1849, p. 8.
2. Property is sacred. *"Cassandrino: But who is going to pay?"*, *Grande riunione*, vol. II, p. 135.

3. There will be no requisitions without presenting an order of the triumvirate. *"Stable hand: With what order are you taking those horses, Excellency? Hero: This is the order, you ugly boor"*, *Grande riunione*, vol. II, p. 398.
4. *"Boy: Mummy, why are they taking our bed away? Mother: Shush, my boy, it's needed for the town gates. Boy: What! Town gates sleep, too!!"*, *Grande riunione*, vol. II, p. 414.

5. Strategy of the Roman Republic. *"MP: It is best to remove anything getting in the way of our cannonballs. Man: The broccoli as well? MP: The broccoli as well. Man: They will be good for the barricades, then."*, *Grande riunione*, vol. II, p. 323.

Roberto Balzani

Synecdoche: The Unforeseen Fate of Evocative Objects

The political objects[1] that have survived the undertow of history have not all had the same fate. Some have been used to document a life and have, therefore, been collected in a subsequent, *post eventum* phase: the memorial meaning attributed to them is therefore posthumous and is determined – in the majority of cases – by belonging to a chronologically concluded "heroic" phase. There are others, conversely, whose value has accompanied the development of a biography. They are objects, or parts of the body, which, after being severed, lost, preserved or reproduced,[2] have given rise to an instant process of identification, however immediately understood, shared and promoted by the protagonists/victims themselves: the synecdoche. This, according to the *Treccani Dictionary*, is the "expressive figure of speech, and traditional rhetorical device, which consists in the transfer of meaning from one word to another on the basis of a relationship of proximity understood as of greater or lesser extension, using, for example, the name of a part for that of the whole or vice versa (*hull* or *sail* for *ship*; *mink* for *mink fur*), etc…".[3] We shall attempt to list the features of this kind of object:

1. They were linked to biographies and, as attributes endowed with a specific evocative function, were therefore already documented during the lifetimes of the protagonists, who actually used them to increase their own personal auras. To borrow a sentence from Jules Michelet related to how historical facts are handed down, we could say that, thanks to the semantic structure of the synecdoche, even these individuals' past is conceived not so much in terms of "narration" or "analysis", but rather "resurrection";[4]

1. For a conceptual and methodological analysis, see "Storia e cultura materiale: recenti traiettorie di ricerca. Interventi di Fabio Dei, Giorgio Riello, Beverly Lemire, Manuel Charpy, Leora Auslander", ed. by Alessio Petrizzo and Carlotta Sorba, *Contemporanea*, 3 (2016), pp. 437-480.

2. On human remains, see in particular *Public Uses of Human Remains and Relics in History*, ed. by Silvia Cavicchioli and Luigi Provero, New York-London, Routledge, 2020.

3. At https://www.treccani.it/vocabolario/sineddoche/, accessed on 28 November 2020.

4. "Que ce soit là ma part dans l'avenir, d'avoir, non pas atteint, mais marqué le but de l'histoire, de l'avoir nommée d'un nomme que personne n'avait dit. Thierry y voyait une *narration* et M. Guizot *une analyse*. J'ai l'ai nommée *résurrection*, et ce nom lui restera" (Jules Michelet, *Le Peuple* (1846), Paris, Flammarion, 1974, p. 73).

2. The association of ideas between an object and character is direct and immediate;
3. The conservation of the object has followed an ordinary pathway: on the one hand, when possible, it has become heritage;[5] on the other, it has also become a story, that is to say, a contemporary memory that settles down as a document and itself becomes an object. The story, in other words, does not simply emphasise the item's importance, but is incorporated into the same device that defines the character's identity.

To avoid being excessively abstract, let us move to some actual cases: the Anglo-Greek helmet of Theódoros Kolokotrónis, a military leader in the Greek War of Independence; the amputated leg of General Antonio López de Santa Anna, one of the protagonists of the Battle of the Alamo, which was turned into a relic for veneration by Mexican citizens and replaced, in the officer's living body, by a wooden one; and finally, Piero Maroncelli's amputated leg, which never became an item of symbolic heritage once severed from the Italian patriot, but which – thanks to a powerful literary tradition – ended up marking the real and fictional existence of the *Carbonaro* from Romagna even during his American exile. It is hardly necessary to point out the varying degrees of symbolic intensity, despite the use of the same rhetorical device: Santa Anna's real leg, although *dead*, was elevated to the rank of a *mixed* object, secular in content but religious in form, even during the general's life. These three cases appear in contemporary sources, and therefore do not qualify as identity or legendary constructs that arose after the mid-19th century.

Out of the many possible examples, these three have been chosen from very different contexts (Greece, Mexico, the Habsburg Empire) which nevertheless converge morphologically on the same narrative/cultural device, made more homogeneous by their shared romantic flavour, by a violence almost transfigured by heroism and by a quasi-classical ethics of sacrifice. Moreover, the period in question, marked by the birth of nations, was conducive to the success of real stories but worthy of the pages of a modern Livy.

The helmet of Theódoros Kolokotrónis (1770-1843)[6] is now kept in the National Museum of the History of Greece in Athens (Fig. 1). Kolokotrónis[7] was born in 1770 and was a Klepht chief, that is to say, the leader of a rural clan from the Peloponnese mountains, devoted to the violent control of its territory. His father had participated in the Orlov Revolt and he himself was anything but an ordinary bandit: rather, he was a gang leader eager to become someone notable. His life changed during the Napoleonic period, when the Mediterranean

5. On the process of transformation into heritage, see *I territori del patrimonio. Dinamiche della patrimonializzazione e culture locali (secc. XVII-XX)*, ed. by Roberto Balzani, Bologna, il Mulino, 2015.

6. For a brief biography, see Dimitris Keridis, *Historical Dictionary of Modern Greece*, Lanham (MD), Scarecrow Press, 2009, *ad nomen*; Richard Clogg, *A Concise History of Greece*, Cambridge-New York, Cambridge University Press, 2013, p. 270.

7. See the romantic biography by Eugène Yéméniz, *La Grèce moderne. Héros et poètes*, Paris, Lévy Frères, 1862, pp. 157-212.

became a war zone. In the early 19th century, after a series of adventures that included participating on the Tsar's side in the Russian-Turkish war, he arrived in Zakynthos (1806), one of the islands once ruled by Venice but which at that time was a small Ionian enclave disputed by both the French and English. Kolokotrónis allied with the side that ultimately won, the British, which, at the end of the French protectorate (1807-1814), set up an autonomous government of seven islands controlled from London. But the British, who did not have sufficient ground troops, tried to form local regiments that would fight under the Union Jack. The effects of these military traditions on local contexts were sometimes unpredictable: in some cases – as confirmed by Hugh Trevor Roper's studies, for example, which examined the creation of Scottish stereotypes between the 18th and 19th centuries[8] – participating in regional/national regiments actually strengthened and transformed the identity of the country of origin. One such example is in the wartime memories of Australian and New Zealand forces immediately after the disastrous but "glorious" campaign of the Dardanelles in 1915.[9]

As for the Greek First Light Infantry Regiment,[10] the limited number of participants in the military events of the early 1810s – 1,000 at most – certainly does not seem to have contributed to a stronger national proto-identity, except for Kolokotrónis, who soon achieved the rank of Major. We should also add that the British gave the uniforms of these quasi-colonial corps[11] what they considered to be an indigenous, very exotic flavour. Kolokotrónis, who later went to Morea and became a military commander in the 1820s revolt,[12] was already used to wearing the helmet of regimental officers, in other words, an English helmet modelled on that of the cuirassiers, saw it as a trait of personal distinction. There was nothing "classic" about the object, but, due to its grandeur and visibility, it allowed Kolokotrónis, especially in the critical phases of the battles, to present himself as a new Leonidas.[13] The further choice of a cross instead of the British insignia on

8. Hugh Trevor-Roper, "L'invenzione della tradizione: la tradizione delle Highlands in Scozia", in *L'invenzione della tradizione*, ed. by Eric J. Hobsbawm and Terence Ranger, Turin, Einaudi, 1987, pp. 19-44.

9. On the campaign and the early veneration of the fallen, there are various contributions, beginning with Robert Rhodes James, *Gallipoli*, Florence, Sansoni, 1968. Anzac Day, the day when the victims of the Turkish are remembered, was first established in 1916 in Australia and New Zealand. For an official outline, see https://nzhistory.govt.nz/war/anzac-day/the-anzacs, accessed on 28 November 2020.

10. See René Chartrand, Patrice Courcelle, *Émigré and Foreign Troops in British Service*, vol. II, *1803-1815*, London, Osprey, 2000.

11. Nikos G. Moschonàs, "I partiti e l'idea dell'unità nazionale nel Parlamento ionio", in *Indipendenza e unità nazionale in Italia ed in Grecia*, conference proceedings in Athens, 2-7 October 1985, Florence, Olschki, 1987, p. 134.

12. See David Brewer, *The Greek War of Independence: The Struggle for Freedom from Ottoman Oppression and the Birth of the Modern Greek Nation*, New York, The Overlook Press, 2001.

13. "Dressed in the Greek fustanella, he wore during the whole of the war, not a fez, but a helmet, declaring that his mind was with the Greeks of old" (Ioannes Gennadius, "Preface" to *Kolokotrones. The Klepht and the Warrior. Sixty Years of Peril and Daring. An Autobiography*, London, Fisher Unwin, 1892, p. xxii); Maurizio Isabella, *Risorgimento in Exile: Italian*

the front of the helmet almost seems an effective ploy to communicate a mixed symbolic value, half ancient and half Orthodox.

Why is this a synecdoche? Because the helmet *was* Kolokotrónis: in his main representations, statues (Fig. 2) and images, it made him easily identifiable. Where he was not wearing it, his previous life as the clan leader devoted to robbery seemed to re-emerge abruptly, revealing to English, French, German or Italian public opinion, beyond the canons of oriental disciplines, the ambiguous and unfathomable nature of at least some of the contemporary Greek patriotism.[14] The synecdoche works because it helped reassure – apparently, at least – the violently Russophobic environments of the West and to Hellenise the outward image of the indigenous revolutionary faction, which was otherwise difficult to distinguish from its Turkish counterpart in terms of its clothes and habits.[15] Religion, in the symbol of the cross, did not resolve contemporary ambiguities and was not in itself sufficient to characterise the broadly "European" identity of the fighters on the field, as the Orthodox faith directed minds towards the north-east, towards St. Petersburg. The classic structure of the Greek myth about their origins, on the contrary, was firmly attached to the body of the continental collective memory. It is obviously impossible to determine whether Kolokotrónis was aware of these subtle cultural details, which would become totally explicit on an intellectual level, even in Greece, only later.[16] But once he accidentally came across British uniforms in the Ionian Islands, it seems reasonable to postulate at least some sort of aesthetic-memorial attraction to the helmet, without any particular narrative complications. In retrospect, however, these decreed its success.

The second case is that of the leg of General Antonio López de Santa Anna (1794-1876), nicknamed *Aquila* (the Eagle) and the Napoleon of the West, President and dictator of Mexico between the 1830s and 1850s and often hotly contested. A hero of independence, originally a liberal and a republican, he showed a more conservative attitude once he came to power. The conflict between centralists and federalists saw him take increasingly authoritarian positions, although these were counterbalanced by reforms.[17] However, compared to his competitors, he developed a particular propensity towards entertaining relations with popular contexts, which was facilitated by his "personalidad charismática". In his case, Will Fowler has spoken of "popularidad mítica", of "Bonapartist political populism",[18] with a tendency towards a spectacularisation that could infect the social arena. In 1838, in a political phase when he did not lead the nation,

Émigrés and the Liberal International in the Post-Napoleonic Era, Oxford, Oxford University Press, 2009, pp. 65-91.

14. See *Philhéllenenismes et transferts culturels dans l'Europe du XIX*[e] *siècle*, ed. by Michel Espagne and Gilles Pécout, special issue of *Revue Geramanique Internationale*, 1/2 (2005).

15. Isabella, *Risorgimento in Exile*, p. 80.

16. Antonis Liakos, "La storia della Grecia come costruzione di un tempo nazionale", *Contemporanea*, 1 (2001), pp. 155-169.

17. Will Fowler, *Santa Anna of Mexico*, Lincoln (NE), University of Nebraska Press, 2007.

18. Will Fowler, "El pensamiento politico de los santanistas, 1821-1855", in *Historia y nación*, Actas del Congreso en homenaje a Josefina Zoraida Vázquez, vol. II, *Política y*

Santa Anna organised the troops when Louis Philippe's French Navy landed in Veracruz on the pretext of forcing the Mexican government to compensate the French traders who had suffered attacks and persecutions in Mexico multiple times since 1828. The intervention was called the "Guerra de los pasteles" (the "Pastry War") because in 1832 a French pastry chef, Monsieur Remontel, had lost a considerable amount of stock following the sack of his shop in Tacubaya at the hands of Santa Anna's officers. Compensation requests were inflated by the Mexican press, which built a case around the event. Xenophobic demonstrations, with summary executions, thefts and forced levies occurred repeatedly due to the political instability of the country, but were undermined, in some regions, by a climate of endemic revolt, aided by the xenophobic attitude of part of the political class. The summary executions of foreigners culminated in Tampico in December 1835 with the shooting by insurgents of twenty-eight people, including two French citizens. Louis Philippe took advantage of this crisis for a military operation actually inspired by his wish to obtain the status of a favoured nation for France, since Great Britain and the United States already held it, and to become a top-level trading partner. The dispatch of a military force led by Commodore Charles Bazoche therefore had a very tangible objective, beyond the apparent irrelevance of the pretext. However, the clash was inevitable and culminated in a few months of hostilities, between 1838 and 1839.[19]

In Veracruz, Santa Anna stood out in his resistance to the invaders. There, as the *Journal des Débats* reported on 20 March 1839 on the basis of news dating to about three months earlier, Santa Anna, because of his injuries, had had his foot and the lower part of his left leg amputated, but the operation was so clumsy "that a part of the bone was still visible", "probablement" requiring further surgery. The *Journal* reported that in Veracruz the outcome of such surgical operations, except in the cases of pirate commanders, was usually ill-fated. "Santa Anna was fortunate to escape", but, it was hoped, for him it would "henceforth be impossible to put himself at the head of any party". This forecast was incorrect. Not only did the general regain control of his body, but also of the politico-military situation, so much so that, once he became President again, he built a special "monument" to the limb he had lost in the *affaire* of 5 December 1838 against the French. It was inaugurated on 27 September 1842 in the cemetery of Santa Paula in Mexico City. As reported by the press, Don Ignacio Sierra y Rosso pronounced a funeral oration appropriate for the occasion, with full military honours by the army corps and fanfares, at the end of a procession through the streets of the capital. The chronicles of Carlos María de Bustamente, an illustrious intellectual of the time, published a few years after the events, reflect the climate of the moment particularly effectively.[20]

diplomacia en el siglo XX mexicano, ed. by Luis Jáuregui and José Antonio Serrano Ortega, Mexico, El Colegio de Mexico, 1998, p. 204.

19. On these events, see Jacques Penot, "L'expansion commerciale française au Mexique et les causes du conflit franco-mexicain de 1838-1839", *Bullettin Hispanique*, 1/2 (1973), pp. 169-201.

20. "Don Antonio Esnaurrizar, Jefe de la Comisaría de México, mandó a erigir una columna en el cementero de Santa Paula, para depositar la pierna de Santa Anna. Erigió dicha

The story is so grotesque that it stuck in the memory and, in 1992, inspired an article by Thomas Calvo, Professor at Nanterre:

> What was Mexican General Santa Anna thinking about on that September day in 1842, as he presided over the national funeral he ordered for his leg, amputated some years before, and which he had therefore dug up on his estate in Manga de Clavo? Was he perhaps thinking of the tragedies of the nation, of which the leg, cut down by a French cannonball, was a sad victim? Did he think, more likely, that it was a heroic leg? Most certainly, he was thinking of himself![21]

This bizarre celebration of a leg is part of the cult of personality and populist politics in which Santa Anna would invest during his long stint in Mexican public life: recent studies have highlighted the role of "fiestas santanistas" in the creation of a popular consensus rooted in a national-personal calendar that was seamlessly conceived and that ranged from the remembrance of the heroic dates of the republic, to the *Te Deum* sung on religious and civil celebrations, and to public ceremonies for the general's birthday.[22] In this context, therefore, the emotional mobilisation is less surprising ("a large public fascinated by the novelty of this unique event", as described by Bustamante), in the wake of a tragicomic event, poised between baroque tradition, classical reminiscences and artistic performance,[23] generated by the evocative act of a power that was not as absolute as it was boundless in its most extreme and apparently absurd (but, precisely for this reason, extraordinary) manifestations. Not only did the "function", as eyewitnesses called it, end up on everyone's lips for days on end, becoming the butt of understandable jokes, but

columna sobre una alta gradería. Sobre un chapitel dorado se colocó una urna o sarcófago, y sobre éste un pequeño cañón de artillería descansando sobre él la águila mexicana. En la base de la columna aparecen cuatro lápidas para otras tantas inscripciones: rodea la columna un enrejado, y en los estremos o esquinas se ven colocadas insignias consulares que precedían en Roma a estos magistrados, es decir, las faces y hachas que simbolizaban su poder… La mañana del 27 de septiembre se hizo un brillante entierro… del miembro de un hombre vivo aún, al que concurrió por la novedad y rareza de la función, la gente más ilustre de México, y un inmenso pueblo, atraído por la novedad de este singular espectáculo… La urna fue colocada por mano del ministro de guerra acompañado del de hacienda. Ínterin se practicaba esta operación bastante arriesgada por los andamios, y espuesta no sólo a que se quebrase los pies, sino a que se matasen los ministros, el Lic. Sierra y Rosso, apoderado y favorecido de Santa Anna, pronunció cerca de la columna y en la galería inmediata que forma los sepulcros, una oración en honor a su héroe y remembrando sus hazañas… Concluido el acto, Esnaurriazar tomó la llave de la urna y delante de mí la entregó a Santa Anna haciéndole una arenga, a la que respondió éste lacónica y tibiamente. Por la tarde fue en un magnífico coche acompañado de gran comitiva de tropas y oficiales para ver el monumento, a donde a de ir el resto del cuerpo el día de la resurrección universal a recoger su pie para presentarse íntegro en el tribunal de Dios". Carlos María de Bustamante, *Apuntes para la historia del gobierno del general Antonio López de Santa Anna* (1845), México, Instituto Cultural Helénico-FCE, 1986, p. 84.

21. Thomas Calvo, "La jambe de Santa Anna", *Matériaux pour l'histoire de notre temps*, 27 (1992), p. 41.

22. Will Fowler, "Fiestas santanistas. La celebración de Santa Anna en la villa de Xalapa, 1821-1855", in *Historia Mexicana*, 2 (2002), pp. 391-447.

23. Luis Alberto de la Garza Becerra, "El entierro de una pata y otras historias santannistas", *Estudios políticos (México)*, 21 (2010), pp. 39-62.

it also fed an almost legendary narrative circuit that storytellers repeated in the public squares.[24]

The fate of the limb that was elevated to the rank of sacred object was not, however, complete. In 1844, during a riot against the former dictator, the crowd removed it from its "secular tabernacle" and dragged it along the streets as an insult. The replacement wooden legs fared no better. In January 1845, Santa Anna, pursued after he tried to escape from where the government had been exiled him, was discovered by natives hunting around the village of Xico, not far from Xalapa, his hometown. "While their dogs barked furiously from the side of the ravine, the Indians came over and found Santa Anna there, who they immediately recognised, thanks to his wooden leg and his physiognomy, which was known to all Mexicans. He had some companions with him, and he had stopped to rest his wooden and cork leg because of the inflammation that such a difficult march had caused to his stump".[25] The *Journal* reported other versions of the events, according to which Santa Anna's capture had taken place thanks to the intervention of local volunteers who had thus saved the general from a tribe of cannibals. This is of little importance. Much more interesting is the fact that the wooden leg became the general's hallmark, his true "identity card".

Santa Anna, moreover, spared no expense in the care of his artificial limb: he had several specimens built, a couple of which have survived to this day. The first, however, seems to have been the work of an American craftsman, New Yorker Charles Bartlett, who allegedly made it for the large fee of $1,300. Its fate is not entirely certain. On 14 April 1847, during the Battle of Cerro Gordo against the Americans,[26] he certainly lost one of them, and the Illinois National Guard, who retrieved it in a carriage along with a treasure of $18,000, immediately seized it as war spoils. For decades veterans demanded 10 cents per visitor to show it, while Barnum wanted it for his collection of extraordinary things.[27] After the First World War, it became state property and is now kept in the Illinois State Military Museum in Springfield (Fig. 3). Until recently, it was exhibited in a rather kitsch setting that re-proposed the "spaghetti western" image of an abandoned carriage with a trunk full of dollars: a scene worthy of Sergio Leone's *The Good, the Bad and the Ugly*. Despite its transformation into a museum exhibit and a "secular relic" of history, which at this stage was no longer Mexican, but American, the leg remains

24. Bustamante, *Apuntes para la historia del gobierno del general Antonio López de Santa Anna*, p. 84.

25. *Journal des Débats*, 20 March 1845, p. 2.

26. A wonderful print (*The Flight of Santa Anna: At the Battle of Cerro Gordo*, Philadelphia, Lith. & pub. by R. Magee, [1847-1848]) with the story of the lost leg can be seen in the collections of the Library of Congress (https://www.loc.gov/resource/pga.11600/, accessed on 28 November 2020).

27. Myra H. Mcilvain, *The Question of Santa Anna's Leg*, 31 October 2014, available at https://myrahmcilvain.com/2014/10/31/the-question-of-santa-annas-leg/, and accessed on 26 November 2020. Also, on the whole story, see the excellent study by Michael Scott Van Wagenen, *Remembering the Forgotten War: The Enduring Legacies of the U.S.-Mexican War*, Amherst (MA), University of Massachusetts Press 2012.

disputed. In fact, in 2014[28] the San Jacinto Battle Monument and Museum in Texas claimed the wooden prosthetic leg so as to render the Battle of the Alamo, a Texan "heroic defeat" at the hands of Santa Anna's troops, more effectively, on the basis of original objects. Shortly after, Santa Anna was in turn defeated by General Samuel Houston's troops in San Jacinto. In 1836, however, at the time of the battle, the general's leg was still firmly in place. The matter even reached the White House in the form of a petition, according to the well-known script of territorial conflicts, but it was not resolved: the objects remain where they were, despite the periodic "pilgrimages" of Texan students, which were still attested to in 2016.[29]

Another of Santa Anna's prosthetic legs is kept at the Museo Nacional de Historia in Mexico City, in this case exhibited as a document of the complex history of Mexican presidencies of the early 19th century and the figures who came to power. There is no rhetoric here, just the confirmation of a narrative that had already established itself successfully in the early 1840s. In 2016, on the website www.tombstonebuilder.com, one Yac Vargas created a provocative virtual image that reproduced the 1842 "cenotaph" almost comically: a plaque commemorates the "wooden leg" of Santa Anna, "hero of the war against France" (but he is not mentioned in the text), which died in 1838. The ironic use of synecdoche could not be greater, thanks to the do-it-yourself, totally digital transformation into heritage that the net allows. To conclude on Santa Anna, it is interesting to note the use of another synecdoche, which was partly connected to the previous one, and already widespread during his difficult season as a leader. After his 1838 amputation, in fact, he was nicknamed "el quinceuñas", "Fifteen-nails", despite the fact he only had fourteen nails left, having also lost a toe in the Veracruz battle. Once again, we find parts of the body used to indicate a person, to name him without pronouncing his name. By making his mutilated physicality a recognisable object, Santa Anna did not only turn himself into heritage, without escaping the multiplier effect of the ironic gaze, but he also consciously constructed a parallel narrative, which in fact has survived better in the Mexican popular and national imagination than the complicated history of the Republic during its first decades of life.

Of the amputated leg that belonged to Piero Maroncelli (1795-1846),[30] the Italian patriot who ended up in the Spielberg Hapsburg prison in Brno, following the repression of *Carbonari* organisations in 1819-1820,[31] we have no trace. He

28. Maggie Galehouse, "Texas Fighting for Santa Anna's Leg", *Houston Chronicle*, 16 May 2014. See https://www.houstonchronicle.com/entertainment/article/Texas-fighting-for-Santa-Anna-s-leg-5483826.php, accessed on 26 November 2020.

29. Will Connors, "The War of Santa Anna's Leg Takes a Big Step Forward", *Wall Street Journal*, 6 November 2016. See https://www.wsj.com/articles/the-war-of-santa-annas-leg-take-a-big-step-forward-1478448713, accessed on 26 November 2020.

30. See, on this, Franco Della Peruta, *L'Italia del Risorgimento. Problemi, momenti e figure*, Milan, FrancoAngeli, 1997, pp. 30-47.

31. Very useful on this topic is Alessandro Luzio, *Il processo Pellico-Maroncelli secondo gli atti officiali segreti*, Milan, Tip. Ed. L.F. Cogliati, 1903. Also *La nascita della nazione. La Carboneria. Intrecci veneti, nazionali e internazionali*, ed. by Giampietro Berti and Franco Della Peruta, Rovigo, Ass. Culturale Minelliana, 2004.

too lost his left leg, like Santa Anna, though not in battle but because of gangrene, which required radical intervention. The terrible operation was performed in June 1828 in precarious conditions and not even by a professional surgeon, but by an Austrian barber. At its end, Maroncelli gave him a rose. The event would have remained unknown and hardly worthy of note had it not ended up, in 1832, in a book that Maroncelli's prison companion, Silvio Pellico,[32] devoted to their Spielberg experience. *Le mie prigioni* (*My Ten Years' Imprisonment*) quickly became a bestseller in Europe and beyond. Pellico described his friend's story with romantic pathos: "Maroncelli was ill with a bad tumour upon his knee. At first the pain was not great, and he only limped as he walked. It then grew very irksome to him to bear his irons, and he rarely went out to walk. One autumnal morning he was desirous of breathing the fresh air; there was a fall of snow, and unfortunately in walking his leg failed him, and he came to the ground. This accident was followed by acute pain in his knee. He was carried to his bed; for he was no longer able to remain in an upright position".[33]

The doctor who went to visit him had his irons removed, but of course it was not enough, nor were the "leeches", "caustics" and other useless applications. Pellico underlined the patient's sweetness and serenity, the manly resignation with which he seemed to meet his fate: "he continued to compose verses, he sang, and he conversed [...]. He lost his powers of digestion, he could not sleep, was reduced to a skeleton, and very frequently swooned away". The torment lasted for nine months, after which the prison administration decided to seek consultation. The Head Physician Pfungen was summoned and issued his sentence: amputation. The physician himself hesitated, given Maroncelli's precarious conditions, but the latter was decided: "and shall I not equally die if I go on, without ending this diabolical torture?" The Spielberg's doctors disagreed and authorisation to proceed was requested from Vienna. Within a week, the affirmative response arrived. Pellico was allowed to assist the sick man. Maroncelli received the sacraments, and then began to sing a hymn. The operation was performed by the barber assisted by a young surgeon, a "student from the Vienna school", who merely looked on and gave directions. The description of the operation is quick, but vivid: the cutting of the muscles, the blood that flowed "in torrents from the arteries" and that was quickly tied with silk thread, the sawn bone.

> Maroncelli never uttered a cry. When he saw them carrying his leg away, he cast on it one melancholy look, then turning towards the surgeon, he said, "You have freed me from an enemy, and I have no money to give you." He saw a rose, in a glass, placed in a window: "May I beg of you to bring me hither that flower?" I brought it to him; and he then offered it to the surgeon with an indescribable air of good-nature: "See, I have nothing else to give you in token of my gratitude." He took it as it was meant, and even wiped away a tear".[34]

32. For an accurate analysis of Pellico's ideas, see Roberto Pertici, "Nazione e religione in Silvio Pellico", *Società e storia*, 106 (2004), pp. 687-704.

33. Silvio Pellico, *My Ten Years' Imprisonment: Translated from Italian by Thomas Roscoe*, London-Paris-New York-Melbourne, Cassell & Company, Limited, 1886, ch. 86.

34. *Ibid*, pp. 152-153. See also *Spielberg. Documentazione sui detenuti politici italiani. Inventario, 1822-1859*, ed. by Luigi Contegiacomo, Rovigo, Ass. Culturale Minelliana, 2010, pp. 72-77.

Compared to Santa Anna, who made his leg *speak* and almost humanised it in its "political" adventures and artificial replicas, *My Ten Years' Imprisonment* emphasised Maroncelli's *absent* leg, because – in the story – it helped perfect the psychological description of the unfortunate patriot from Romagna. Without the amputation, we would not have known that he was courageous, resolute, romantic, faithful to religious tradition, generous. His detached limb works as a synecdoche because through his reaction it reveals, in this case thanks to a skilful narrative device, human contents that are otherwise unfathomable, and which make Maroncelli a character heroic in his own way.

The first to understand the potential of the synecdoche was a young Giuseppe Mazzini,[35] who, as early as 1833, while reconstructing the unfortunate life of Enrichetta Castiglioni who had died in an Austrian prison due to illness, noted for the readers of the fourth issue of *Giovine Italia*: "Only, to refine the hypocrisy, when everything turned to the worst, [and] his case was desperate, [and] it was impossible to carry him outside, [then] permission came, a kind of bitter irony, which few would believe, if Maroncelli's leg, committed to the surgical operation, with Vienna's permission, when gangrene had already advanced, was not irrefutable evidence of the customary procedure".[36]

The "customary procedure" was relieving the harsh prison regime *in extremis* by administrative and bureaucratic means, "because the Governor of Spielberg", he would repeat in 1845 in an open letter to Sir James Graham, British Minister of the Interior, "having received his prisoner with two legs, was obliged to give him up in the same condition, and therefore could not allow the operation to take place until he had received a sanction from Vienna".[37] The Spielberg's documents appear to confirm the tone, both tragic and grotesque, of Mazzini's reconstruction: a document dated October 1828 confirmed the request, by the superintendent and the prison doctor, for "a state-of-the-art wooden leg" for the convalescent inmate.[38] The limb interested the revolutionary leader much more than Maroncelli's ideas, which he immediately felt to be alien. Through its painful separation from the body, it accused the Hapsburg repressive system and revealed its ice-cold cruelty. The transformation of the leg into heritage for the benefit of the imaginary museum of objects that the Italian exiles would establish in exile to preserve the genealogical memory of the conspiracy is therefore attested to early on.

35. Roberto Balzani, "Il mito di Maroncelli", in *Piero Maroncelli. L'itinerario di un romantico dalla Carboneria al Fourierismo, nell'età della Restaurazione*, ed. by Flavia Bugani, Forlì, Comune di Forlì, 1997, pp. 85-106.

36. "Soltanto, per raffinamento d'ipocrisia, quando ogni cosa, volta alla peggio, disperato il caso, riesciva impossibile trasportarla al di fuori, venne un permesso, specie d'amara ironia, che pochi vorrebbero credere, se la gamba di Maroncelli, commessa, per concessione di Vienna, all'operazione chirurgica, quando la gangrena era già formata, non fosse irrecusabile documento del consueto procedere". Giuseppe Mazzini, "Una memoria" (1833), in Giuseppe Mazzini, *Scritti editi ed inediti*, vol. III, Imola, Galeati, 1907, p. 173.

37. Giuseppe Mazzini, "Italy, Austria, and the Pope: A Letter to Sir James Graham, Bart." (1845), in Giuseppe Mazzini, *Scritti editi ed inediti*, vol. XXXI, Imola, Galeati, 1921, p. 303.

38. *Spielberg. Documentazione*, p. 80.

The same can be said of the story of the amputation. *My Ten Years' Imprisonment* was immediately translated into French (there were four editions in 1833 alone) and into English by Thomas Roscoe, also in 1833. A more accurate American edition was published in Cambridge (Massachusetts) in 1836 and reviewed in January 1837 by the *North American Review*. In August, Federico Confalonieri, also in the United States, wrote to Giuseppe Arconati and reported with amazement that he had "found *My Ten Years' Imprisonment* in everyone's hands in all the provinces he travelled through, on the banks of the Saint Lawrence, the Mississippi and in the huts of Chichingar". Confalonieri benefitted from the volume's popularity, triggered by the "remarkable" "political-moral" phenomenon of "Martyrdom for the cause of the improvement of Humanity".[39] Whereas Confalonieri was "celebrated in an oppressive way", Maroncelli, who chose the North American republic as his homeland, nevertheless had greater problems surviving, despite the notoriety that followed him due to his transformation into a fictional hero. Perhaps he was the first of a series of Italians transfigured and "consumed" by Anglo-Saxon popular culture during the *Risorgimento*.[40]

Maroncelli's leg, therefore, survived quite well in the cultural memory of the 19th and 20th centuries, not only in Italy but across Europe. In Brno, at the Spielberg, an attempt has been made to give physicality to Pellico's story by exhibiting the withered rose the patriot gifted his surgeon (Fig. 4). Since no other credible evidence is available, the other romantic object central to the narrative was chosen.[41] The "name of the rose", at this point, is Maroncelli's. Is this another (weak) synecdoche for the benefit of tourists?

39. For information and quotes, see Luisa Cetti, "Piero Maroncelli. Lettere dall'America, 1834-1844", *Il Risorgimento*, 3 (1993), pp. 338 and 341. See also Angeline H. Lograsso, "Piero Maroncelli in America", *Rassegna storica del Risorgimento*, 15 (1928), pp. 894-841.

40. See, on this, Elena Bacchin, "Felice Orsini and the Construction of the Pro-Italian Narrative in Britain", in *Britain, Ireland and the Italian Risorgimento*, ed. by Nick Carter, London, Palgrave, 2015, pp. 80-103.

41. Andrea Lessona, "Fortezza dello Spielberg, prigione d'Europa", *Il Reporter*, 16 December 2014 (http://repubblicaceca.ilreporter.com/fortezza-dello-spielberg/la-rosa-di-piero-maroncelli-nella-fortezza-dello-spielberg-andrea-lessona/, accessed on 28 November 2020).

1. Kolokotrónis's helmet. National Historical Museum of Greece, Athens.
2. The hero on his horse. He is recognisable thanks to his plumed helmet. Athens, Greece.

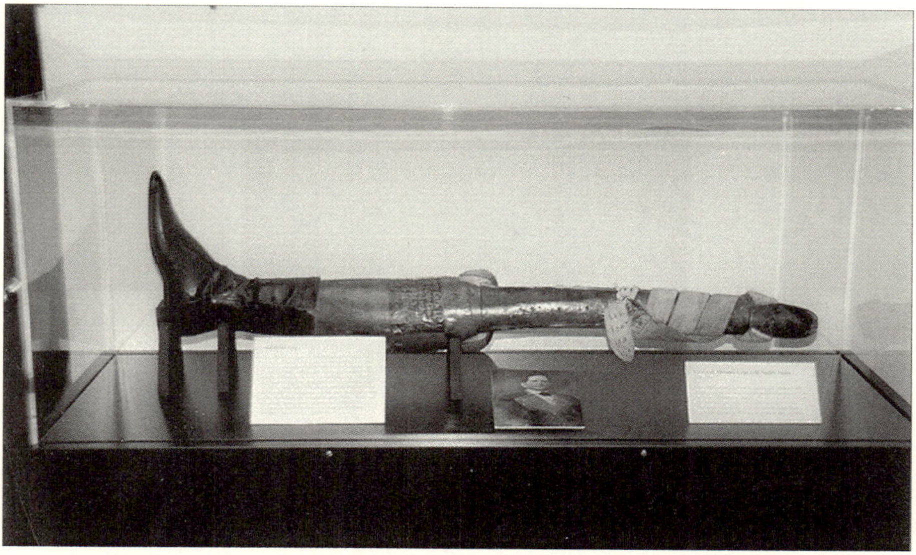

3. Santa Anna's wooden leg, an American spoil of war. Illinois State Military Museum, United States of America.
4. Maroncelli's rose at the Spielberg. Spielberg's Castle, Brno.

III

Objects as Relics and Memory

Silvia Cavicchioli

The Politics of Memory: Heirlooms and Relics of Patriots, Fighters and Martyrs of the Italian *Risorgimento*

1. *Seeing the* Risorgimento

The following pages are a preview of a larger work devoted to patriotic memorabilia and offer some reflections, accompanied by examples, on a particular set of objects: the relics of the many martyrs and patriots who featured in exhibitions and museums of the *Risorgimento*, ever since they were first established.

The narration of the national *Risorgimento* was in fact also built thanks to a massive movement of peculiar memorabilia and the attention generated by their symbolic potential. This historiographical topic has been acknowledged as relevant: in fact, the study of relics continues to attract attention from the scientific community as shown, among others, by the international projects developed by the Universities of Limoges and Poitiers on the matter of *reliques politiques*.[1]

It is not appropriate to focus here on the historiographical importance of material culture and the centrality of the *Social Life of Things*.[2] However, I would like to strongly reiterate how indispensable material studies and the methodologies for studying political objects are for the historical investigation of a period that saw the growing importance of both public opinion and the cult of personality, expressed by acknowledging and acclaiming contemporary celebrities of every political affiliation and national origin.[3]

These approaches allow us to better understand, for example, the euphoria of those Tuscan noblewomen who, during the journey by Radetzky across the Grand Duchy in June 1849, rushed to see him and pay homage to him and competed to grab "the feathers that adorned his hat, to keep them as venerable relics", as

1. *Reliques politiques*, ed. by Albrecht Burkardt and Jérôme Grévy, Rennes, Presses Universitaires de Rennes, 2020.

2. *The Social Life of Things: Commodities in Cultural Perspective*, ed. by Arjun Appadurai, Chicago, Chicago University Press, 1986.

3. "Storia e cultura materiale: recenti traiettorie di ricerca. Interventi di Fabio Dei, Giorgio Riello, Beverly Lemire, Manuel Charpy, Leora Auslander", ed. by Alessio Petrizzo and Carlotta Sorba, *Contemporanea. Rivista di storia dell'800 e del '900*, 3 (2016), pp. 437-480; Enrico Francia, "Oggetti patriottici. Una ricerca sulla cultura materiale del Risorgimento", *Passato e Presente*, 35 (2017), pp. 37-44.

Licurgo Cappelletti wrote.[4] Or they allow us to contextualise the gesture of Count Cavour who, on 1 August 1860, at the time of Garibaldi's expedition to Sicily, sent as a gift to Emanuele d'Azeglio a lock of the hair (Fig. 1) of his eternal enemy, the "Hero of Two Worlds", which he had obtained at the glorious peak of an already legendary life.[5]

But in addition to the fame of heroes and celebrities, these objects made the narration of the major events of the 19th century tangible, simplifying its story for the general public, supporting the new times and the need for a *Risorgimento* which could "be seen", in place of memory and words. A demonstration of this is offered by one of the many attempts to rehabilitate memories, where republican conspirators became martyrs of the unified homeland. In 1882, the director of the prison located in the Castle of San Giorgio in Mantua turned into a tourist attraction, complete with an exhibition of memories and portraits, one of the cells where the martyrs of Belfiore and other prisoners, including Felice Orsini, had been imprisoned. On the windowsill of the sell he placed "a very small saw" to give "visitors an idea of the way in which the bars had been sawn" by the famous prisoner in his daring escape, as Mantuan scholar Don Attilio Portioli reported in a local newspaper.[6] Two years later he lent the piece sawn off by Orsini to the Turin Exhibition,[7] along with some other prison objects of his, lent by a collector of national memorabilia who had bought them from a prison warden who had fallen on hard times; by a former fellow prisoner; by a local scholar: all actors in contexts at the centre of my research. Those memorabilia were able to recreate, 300 kilometres away and in an ephemeral context, the dramatic and emotional narration of Orsini's imprisonment, escape and martyrdom.

Those cited above are examples of how, before breaking into and occupying public space and becoming political tools, individual objects and entire collections had moved from private contexts into public circuits, assuming different meanings from those they had held originally. These pages aim to reconstruct the many threads of those pathways, through an analysis of the origin, conservation and exhibition of relics and through a study of the various agents that played a primary and active role *par le bas*, thus from a social rather than political-institutional point of view.

I selected these objects from the large set of "*memorie patrie*" (as the various sets of *Risorgimento* memorabilia – heirlooms, documents, weapons, clothes, medals, portraits, drawings, photographs, etc – were commonly known in their broadest sense). In the 19th century, they were objects selected as eloquent

4. Licurgo Cappelletti, *Austria e Toscana. Sette lustri di storia*, Turin, Fratelli Bocca, 1917, pp. 285-286.

5. Historical Archive of the City of Turin, *Affari Gabinetto del Sindaco*, cart. 129, f. 1, sf. 3, ssf. 15, letter from Emanuele d'Azeglio to the Mayor of Turin, 9 November 1886, and his reply.

6. Attilio Portioli, "Le carceri politiche del Castello di S. Giorgio in Mantova", *Il Mendico*, 14 (16 July 1882), p. 7. See also Costanza Bertolotti, Gian Luca Fruci, Alessio Petrizzo, *Icone politiche. Celebrità e nuovi media al tempo del Risorgimento*, Mantua, PubliPaolini, 2018, pp. 17-23.

7. *Catalogo degli oggetti esposti nel padiglione del Risorgimento italiano*, vol. II, *Oggetti*, Milan, Dumolard, 1888, p. 198.

materials particularly suited to narrating the *Risorgimento* as a collective sacrifice and to inducing feelings of gratitude and patriotism; nowadays, they are highly symbolic items, suitable for reflections on the transfers of their literal and semantic meanings and endowed with extraordinary intrinsic symbolic power. This power of relics is highlighted, for instance, in a surprising episode that occurred in Venice during the insurgence of 1848, an episode that also shows the sense of a profound continuity between the widespread presence of the ancient relics that came from elsewhere to the lagoon city and the contemporary civil relics. At that time, General Antonini's arm (amputated after the battle of Monte Berico, embalmed and presented as a "relic of the Nation") was thought to be set in an urn in the church of San Biagio in the Arsenale, to replace (with oppositional value) the heart of Archduke Frederick of Austria, former commander of the Venetian navy, who had died prematurely the year before.[8] The symbolic meaning also emerged from the wooden spoon Giorgio Pallavicino Trivulzio used during his long detention in the Spielberg prison: it was kept "in a private display case in his study in San Fiorano" and was then donated by his daughter Anna d'Angrogna to the Museum of the *Risorgimento* in Milan.[9] When the item was mentioned during the solemn commemoration of the former conspirator, pronounced upon his death in 1878 in the Italian Senate, it acquired a different status, shifting from a "simple" secular relic to a symbol of national reconciliation.

2. *The lay relics of the homeland*

> Mr Michele Baccoli, a hotelier in Condino, has delivered to the National Risorgimento Museum in Brescia: some left-overs from the breakfast (bread and cheese) Giuseppe Garibaldi had on the morning of 20 May 1866 in Monte Suello; the glass and tablecloth he used on the aforementioned occasion. [...] And then they shout that we Catholics are superstitious. If they, Garibaldi's fanatical admirers, are not the ones who are superstitious, we really do not know what superstition is.[10]

The parody in the Catholic press of 1889 which, by stigmatising the secular canonisation of the fathers of the nation and pro-Garibaldi fetishism, mocked the relics of the *Risorgimento*, on the one hand raises the crucial question of the coexistence of practices, languages and communication codes seen as sacred in political contexts that were not only secular and liberal but which also had democratic, harshly anti-clerical and even masonic senses and connotations.

8. This civil relic had been kept by "republican countess" Maddalena Montalban Comello for a long time, and it was then showed in the Museo Civico Correr in Venice. It finally reached the Art Gallery in Varallo. See Carlo Arrigoni, "Un cimelio chirurgico-risorgimentale: il braccio destro del generale Giacomo Antonini visto a più d'un secolo dall'amputazione", *Minerva chirurgica*, 11 (1954), p. 10.

9. Private Archive Barbiano di Belgiojoso, San Fiorano (LO), Will of Anna Pallavicino Trivulzio d'Angrogna, 10 June 1919.

10. The quote from a Catholic newapaper is taken from: "La vita che si vive", *Gazzetta Piemontese*, 13 November 1889, pp. 2-3.

On the other hand, it refers to the extent and pervasiveness of materiality and reliquary rhetoric in the museum displays of homeland history in the last twenty years of the 19th century. At that time, in fact, the first civic collections on the *Risorgimento* and the temporary exhibitions displayed large quantities of patriotic relics. At the end of the 19th century, bloody bandages, torn uniforms and bone fragments had become common elements in the burgeoning *Risorgimento* museums, central features in the construction of a civil religion of the homeland. Their proliferation and spread, which in some cases took on traits of authentic fetishist degeneration, not only testifies to the importance gained by material goods in the communication of a political message, but also to the symbolic and totemic value attributed to these items and their transformations over time. The same observations that apply to Christian relics are also valid for the secular relics linked to the political processes of the 19th century: both in a latent state of passive conservation and in an active one, in a circuit of exhibition and secular veneration, they appeared to become imbued with symbols and meanings, powerful vectors of "*configurations historiques différentes*".[11] Thanks to their intrinsic capacity to connect distant spaces and times, they therefore represent an excellent key through which to examine the *longue durée* of these phenomena.

The study examines several hundred objects held in museums of the *Risorgimento* and in Italian civic museums, or displayed in temporary exhibitions between 1861 and 1911, with a summary offered here through selected examples. My intent was to verify the accumulation of political and memorial meanings in these relics that ran through the *Risorgimento* and continued right up to the eve of the First World War, after the Jubilee of the Homeland in 1911: from Italy's entry into the war and the idea of building a "live" myth, a twist would take place in exhibitions about the *Risorgimento*, with the inclusion of photographs of the fallen, agendas, military postcards, diaries and letters from the front.[12]

Shifting our focus on patriotic objects does not only allow us to analyse the paraphernalia and material equipment of the discursive, narrative, expository practices of the *Risorgimento* story in depth. It also means that we overturn the dominant point of view, from the container to the content, revealing new and partly unexpected elements. It is therefore necessary first to define the type of producers of memorabilia and relics that are the subject of this research: which protagonists of the Italian *Risorgimento* are we referring to? We could reply with the words Francesca Zambusi Dal Lago used in 1870 in a letter to Gualberta Beccari to describe the Veronese martyrs from 1848 to 1866, as those who had sacrificed themselves "for the nation's independence, on the bloody fields, in prison or on the most painful gallows".[13] Homeland martyrs had featured among the victors and the vanquished: regulars and volunteers fallen in the war; conspirators and

11. *Reliques modernes. Cultes et usages chrétiens des corps saints des Réformes aux revolutions*, ed. by Philippe Boutry, Pierre Antoine Fabre and Dominique Julia, Paris, Éditions de l'EHESS, 2009.

12. *La Grande Guerra in vetrina. Mostre e musei in Europa negli anni Venti e Trenta*, ed. by Massimo Baioni and Claudio Fogu, *Memoria e Ricerca*, 7 (2001).

13. *La Donna*, 12 June 1870.

revolutionaries; heroes and patriots. Both sides had worked on their memories with different messages and languages, adopting the leitmotif of heroic sacrifice and martyrdom as a new device of mass politicisation, substantiated in the numerous popular martyrologists.[14]

Leaving aside the broader sense of the term, as a sacrificial representation of the violent killing of the righteous by an oppressive power, the definition of patriotic martyr shows some variation and incorporates different forms of political suffering.[15] The absence of a bloody death did not affect the virtuous aura of those who had been ready to sacrifice themselves for their homeland. In the construction of the national discourse, those who had undergone a series of shared generational experiences – such as imprisonment and exile – managing to survive and, subsequently, bearing the physical and moral signs of the wounds inflicted by oppressive regimes, were also, therefore, considered martyrs. These included, for example, Giorgio Pallavicino Trivulzio or Eleuterio Felice Foresti, frequently referred to as the Spielberg's "martyrs". Historian Atto Vannucci first included the figure of the exile within the dimension of martyrdom, and the term expanded to include a particular category, that of survivors or "living martyrs".[16]

On a different political side, even the moderates adopted the same communicative codes. Charles Albert of Savoy's lonely death in exile allowed the liberal ruling class to turn the former king from a magnanimous monarch who had granted the Statute into a martyr of the *Risorgimento.* This was a transformation that helps to understand why, rather than the table on which the Statute had been signed, the 1884 Exhibition and then the Museum of the *Risorgimento* in Turin exhibited the bedroom where he had lived his last moments in Porto and which, with his funeral mask on display, became the place of pilgrimage as much as his tomb in Superga.

For this reason, it has been useful and necessary to broaden the field of investigation and at the same time the concept of martyrdom, with the addition of aspects of suffering and self-denial, also including a wider range of people, and therefore of objects, in the political and comparative analysis. Following the methodological approach of similar research,[17] an inclusive and flexible perspective has been adopted for the latter, starting from actual bodily relics, or their parts and fragments, on the model of the Christian *ex ossibus* and *ex piliis* relics, which include hair, teeth, nails, bones, organs and bodily tissue: from

14. Maurizio Ridolfi, "Martiri per la patria", in *Gli italiani in guerra. Conflitti, identità, memorie*, vol. I, *Fare l'Italia. Unità e disunità nel Risorgimento*, ed. by Eva Cecchinato and Mario Isnenghi, Turin, UTET, 2008.

15. Pierre-Marie Delpu, "Une religion politique. Les usages des martyrs révolutionnaires dans le royaume des Deux-Siciles (années 1820-années 1850)", *Revue d'histoire moderne et contemporaine*, 64/1 (Jan.-March 2017), pp. 7-31.

16. Fulvio Conti, *Italia immaginata. Sentimenti, memorie e politica fra Otto e Novecento*, Pisa, Pacini, 2017, pp. 64-69; Lucy Riall, "Martyr Cults in Nineteenth-Century Italy", *The Journal of Modern History*, 82 (2010), p. 268.

17. "Relics and Remains", ed. by Alexandra Walsham, *Past and Present*, Supplement 5 (2010), pp. 9-11.

the blood clot of an anonymous soldier who fell at the battle of Mentana (Fig. 3), to the vertebra of the martyr of Belfiore (Fig. 4), to a piece of Carlo Poerio's aorta.[18]

By extending the category of patriotic relics by contact, determined by the proximity with charismatic individuals in the moment of the maximum expression of their virtues, heroism and sacrifice, I have included objects worn and touched by martyrs, personal effects and/or items linked to their deaths, their funeral attires and instruments of martyrdom. The different sub-categories include clothing, uniforms, headwear, footwear, accessories, fabrics either torn, perforated or damaged by gunshots, stained with blood (in the set of relics *ex tela imbuta sanguine*) and very often cut, where it had been necessary to intervene urgently on an injured body (one such example is the jacket "with its sleeves cut so as to take it off him" and the trousers "completely unstitched to take them off him and still stained with mud and blood" of Colonel Cesare Boldrini, who died in Bologna in 1849).[19] I then included inorganic mineral and vegetable materials, mainly stone relics, trees and clods of earth, where the act of heroism had left everlasting traces, closely mimicking the sacred *ex rupe praesepi* relics of the Christian religion and the miraculous rocks of the Islamic and Indian worlds[20] (a fragment of the almond tree from Villa Glori under which Enrico Cairoli died (Fig. 6); a clod of earth soaked in the blood of Ugo Bassi, already exhibited in Bologna in 1888 and then transferred to the city's Museum of the *Risorgimento* together with another clod taken from his grave by his doctor friend Didaco Facchini;[21] or even splinters from the tree on which Garibaldi, injured in Aspromonte, had leaned, whose uncontrolled proliferation closely resembles that of the wooden fragments of the cross of Christ, which had provoked Erasmus' criticism).

Even torture instruments became objects of veneration, in parallel with what had happened since the age of the Counter-Reformation: chains, fetters, nooses, entire scaffolding structures, and, together with them, the symbols of imprisonment, keys to cells, mourning veils, handkerchiefs, cutlery and crockery, decks of cards and matches. Assuming then that secular relics, like those of Christianity, in their physicality are "only contingent material objectifications of ideas and gestures endowed with their own specific and historicisable origins",[22] we have considered the temporal dimension as an important variable: possession in the moment of agony preceding martyrdom, or the natural death of "living martyrs" and of protagonists who did not take part in the fight on the battlefields, both transform an object into a relic. The investigation therefore regarded memorabilia related to the moment of illustrious men's decease and linked to their bodies: fragments of

18. See other interesting examples in Marco Pizzo, *Visita al Risorgimento. Il Museo Centrale del Risorgimento di Roma*, Rome, Gangemi, 2005.

19. *Catalogo degli oggetti esposti*, p. 185.

20. Ugo Fabietti, *Materia sacra. Corpi, oggetti, immagini, feticci nella pratica religiosa*, Milan, Raffaello Cortina, 2014.

21. Archive of Bologna's Museum of the *Risorgimento*, *Fondo Belluzzi*, *Traversata*, f. 5, letter from Ettore Marziali to Carlo Corticelli, 8 February 1897.

22. Luigi Canetti, *Frammenti di eternità. Corpi e reliquie tra Antichità e Medioevo*, Rome, Viella, 2002, p. 14.

sarcophagi, mortuary decorations and grave goods, sheets and funeral drapes (the drape that "covered him when he was sick and dead" also allowed the narration of Garibaldi's death to be included in the 1884 Exhibition).[23] A separate subset is represented by death masks, relics by contact *par excellence* and metonymic representations of the deceased.[24]

The analogies with an essential aspect of what is commonly called the cult of holy bodies, the veneration of relics, is, on the classification level of communicative codes and methods of conservation, sometimes surprising and reminiscent of the essential core of that cult, that is to say the types of relationship and exchange between the living and the dead[25] (and between the living and the revenants). Preserving, wearing, handing down the relics of fellow prisoners, political leaders and exiled conspirators meant perpetuating their belonging to a political family. In this sense, even more than in the epistemic aspects, we are interested in the performative dimension of the ritualistic contexts (often masonic) and pathways of objects. Two examples will help to clarify this: piliferous relics, widespread in popular tradition, easy and abundant to obtain and keep – in fact, less prone than others to decompose and, as such, apt to keep the heroic and patriotic virtues unaltered – also allowed the establishment of chain relationships. So it was in the case of highly symbolic relics such as Goffredo Mameli's hair, whose thick locks were first cut during embalming and then before subsequent transfers, when they took different directions; one, for example, was donated in 1872 by Agostino Bertani to Genoa's Circle of Mazzini supporters *Pensiero e Azione* (*Thought and Action*) as compensation for the failure to repatriate the remains of their martyr.[26] In 1849, even Nino Bixio had obtained a lock of the martyr's hair, which he kept as a sacred relic and then donated to Mazzini in 1862, who in turn handed it back to Giuseppe Dolfi. In 1870, he gave it to Giuseppe Mazzoni, who bequeathed it to his son-in-law Nicola Guerrazzi, who exhibited it, in a medallion, in a pride of place in his home in Tuscany, where many Mazzini supporters had found shelter.

A similar symbolic dislocation happened with Carlo Cattaneo's shawl, which "wrapped his body" in 1869 and which "Giuseppe Mazzini cherished as a memory of him and covered him whilst sick and once he had died" in 1872.[27] Collected by Bertani, who had assisted both of them as they lay dying, the

23. "Drappo garibaldino", *Torino e l'Esposizione del 1884. Cronaca illustrata della Esposizione nazionale-industriale ed artistica del 1884*, 29 (1884), p. 226.

24. Jonathan Barbier, Bruno Bertherat, "La République et ses masques. Culte du grand homme et culture matérielle (de la Ire à la Ve République)", *Cahiers Jaurès*, 219-220 (2016), pp. 119-143.

25. Krzysztof Pomian, "Histoire culturelle, histoire des sémiophores", in *Pour une histoire culturelle*, ed. by Jean-Pierre Rioux and Jean-François Sirinelli, Paris, Seuil, 1996, pp. 73-100.

26. Archive of Milan's Museum of the *Risorgimento*, *Carte Bertani*, cart. 52, pl. 39, n. 17, letter from the Circolo Pensiero e Azione to Bertani, 12 June 1872; Silvia Cavicchioli, "I resti dei vinti. I martiri della Repubblica romana (1849-1879)", *Il Risorgimento. Rivista di storia del Risorgimento e di storia contemporanea*, 2 (2017), pp. 37-84. Other locks of Mameli's hair (Fig. 2a and Fig. 2b), as well as Mazzini's and others', are preserved in the Genoa's Museum of *Risorgimento*. I thank the director Raffaella Ponte for her great courtesy.

27. Alberto Mario, Jessie Mario, *Carlo Cattaneo. Cenni e reminiscenze*, Rome, Casa editrice A. Sommaruga, 1884, p. 162.

woollen cloth also wrapped the body of a faithful friend of Mazzini, Maurizio Quadrio, before being bequeathed to Adriano Lemmi, whose son Emilio donated it in 1932 to Genoa's Istituto Mazziniano.

It is now necessary to start from the first agents in the gathering and conservation of patriotic relics, focussing on the contexts in which their recovery took place without raising the certainly important question of their authenticity. In this investigation, the relics interest us as carriers of symbols, therefore in their mythopoetic value, which we will attempt to discern and decode, without claiming to ascertain facts, but only symbolic values. In fact, as Jan Assmann has pointed out, "the figures of memory in a retrospective self-modelling possess their own truth, the study of which requires its own methodology: mnemo-history. Archaeological evidence cannot verify or refute these figures of memory, their truth lies elsewhere".[28]

3. *The struggles of the* Risorgimento

As Roberto Balzani has pointed out, the "war possibilities" that could validate a call to arms as a parameter of love for one's country were very numerous, given the time span of the unification process, lasting from Napoleon's campaigns to the taking of Rome.[29] Consequently, the number of memorial objects linked to the *Risorgimento* as an experience of war with regular troops and voluntary corps is in itself huge.

The spontaneous collection of memorabilia from the battlefields by civilians, both at the end of a conflict and in pilgrimages in search of such objects,[30] was as old a practice as that of war. Whilst young Alessandro, nephew of Antonio D'Alessandri, the author of rare photographs of the battlefield, brought an entire collection of them from Mentana to Rome,[31] the tourist-patriotic pilgrimages to San Martino and Solferino generated a spread, and also a trade, of considerable size.

More generally, a remarkable collection of memorabilia, weapons and ammunition was produced at all levels – from the top military hierarchies to simple private soldiers – both of comrades and stolen from the enemy as war trophies, a contemporary revival of the *spoglia opima*, even as artistically reworked objects.[32]

There are many examples, from cannonballs collected on the battlefield of San Martino through the direct involvement of King Victor Emanuel II, to the

28. Jan Assmann, *Mosé l'Egizio. Decifrazione di una traccia di memoria*, Milan, Adelphi, 2000, pp. 31-33.

29. Roberto Balzani, "Le 'sacre memorie' risorgimentali", in *Forze armate e beni culturali. Distruggere, costruire, valorizzare*, ed. by Nicola Labanca and Luigi Tommassini, Milan, Unicopli, 2007, pp. 141-142.

30. Alberto Mario Banti, *La nazione del Risorgimento. Parentela, santità e onore alle origini dell'Italia unita*, Turin, Einaudi, 2000, pp. 174-176.

31. Silvio Negro, *Seconda Roma. 1850-1870*, Vicenza, Neri Pozza, p. 395.

32. A few examples are in Silvia Cavicchioli, "Crimean War: politiche della memoria e nuove forme di democratizzazione nella costruzione delle identità nazionali", *Contemporanea. Rivista di storia dell'800 e del '900*, 2 (2021), pp. 177-209.

storage of Austrian weapons and ammunition in barracks, up to the trophies won during the fight against brigands (such as amulets containing "the hair of Pope Pius IX or the Lilies, coat of arms of King Francis of Bourbon"),[33] almost always displayed in *Risorgimento* exhibitions by officers of the regular army, former soldiers and veterans' societies.

As in a mirror image, Austrian barracks also stored *italienische trophaen* such as panoplies of flags and weapons taken from the enemy in the battles of 1848-1849: for example, the "*Radetzky Reliquien*", subsequently exhibited in the second weapons room in the Heeresmuseum in Vienna and photographed as propaganda postcards during the First World War.[34] Round-trip trophies were the two keys of the Sforza Castle in Milan, removed in 1848 by Anton Ritter von Burlo, a major in the *Kaiser-Jäger* who had protected the Austrian retreat from Milan in 1848: they were exhibited in the Kaiserjäger Museum in Innsbruck, founded in 1880, and recovered after the armistice of Villa Giusti in 1918 to be donated to the Museum of the *Risorgimento* in Milan.

Other contexts that favoured the direct recovery of relics were the scenes of executions. The spread of the popular practice of hoarding parts of the bodies of the executed, the executioner's instruments or bloody clothes as propitiatory items for their thaumaturgical and salvific value lasted right up to the modern age.[35] The people of Cosenza, for instance, had fought over the hair of the Bandiera brothers, the bullets "still covered in blood", the cloths that had covered the faces of the condemned men.[36]

The imprisonment of patriots was also a context that produced vast quantities of memorabilia. The personal objects of men sentenced to death, as the only and final material link with earthly life, were invested with a profound symbolic value. The collectors were first and foremost their fellow prisoners who had survived the gallows. Driven by the sharing of political ideals, a long friendship, but also the inevitable feelings of guilt, the survivors, who had seen their death sentences changed into long detention, became faithful executors of their companions' last wishes: for example Roberto Marin, who lent to the 1884 Turin Exhibition the personal objects that Pietro Fortunato Calvi had manufactured during his imprisonment.

Entrusted to cellmates (often the future intermediaries with family members), sought after and appreciated even by wardens for their remembrance or expiatory value, bloody bandages and handkerchiefs, notebooks and playing cards joined the direct and indirect instruments of torture. This context highlights two aspects, among others. The martyr's self-awareness, through which he

33. *Catalogo degli oggetti esposti*, p. 246.

34. Central Museum of the *Risorgimento*, Rome, Sezione iconografica, (CA 5) 2901.

35. Fulvio Conti, "Le urne dei forti. Religioni politiche e liturgie funebri nei secoli XIX e XX", in *Rituali civili. Storie nazionali e memorie pubbliche nell'Europa contemporanea*, ed. by Maurizio Ridolfi, Rome, Gangemi, 2006, pp. 117-118; Luigi Lazzerini, "Le radici folkloriche dell'anatomia. Scienza e rituale all'inizio dell'età moderna", *Quaderni storici*, 29/1 (1994), pp. 206-226.

36. Felice Venosta, *I fratelli Bandiera e loro compagni martiri a Cosenza. Notizie storiche*, Milan, Carlo Barbini, 1863, pp. 97, 105, 108-109.

entrusted the relic with intangible meanings and messages (Tito Speri's testament is an example of this); and the wide range of recipients who, by including priests and prison guards, allowed the objects to be spread far beyond the networks of family or political brotherhood. The most important case in 19th-century history, Napoleon's death in St Helena, had proved this. From this remote island, not only had the faithful such as Las Cases or General Bertrand returned to Europe with objects belonging to the illustrious exile, but so had the English, aware of the very high value of the deposed emperor's (and most famous contemporary's) memorabilia, which years later would be displayed in the great exhibition of the Revolution and the Empire.[37]

The beneficiaries of these bequests also included the comforters and saviours of souls, in charge of collecting confessions during periods of detention and giving blessings before executions, such as Monsignor Martini, who in the chapel of the Mantuan prisons received the personal objects of the martyrs of Belfiore, which would later endow the rooms of the *Risorgimento* museum in Mantua,[38] or Abbot De Rose, one of the twelve comforters of the Bandiera brothers and their companions.[39]

And this is how, paradoxically, ministers of religion and priests became, often in spite of themselves, unwitting guardians of lay relics which subsequently became appropriate guarantees, aiding their patriotic rehabilitation (whereas in the museums of the *Risorgimento* the insistence on the presence of confessors would be used to explain that the patriots had loved their country as believers: there was no contradiction between love of the homeland and the Christian faith).

Not only were the parish priests and ministers of the brotherhoods charged with preparing prisoners for a "good death" as the recipients of symbolic objects, but their own spiritual instruments also became relics, such as the "Christ used by Father Marraccini to comfort the final moments of Attilio Frosini, shot in Pistoia in 1849",[40] or the "fine and beautiful miniature of the Madonna, kissed by the twenty-one volunteers" shot in the Buonconsiglio pit in Trento on 16 April 1848, kept by Father Bonuzzi.[41]

Alongside comforters, jailers were the only other people to whom prisoners could leave personal objects, letters, drawings, in the hope that they would be kept or subsequently delivered to family members. An emblematic case is that of the deputy-chief warden of Mantua's prisons, Stefano Tirelli, who had gathered

37. *Exposition historique et militaire de la révolution et de l'empire, Catalogue*, Paris, Galerie des Champs-Élysées, 1895; Arianna Arisi Rota, "Tra desiderio e nostalgia. Declinazioni visive del culto napoleonico nell'Italia della Restaurazione", *Mélanges de l'École française de Rome – Italie et Méditerranée modernes et contemporaines*, 130/1 (2018), pp. 17-29.

38. Gabriele Fantoni, *I fasti della Guardia Nazionale del Veneto negli anni 1848 e '49. Memorie storiche*, Venice, Grimaldo, 1870, p. 110.

39. "Per la memoria di Domenico Lupattelli", *Archivio Storico del Risorgimento Umbro*, 4 (1907), pp. 275-277.

40. *Catalogo della mostra dei ricordi storici dell'indipendenza italiana dal 1796 al 1870 tenuta in Pistoia nell'estate 1899*, Pistoia, Tip. di Giuseppe Flori, 1899, p. 14.

41. Claudio Cesare Secchi, "Luigi Blondel, nipote di Alessandro Manzoni, fucilato a Trento il 16 aprile 1848", *Studi trentini di scienze storiche*, 3 (1956), p. 282.

personal mementos seized from the Belfiore conspirators and other inmates. In 1880, before being admitted to a Beggars' Shelter, he offered them to curator of Mantua's monuments Francesco Tamassia,[42] who lent them to the 1884 Exhibition (finally donating them to Mantua's burgeoning Museum of the Risorgimento).

This example refers to a crucial point in this research: with the transition from history to memory of the *Risorgimento*, the circulation of relics, whether real or presumed, ended up feeding the collectors' and antiques market, with a direct impact on the creation of the first museums. One of the greatest Turin collectors, Antonio Clemente, who lent a large number of memorabilia to the 1884 Exhibition, had prepared his own catalogue for the sale of such objects.

In the medium term, these phenomena brought with them the inevitable production of fakes and enhanced the already considerable needs for authentication. In fact, especially among democrats, the need for the certification of relics had developed very early on, and in the case of Garibaldi it turned into a real obsession.[43] It was not just a matter of ascertaining, for monetary purposes, the authenticity of memorabilia against the increasingly widespread risk of counterfeiting. The great families of Mazzini's and Garibaldi's supporters needed to verify the origin and legitimacy of the relics in order to grant truthfulness to events and individual sacrifices, so that they would not only be remembered but also not diminished or denied. The relics stained with the blood of patriots acted not only as reminders, but as demonstrations. The certificates also became part of each story, multiplying its *effet de réel*.

The people invested with this task included doctors, who played the role of historical eyewitnesses in different contexts. An emblematic example is the information on the siege of Rome given by Doctor Pietro Ripari to novelist Francesco Domenico Guerrazzi. Because of their easy and direct access to the bodies of celebrated contemporaries, to the wounded or dead bodies of patriots, physicians were, directly or indirectly, powerful keepers, authenticators and distributors of relics. For some, it was a matter of an impromptu acceptance of patriotic memorabilia *in limine mortis*. For others, more "militant" doctors, it was a personal mission. Alongside Agostino Bertani, who played an active role in the collection of relics of the martyrs of the Roman Republic,[44] stood the entire group of Garibaldi's doctors: Timoteo Riboli, Giovanni Prandina and Ferdinando Zannetti. Far from them, and with very different objectives, were Efisio Marini (responsible for solidifying Garibaldi's blood), Gerolamo Segato and Angelo Motta, who, at the height of Positivism, exploited the full

42. Stefano Benetti, Elena Paladini, "Le collezioni di storia di Francesco Tamassia e di Marco Guastalla", at www.museiperlastoria.com, pp. 4, 6.

43. Dino Mengozzi, *Garibaldi taumaturgo. Reliquie laiche e politica nell'Ottocento*, Manduria-Bari-Rome, Lacaita, 2008; Mauro Passarin, "Garibaldi al Museo: la "Donazione Cariolato" di Vicenza", *Venetica*, 22 (2010), pp. 127-136.

44. Silvia Cavicchioli, "The Remains of the Vanquished: Bodies and Martyrs of the Roman Republic from the Risorgimento to Fascism", in *Public Uses of Human Remains and Relics in History*, ed. by Silvia Cavicchioli and Luigi Provero, New York, Routledge, 2020, pp. 208-229.

potential of the new techniques of conservation of human remains (embalming, mummification, metallisation, petrification) to create collections where a sort of *sensé macabre* often prevailed.[45]

Doctors were also present in another instance of intense relic production, namely the exhumation of the remains of martyrs and fallen soldiers, a widespread practice in the 19th and 20th centuries. There are countless examples of this, from the transfer of Andrea Vochieri's remains, which allowed for the recovery of the skull and jaw of the Giovine Italia martyr, then welcomed by the Civic Museum in Alessandria,[46] to the Venetian patriots who took the "Drape and crown used when transporting Daniele Manin's ashes from Paris to Venice", later exhibited in the Hall of Patriotic Memories of Casa Correr.[47]

The collective exhumations carried out during the construction of the *Risorgimento* ossuaries, from Bicocca to Custoza, above all put a large quantity of weapons, ammunition and relics into circulation, to represent the memories preserved by the societies of veterans of homeland battles in their own locations.

One of the most impressive operations was the recovery of the remains of the fallen at the battles of Solferino and San Martino, sponsored in the spring of 1870 by the Society responsible for building the ossuary. In the following years, it was precisely the Society of Solferino and San Martino that promoted a museum with the same name in a hall of the Civic Museum in Padua, exhibiting weapons and flags "collected on the battlefield" and other "objects taken from the corpses",[48] a selection of which was used to make up the two great trophies in the room named "of the Battle of San Martino" in the 1884 Temple of the *Risorgimento*.[49]

An examination of the people most closely involved in relic conservation cannot ignore experts of local history and scholars, belonging to liberal groups, sometimes with a past of direct political participation and, above all, with a role in preserving the memories of the homeland and especially in the practice of transferring and repatriating patriotic remains. Some of them considered the collection of objects and material evidence to be complementary to historical reconstruction, such as Cesare Romiti from Osimo who, along with narrating the events in the life of *Carbonaro* Cesare Gallo, from Macerata, also recovered his personal objects, subsequently exhibited at the Vittoriano in Rome in 1911.[50]

For some who aspired to political roles, the ability to boast about having played a part in the recovery and possession of secular remains and relics, seen as identity belongings similar to the other political objects examined in this volume,

45. Alberto Carli, "Il valore educativo e la rilevanza formativa dei preparati anatomici tra XVIII e XX secolo. Alcuni brevi spunti", *Rivista di Storia della Medicina*, 1-2 (2010), pp. 1-10.

46. Ersilio Michel, "Il Museo civico di Alessandria", *Rassegna Storica del Risorgimento*, (1917), p. 197.

47. *Guida illustrata del Museo Civico Correr di Venezia*, Venice, Premiata Tip. Emiliana, 1909, p. 144.

48. Ersilio Michel, "Il Museo di Solferino e San Martino in Padova", *Rassegna Storica del Risorgimento*, (1915), pp. 621-622.

49. *Catalogo degli oggetti esposti*, p. 215.

50. *Mostra del Risorgimento-Roma 1911, Elenco dei documenti e degli oggetti esposti*, ed. by Vittoria Buonanno, Milan-Rome-Naples, Albrighi, Segati & C., 1913, pp. 32-33.

became a kind of patriotic self-certification to be exhibited publicly at various political events. This was the case with the Cosenza lawyer and scholar Francesco Lattari, who was exiled and imprisoned several times and who, already active in the recovery of the Bandiera brothers' remains, in 1848 had obtained Emilio Bandiera's cap from prison superintendent Gioacchino Gaudio, precisely when he stood for election in the province of Cosenza, in the Kingdom of Naples. This also happened with Sienese patriot Luciano Ravaggi, portrayed in the *Risorgimento* rooms of the town hall, who could publicly boast of possessing "Garibaldi's mattress wool soaked in his blood".[51]

If many of them accumulated collections that were destined to become the main supply and information channels of local history museums, some authors of martyrologies also played an active role in the distribution of relics. Their works had great editorial success, thus helping spread the praise of personal sacrifice at the centre of Mazzini's political creed. In addition to the printed pages, their contribution also consisted in their interest in some symbolic objects related to sacrifice, as in the case of Felice Venosta, who, as an expert, authenticated the "piece of shroud in which Carlo Cattaneo's body had been wrapped in 1869" (the body had been exhumed in 1884, preserved under glass and then exhibited in Turin).[52] Or in the case of Garibaldi's supporter and patriot from Vicenza, Gabriele Fantoni, the author of a *Compendio di storia d'Italia ne' suoi martiri* (1866) (*Compendium of the History of Italy and its Martyrs*) and one of the greatest promoters of, and donors to, the museums of the Veneto region.[53]

4. *Contexts, actors and pathways of conservation*

The first instances of conservation of, and exposure to, mementos of the *Risorgimento* took place in private and, in some cases, clandestine contexts. Alongside the traditional forms of family mementos, which were typical of romantic sensibilities – such as the keeping of locks of hair, fragments of fabric, jewellery, miniature portraits, personal fetishes[54] – individuals and families also retained the evidence of patriotic sacrifice. These were objects kept in prominent positions within the home and, on particular occasions, such as celebrations, they were exhibited and enjoyed by extended audiences.

One such example was the "sacred reliquary" of the Leati brothers from Ferrara: built up between 1848 and 1867 as their heroic career progressed, it displayed a bayonet bent during the fight in Vicenza (which belonged to

51. *Inaugurazione del monumento a Garibaldi. Mostra di ricordi patriottici*, Siena, Tip. Cooperativa, 1896, p. 39.

52. *Catalogo degli oggetti esposti*, p. 86

53. Ersilio Michel, "Gabriele Fantoni", *Rassegna Storica del Risorgimento*, 1 (1914), pp. 189-190.

54. Gian Luca Fruci, Alessio Petrizzo, "Visualità e grande trasformazione mediatica nel lungo Ottocento", in *Il lungo Ottocento e le sue immagini. Politica, media, spettacolo*, ed. by Vinzia Fiorino, Gian Luca Fruci and Alessio Petrizzo, Pisa, Edizioni ETS, 2013, pp. 14-17.

Themistocles), the red wool shirt punctured by two bullets "and still soaked in blood"[55] and the blood-stained trousers that had belonged to Vincenzo, who fell in the battle of Bezzecca, and was maintained by their heirs as a symbol of a tradition of sacrifice for one's homeland. It was transferred in its original form from the family home to Ferrara's civic collections, then to the Italian Exhibition of 1884 and finally to its definitive museum display, inaugurated in Ferrara in 1903.

Women often played prominent, socially recognised roles as protectors and guardians of family heirlooms, with a crossover between private and public roles and often a bequeathing of responsibilities from mothers to daughters, or mothers-in-law to daughters-in-law, as in the case of Anna Koppmann Pallavicino Trivulzio and her daughter in managing the material memories of their husband/ father Giorgio. Women also exchanged the relics of husbands and children now risen to symbols of national sacrifice, such as Carmelita Manara and Ermellina Dandolo; or women like Giuseppina Morosini, who at the 1884 Exhibition reconstructed the sacrifice of her brother and his companions, who had died in the siege of Rome as a reliquary unit. Women also attended the protagonists of the *Risorgimento* right up to their deathbeds and welcomed precious bequests, like Janet Nathan Rosselli, who remained close to Mazzini right up to his death and in 1884 entrusted his relics to the Roman Commission for the Turin exhibition. Women thus ended up contributing significantly to the growth of the patriotic collections of important museums. If at first glance their presence would again seem to suggest their subsidiary and subordinate relationship compared to the male figures of the *Risorgimento*, in actual fact from documents and correspondence it emerges that most of the time their role was aware and active, driven by their courage and determination. In many cases, family collections turned into authentic museums, as in the example of Felicita Bevilacqua and her husband Giuseppe La Masa, who set up a sort of private chapel in their home "devoted to the preservation-veneration of the family's memorabilia" and ultimately took steps to ensure that the family's documents and objects they had preserved found places in the burgeoning *Risorgimento* museums.[56]

Other contexts of conservation and exhibition were military ones. Fighters were often the first to collect the personal items of fallen comrades, to deliver them to family members. The museum display cases do not mention the names of these first, fundamental keepers, whose identity only the consultation of documentary sources can reveal. Lieutenant Lorenzo Bigotti and Major Giuseppe Bianchi brought to Baron and Baroness Savio a lock of their son Alfredo's hair and a stone stained in their other son Emilio's "generous blood",[57] respectively from Ancona and Gaeta. The latter was subsequently given to Turin's museum.

The relics collected in the field ended up, either immediately or later on, with the collections of the societies of veterans of homeland battles.

55. *Catalogo degli oggetti esposti*, p. 284.

56. Elena Sodini, *Le carte di Felicita Bevilacqua: famiglia, nazione e patriottismo al femminile in un archivio privato (1822-1899)*, Verona, Cierre, 2010.

57. "Memorie della baronessa Olimpia Savio", ed. by Raffaello Ricci, Milan, Fratelli Treves, 1911, pp. 339-340.

Although different in terms of their regional origin and political inspiration, the associations of former fighters worked for the cause of shared memories and the conservation of memorabilia. One example is the extremely active Association of Vicenza Volunteers, which collected a wealth of objects from the battle of Monte Berico that included, with oppositional meaning, even the relics of Austrian prince Wilhelm Karl Thurn und Taxis, mortally wounded in the battle to recapture Vicenza. As we have seen, they created their own museums, such as that of the Volunteers' Society of the City and Province of Padua.[58] In these places, the relics recovered from bloody battlefields were often framed, such as aide-de-camp Cipriani's sabre, with its blade broken by a bullet, or the buttons of the uniform he was wearing when he burned to death in 1848, exhibited in Siena in 1896 by the Regional Veterans' Committee of Florence.[59]

The actions of the associations of veterans and former fighters were paralleled by the conservation in the army corps, which kept relics in their barracks and regimental halls. This was the case with the *Bersaglieri* Corp, which brought individual collections together to the Historical Museum inaugurated at Porta Pia in 1904. This process was entirely similar to what happened beyond the Alps: at the Paris Exhibition of 1889, "the frame preserved piously by the 46th Infantry and which contains a few small objects collected from the body of the most illustrious of its soldiers: La Tour d'Auvergne, the first Grenadier of France" stood out.[60] Here, too, the classic elements of the construction of a military epic were at play: the compassionate gesture of fellow soldiers towards their commander's relics; the religiously preserved objects as proof of the heroism and sacrifice of those who, even before dying, had already risen to the national pantheon.

5. *Exhibition pathways*

Before becoming exhibits in popular public contexts, the memorabilia of war heroes and the relics of martyrs had been elements in dramatic and emotional stories that had united their keepers: widows of generals and comforters of prisoners, comrades-in-arms and exiles who had survived the gallows, military doctors and fellow prisoners. They had been intermediaries in personal relationships, rings in chains that linked the dead to the survivors, means designed to generate a range of feelings and attitudes: memory, pain, affection, gratitude, desire for emulation, the extolling of military and chivalrous virtues. Their conservation had followed the well-established pathway of one of the most rooted and widespread anthropological and cultural foundations: the cult of the dead.

Private narration then experienced an initial development in expanded forms of sharing on semi-public and commemorative occasions, within the home, in

58. Mario Zangrando, *Veterani del Quarantotto a Padova. Biografia collettiva di una società di ex combattenti*, Thesis, Supervisor Prof. Carlotta Sorba, University of Padua, 2008-2009.

59. *Inaugurazione del monumento a Garibaldi*, p. 35.

60. *Catalogue Général Officiel, Exposition rétrospective du Travail et des Sciences Anthropologiques, Section V, Arts Militaires*, Paris, Imprimerie L. Danel Lille, 1889, p. 118.

military barracks, in veterans' meetings, assuming the language and codes of the secular cult of Christian martyrs and the ways and means of venerating the great men of the past, in turn based on the heroic relics of the classical world.

Although acted out in essential forms, and in self-celebratory and self-referential ways, the first staging of the relics allows for some general considerations. We often find ourselves in the presence of real reliquary compositions, where the objects were combined with other elements, generally those that had caused the martyrdom, and assembled in containers, displays, reliquaries, frames not exclusively designed to preserve the objects but an integral part of them. Such multi-material compositions reflected a first, albeit minimal and didactic, mediatic level. They preserved a memory and communicated a message (*exemplum*) for internal use, to arouse emulation in the different generations and to convey the sense of family continuity at the service of the homeland. When placed in official environments, they spread the essential forms of a patriotic story. Even in their private and semi-public dimension, they alluded to acts of heroism and sacrifice as codes and communicative devices that adopted a dramatic and emotional language, one that was maintained in the moment of transition to the first public contexts: those of civic museums. As natural precursors of the *Risorgimento* collections, from the time of the country's unification they became points of convergence for the intentions of the patriots' families, on the one hand, which were happy to donate and thereby to increase their status and social recognition, and the military groups and municipalities, on the other, that, by exhibiting many episodes of local heroism, could thus provide evidence of their own "small homeland's" participation in the great national construct and certify their patriotism with the blood of martyrs.

Subsequently, in the Turin Exhibition of 1884, in those that followed and in the *Risorgimento* museums that drew momentum from them, the growing reliquary custom, which was applied to the cult of the protagonists and martyrs of the nation-building process, flowed with all its evocative strength into the public spaces designed to celebrate those events. It also supported the burden of official patriotic pedagogy, alongside a number of other means and channels used to consolidate a national identity, put in place to "make the Italians" and teach the "religion of the homeland" (patriotic festivals, monuments, toponymy, school textbooks). These grassroots modes of inclusion, prompted by a call for donations made by former democrats who had become curators of the Temple of the *Risorgimento* in the Turin exhibition (Freemason Tommaso Villa; former Garibaldi supporters Giovanni Camozzi-Vertova, curator of the catalogue of medals, and Oreste Baratieri, curator of the pavilion; former Garibaldi supporter and democratic deputy Enrico Guastalla, a military man and Freemason, curator of the catalogue of objects) to families, veterans' societies and municipalities, favoured the emergence of a sacrificial atmosphere. It was immediately central and foundational to the various expressions of suffering and martyrdom, since, in the wealth of serial and anonymous objects collected in Turin, Pavia, Milan, Bologna, Perugia, Mantua, Rome or Palermo, significant kernels of objects that had previously been exhibited and that already bore the evident signs of the patriotic stigmata stood out. The martyrial message, settled in the dynastic-military rhetoric of the nation, lost part of its political significance but gained on a moral level, creating a contamination between democratic-popular and liberal-moderate representations. The unitary and conciliatory idea, forged by memories based on grief and pain, transformed the Temple of the *Risorgimento* into a place for the emotional and cultural recomposition of the injuries and collective traumas produced by the struggles of the *Risorgimento*. Garibaldi's pierced boot, a material visualisation of the deepest wound, the fratricidal war between Italians, was one of the most eloquent symbols, while the battles of Curtatone and Montanara, Novara and Custoza were re-labelled as "glorious defeats", necessary steps towards a predestined nation.

The 1884 Turin pavilion became the founding model of a new style of historical museum. There lay the beginning of the chaotic stacking of objects that would characterise most of the public collections of the *Risorgimento* for a long time, also showing its obvious limitations.[61] At the dawn of the 20th century, new concepts of museum display, with a significant change in the ways patriotic relics were gathered and exhibited, marked the beginning of their loss of meaning. This culminated in their transformation into simple and anonymous "fragments", as Roberto Balzani has recently and very effectively highlighted, once again raising the issue of their current opportunities to be used as museum artefacts.[62]

61. Massimo Baioni, *Vedere per credere. Il racconto museale dell'Italia unita*, Rome, Viella, 2020; Silvano Montaldo, *Celebrare il Risorgimento. Collezionismo artistico e memorie familiari a Torino, 1848-1915*, Turin-Rome, Comitato di Torino dell'Istituto per la Storia del Risorgimento Italiano-Carocci, 2013; Umberto Levra, "Il Museo Nazionale del Risorgimento Italiano. Dalla primazia piemontese alla contestualizzazione europea dei processi di nazionalità (1878-2011)", *Annali dell'Istituto storico italo-germanico in Trento*, 46 (2020), theme: *Luoghi controversi della memoria – I musei nazionali europei*, ed. by Silvia Cavicchioli and Gabriele Clemens, pp. 25-40.

62. Roberto Balzani, discussant on panel "Oggetti patriottici. Cultura materiale e politicizzazione del quotidiano nell'Ottocento italiano", coordinated by Enrico Francia and Carlotta Sorba, Cantieri di Storia, SISSCO, Viterbo, 2015; Maria Vittoria Marini Clarelli, *Pezzi da museo. Perché alcuni oggetti durano per sempre*, Rome, Carocci, 2017.

2a

2b

1. Garibaldi’s lock of hair donated by Camillo Cavour to Emanuele d’Azeglio on 1 August 1860. Museo Nazionale del Risorgimento Italiano, Turin.
2a. Composition with lock of Goffredo Mameli’s hair preserved by his assistant nicknamed Pius IX. Istituto Mazziniano-Museo del Risorgimento, Genoa.
2b. Lock of Goffredo Mameli’s hair donated by his mother to Agostino Bertani on 9 June 1872. Istituto Mazziniano-Museo del Risorgimento, Genoa.

3. Glass vial with the blood of a martyr from Mentana. Museo Centrale del Risorgimento, Rome.
4. Vertebra of Angelo Scarsellini, martyr of Belfiore. Museo Centrale del Risorgimento, Rome.

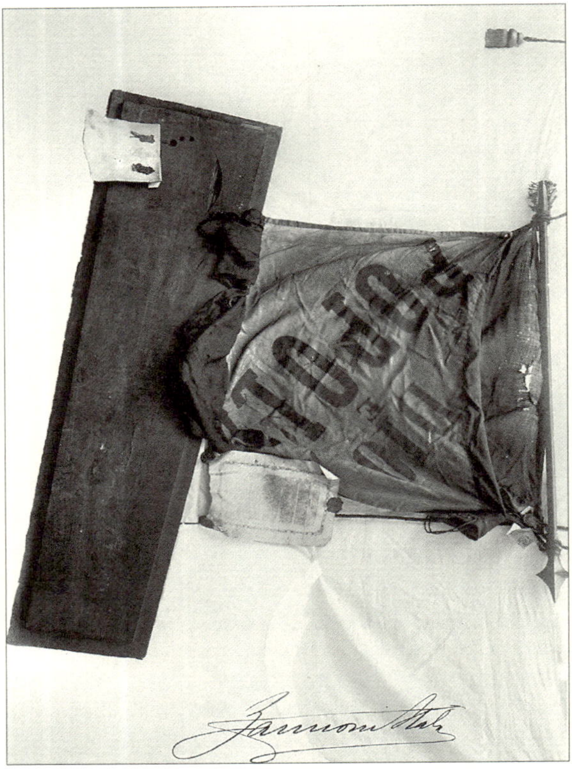

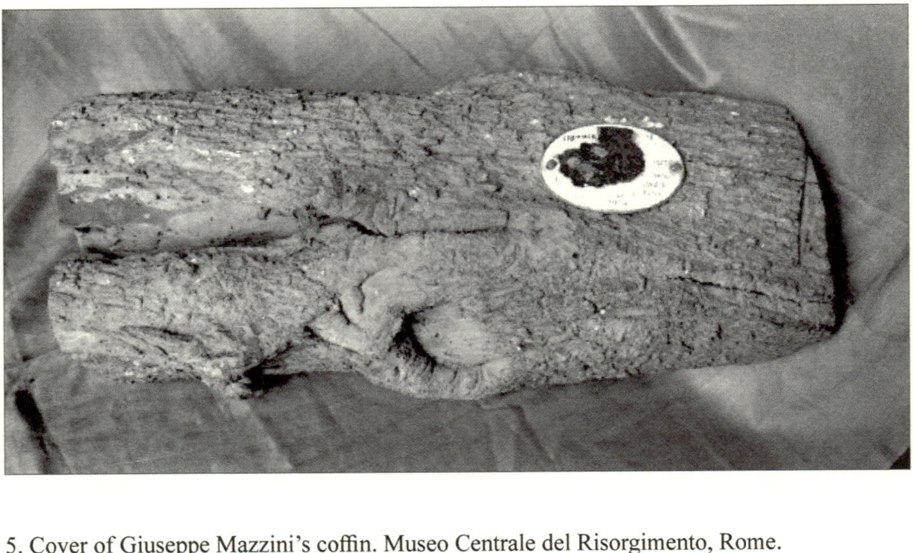

5. Cover of Giuseppe Mazzini's coffin. Museo Centrale del Risorgimento, Rome.
6. Fragment of the almond tree from Villa Glori in Rome under which Enrico Cairoli died on 23 October 1867. Museo Centrale del Risorgimento, Rome.

Marina Tesoro

Adelaide's Buttons: Fetishism, Domestic Cult and Museum Heritage in the Pavia *Risorgimento*

1. *Introduction*

The present case study is worthy of attention as a significant example of typical Romantic era memorial culture and practice, characteristic of Western societies from the early decades of the 19th century onwards. At the same time, the history of the items belonging to the Cairoli family of Pavia, precociously transformed into a museum, presents certain exceptional characteristics and may add valuable particulars to the history of the Italian *Risorgimento* from the material studies point of view.

Adelaide Bono Cairoli was a woman who, however unwillingly, displayed both a very strong personality[1] and awareness of the fact that martyrdom lay at the heart of patriotic and nationalistic discourse.[2] For this reason, in order to lend a sense of purpose[3] to the deaths of four of her children – Ernesto, Luigi, Enrico and Giovanni – in rapid succession over a ten-year period as followers of Garibaldi,[4] she decided to politicise both their sacrifice and her own suffering as a bereaved mother. A fifth son, Benedetto, lived to become an important political

1. The most recent scholarly contributions on this figure are: Marina D'Amelia, *La mamma*, Bologna, il Mulino, 2005, pp. 74-82; Azzurra Tafuro, *Madre e patriota. Adelaide Bono Cairoli*, Florence, Firenze University Press, 2011.

2. Alberto Mario Banti, *La nazione del Risorgimento. Parentela, santità e onore alle origini dell'Italia unita*, Turin, Einaudi, 2008. The author includes Adelaide's published epistulary, *Adelaide Cairoli e i suoi figli. Lettere dal 1847 al 1871*, ed. by Erminia Ghiglione Giulietti, Pavia, Renzo Cortina, 1960, in the sample of 33 memoires and letters of men and women who played a significant role in the construction of the "canon of the Risorgimento", pp. 32 and 54-55.

3. Roberto Balzani, "Alla ricerca della morte 'utile'. Il sacrificio patriottico nel Risorgimento", and Lucy Riall, "'I martiri nostri son tutti risorti'. Garibaldi, i garibaldini e il culto della morte eroica nel Risorgimento", in *La morte per la patria. La celebrazione dei caduti dal Risorgimento alla Repubblica*, ed. by Oliver Janz and Lutz Klinkhammer, Rome, Donzelli, 2008, pp. 3-21 and 23-44.

4. Ernesto on 26 May 1859 in the Battle of Biumo, near Varese; Luigi on 18 September 1860, dying of typhus in Naples after joining his brothers and the General in Sicily; Enrico on 23 October 1867 at Villa Glori, during the Monti Parioli expedition in the failed Garibaldian attempt to free Rome; Giovanni on 11 September 1869, as a consequence of the wounds received in the same battle.

leader sitting on the left side of national Parliament. She turned herself into an entrepreneur of memory and elaborated a project of patriotic pedagogy with a democratic bent. In essence, she became the first high priestess of what developed into a lay cult. By using her own body and objects of all kinds, including everyday items that she kept at home and continued to collect, she sanctified the memory of her "heroes" and "martyrs" and ensured that this memory would be handed down to future generations. In her villa in the countryside near Pavia, she took it upon herself to create a museum linked with a garden funerary chapel where her sons were buried. She called it "our domestic mausoleum".[5] In reality, Adelaide was looking beyond the confines of the family, in the hope of bequeathing an example upon the new nation of Italy.

After her death, and as the years passed, the religious value attributed to the items she had collected and displayed gradually faded. The objects of the Cairoli household underwent a semantic shift: what had at first been fetishes and relics of religious value afterwards became material traces, indicative of a Garibaldine political identity that was still very much alive at least until the First World War. Today these objects are recognised both as historical documents suitable for collocation in a public museum, and as peculiarly useful sources for historical analysis in the field of material culture studies pioneered, among others, by Arjun Appadurai.[6]

2. *The mourning body*

A portrait by the Pavian artist Pacifico Buzio, painted many years after her death, presumably from a photograph,[7] shows Adelaide Cairoli in advanced old age (Fig. 1). In the later years of her life, Adelaide had become a "celebrity"[8] and, it may be said, was entering into the dimension of myth. Her personal and political

5. Concerning the rhetorical formulae and modes of communication adopted within the family, see Marina Tesoro, "Lessico familiare: sentimenti e politica nei rapporti tra i cugini Cairoli e Cavallini", in *Patrioti si diventa. Luoghi e linguaggi della pedagogia patriottica nell'Italia unita*, ed. by Arianna Arisi Rota, Monica Ferrari and Matteo Morandi, Milan, FrancoAngeli, 2009, pp. 115-130.

6. *The Social Life of Things: Commodities in Cultural Perspective*, ed. by Arjun Appadurai, Chicago, Chicago University Press, 1986. For a recent discussion, see "Storia e cultura materiale: recenti traiettorie di ricerca. Interventi di Fabio Dei, Giorgio Riello, Beverly Lemire, Manuel Charpy, Leora Auslander", ed. by Alessio Petrizzo and Carlotta Sorba, *Contemporanea. Rivista di storia dell'800 e del '900*, 3 (2016), pp. 437-480.

7. Gigliola De Martini, "L'immagine di Adelaide Cairoli", *Museo in rivista*, 1 (1998), pp. 180-184. A photograph that portrays Benedetto and Adelaide, here in similar attire to that of the painting, bears this dedication on the back side: "To the most kind Zoja family. Pacifico Buzio. Painter. January 1st, 1896". Adriana Panizza, who had been engaged to Luigi and, following his death, had married the doctor Giovanni Zoja, always nurtured a great fondness for the Cairolis, as did her husband. Buzio's handwritten annotation allows us to suppose that it was they who commissioned the painting.

8. Costanza Bertolotti, Gian Luca Fruci, Alessio Petrizzo, *Icone politiche. Celebrità e nuovi media al tempo del Risorgimento*, Mantua, Istituto Mantovano di Storia Contemporanea, Istituto

story had earned her the status of a symbol, among the most potent of the Italian *Risorgimento*, but one that was progressively redefined as time passed: mother of citizens, mother of heroes, sacrificial mother and the *mater dolorosa*. This portrait, like many other visual documents of various kinds that concern her, realistically reflects the modes of self-representation adopted by Adelaide in both the private and public sphere. Her mourning and suffering, as expressed by the colour of her clothing and the afflicted expression on her face, are compensated by the pride of being able to show, worn on her own body, the marks of a unique individual and family history that was, at the same time, paradigmatic. The four buttons of her blouse bear miniatures of the four sons who fell for the cause of nationhood; the two golden bracelets – the ones "I always wear", as Adelaide wrote in her will[9] – bear the portraits of Ernesto and Luigi; the ring on her right index finger is probably the one containing a splinter of bone extracted from Enrico's forehead after he was injured in the Battle of Palermo on 27 October 1860. Along with the ornaments shown in the Buzio painting, Adelaide used to lighten her mourning with other mementoes or outright relics, such as medals and brooches, which also bore images or bone fragments or locks of hair from her sons.

In the Western world, the norms for mourning had become established over hundreds of years and were still rigorously observed in the 19th century, especially in bourgeois and aristocratic circles. There were precise prescriptions concerning the length of the mourning period, the colours and fabrics that could be worn, as well as the headdresses and ornaments. An industry specialising in mourning clothes and jewellry had blossomed.[10] In reality, the custom of wearing jewels bearing traces, even material ones, of the deceased family member[11] was neither recent nor unusual, but in the latter forty years of the century, coinciding with Queen Victoria's long widowhood, the fashion of mourning jewels spread from Great Britain to Europe and the United States. In the present day, traces of this custom may still be observed.[12] On the one hand, it is rooted in the Christian

Superiore Carlo d'Arco e Isabella d'Este, 2018. See also *Il lungo Ottocento e le sue immagini. Politica, media, spettacolo*, ed. by Vinzia Fiorino, Gian Luca Fruci, Alessio Petrizzo, Pisa, ETS, 2013.

9. Adelaide Bono Cairoli's handwritten will, Archivio storico civico di Pavia, Fondo Cairoli, cart. XXVI, n. 6.

10. Lou Taylor, *Mourning Dresses: A Costume and Social History*, Abingdon-New York, Routledge Revivals, 2009. At the Metropolitan Museum of Art in New York, the exhibition "Death Becomes Her: A Century of Mourning Attire" (11 October 2014-1 February 2015) retraced the evolution of funerary fashion from 1815 to 1915. Visit https://www.metmuseum.org/press/exhibitions/2014/death-becomes-her.

11. In the case of Adelaide, the bone splinters were used for jewels while her children were still alive.

12. Caroline Goldhorpe, *From Queen to Empress: Victorian Dressess 1837-1871. An Exibition at the Costume Institut*, New York, Metropolitan Museum of Art, 2009, pp. 69-78; John Plunkett, *Queen Victoria: First Media Monarch*, Oxford, Oxford University Press, 2003; Maureen DeLorme, *Mourning Art and Jewelry*, Atglen, Schiffer Publishing, 2004. The fact that the practice of remembrance jewels is still very much alive is demonstrated by the existence of large numbers of funeral agencies that sell such products via catalogue and online. For example, see www.oflalatrocielo.it/un-gioiello-e-per-sempre.

tradition of saintly relics,[13] and on the other hand, it expressed the mysticism and new way of thinking about death in the era of 19th century Romanticism.[14] Garibaldi had proven himself to be a true champion of the fetishist use of relics pertaining to himself and his volunteers, which he painstakingly collected, multiplied and distributed widely.[15]

Adelaide, like her children, had distanced herself from the Catholic religion, but its mark is still clearly evident upon them, both in their lexicon (references to angels, to heaven and to the martyrology of the saints are frequent) and in their practices. The family wished to imitate the communicative example set by the General, knowing well that by interweaving the family myth with Garibaldi's planetary myth, it could make the leap into history and posterity. Garibaldi, for his part, had nurtured the myth of Mother Cairoli and her children by means of a great many proclamations, speeches, letters and exchanges of gifts.[16]

If, on the one hand, the way in which Adelaide presented herself reflected a Catholic heritage and was in harmony with the sensibilities of the time, on the other hand it hinted at the existence of a well-constructed project, to which the concept of "the social and civic pedagogy of the beautiful death" was well suited.[17] What is certain is that by wearing the signs of her dead sons' martyrdom upon her sleeve and publicising her mother's suffering, she sought to create an articulated memorial and educational system of a sanctifying nature. Initially, the museum-temple was conceived by Adelaide as a way to console and unite her family in a common memory and shared value system, but it soon came to be seen as something to bequeath upon the nation, in order to cultivate the memory and practice of the cult of the Cairolis. We find testimony of this in a text by Giacomo Oddo, popular narrator of the adventure of the One Thousand,[18] who visited "Mother Cairoli" in her townhouse in Pavia, first in 1867, after the death of Enrico, and a second time in 1869, after the death of Giovanni.

> Who has seen the House of Cairoli in Pavia? Within, it is a temple; a temple hallowed to the martyrs of Italic freedom! The walls are hung with the portraits of the brave, upon the

13. Roberto Mancini, "Il dono di sangue. Identità nazionale italiana e impegno bellico da Garibaldi alle prime imprese coloniali", in *Una nazione da inventare. Le guerre di indipendenza alle origini della Fratellanza Militare*, ed. by Roberto Mancini and Marco Pignotti, Florence, Nerbini, 2011, p. 44, clarifies the distinction between religious and profane relics.

14. Emmanuel Fureix, *La France des larmes. Deuils politiques à l'âge romantique (1814-1840)*, Seyssel, Champ Vallon, 2009, pp. 43-46. See also *La politica dei sentimenti. Linguaggi, spazi e canali della politicizzazione nell'Italia del lungo Ottocento*, ed. by Marco Manfredi and Emanuela Minuto, Rome, Viella, 2018.

15. Dino Mengozzi, *Garibaldi taumaturgo. Reliquie laiche e politica nell'Ottocento*, Manduria-Bari-Rome, Piero Lacaita, 2008, pp. 63-98. See also Lucy Riall, *Garibaldi. L'invenzione di un eroe*, Rome-Bari, Laterza, 2007.

16. Marina Tesoro, "Pavia città garibaldina", in *Garibaldi, Pavia e Palermo. L'Italia in cammino*, ed. by Arianna Arisi Rota and Marina Tesoro, Como-Pavia, Ibis, 2008, pp. 69-88.

17. Fureix, *La France des larmes*, p. 45

18. Giacomo Oddo, *I Mille di Marsala. Scene rivoluzionarie. Opera dedicata a Venezia*, Milan, Giuseppe Scorza di Nicola, 1863. This work enjoyed two reprints, in 1866 and 1870.

> tables stand their photographs, alongside baskets of flowers and wreaths of glory. The one priestess of this temple is Adelaide Cairoli-Bono [...]. The rings upon her fingers and the bracelets upon her arms bear not gemstones, but something far more precious still, the bones of the martyrs set in gold. Awestruck, whoever you may be, you feel small in her presence, and your tongue fumbles for words.[19]

Adelaide had wanted to situate her own living body, complete with traces of her sons, at the centre of this mystical and memorial complex. Ever since she had been a young wife and mother, she had compulsively conserved family mementoes and everyday objects: her children's notebooks, drawings and toys, her husband's medical tools, letters, political and personal documents, photographs and albums. The death of Ernesto in the field brought about a change in this habit. It was Garibaldi's motto, "Saint Cairoli!" that illuminated her. In the teeth of the Church, which would have liked to stop the usage of a term that it felt lay solely within its bailiwick, Adelaide imposed the burial of Ernesto in the unhallowed chapel beside the family villa in the village of Groppello Lomellina and demanded that the tombstone be inscribed with the General's motto. From that time onwards, when the first death was followed by others, she took the reins of the funeral celebrations, which were used as a "public theatre of suffering",[20] capable of evoking and expressing political emotions. The highly evocative nature of these ceremonies was enhanced by the fact that the remains of her sons came from afar: Ernesto's from Varese; Luigi's from Naples; Enrico's from Rome; and Giovanni's from Belgirate, on Lago Maggiore, where the third family residence was. The funeral notices the family had made for each of the deaths bore their effigies, so as to impress them upon the sight and sentiments of those who participated in the rites. A painting dedicated to Adelaide by the students of the University of Pavia portrays with realistic details the funeral procession of Enrico and one of his brothers in arms, a fellow citizen.[21]

After the first death in 1859, Mother Cairoli dedicated herself to the mission of transforming their private home in Groppello into a lay temple, while the tombs became so many "altars" upon which to practice the religion of nationhood, following the precious confirmation received from Mazzini (Fig. 2).[22]

3. *Building the temple*

Aware of the communicative force and symbolic potency of both images and, above all, objects, Adelaide established in her home a sort of exhibition made of

19. Giacomo Oddo, *La famiglia Cairoli nel Risorgimento d'Italia*, Trieste, Tipografia Herrmanstorfer, 1869, p. 21.

20. Fureix, *La France des larmes*, p. 66.

21. Arianna Arisi Rota, Marina Tesoro, "Au-delà des frérs Cairoli: la fraternitè a Pavie", in *Frérs de sang, frérs d'armes, frérs ennemis*, ed. by Catherine Brice, Rome, École française de Rome, 2017, pp. 285-286.

22. Mazzini's letter, dated 14 October 1869 and Adelaide's reply can be found in Maria Magni, *Adelaide Cairoli*, Turin, Società subalpina, 1943, pp. 318-319.

paintings with her sons as subjects, commissioned or bought by her,[23] funeral notices, photographs and frames, together with a quantity of things that were now, however, selected according to different criteria than in the past. Any object belonging to, or that had simply come into contact with, one of her sons became a relic. She used the term "relic" frequently and in a broad sense. Relics included bodily remains, such as bone splinters or blood stains on clothes or uniforms, or a strip of bandage used to dress the wound the General received in Aspromonte, kept in a brooch by Enrico, who was a doctor and with Garibaldi at the time of injury; a great profusion of locks of hair in lockets; and her own tears on the letters she wrote to her sons and friends, which had made the ink run. Inanimate objects that bore witness to the moment of death were also relics, such as an almond branch gathered at Villa Glori. Objects that accompanied physical pain were, too, such as her fifth and surviving son Benedetto's crutch. Clothing worn during battle were also relics, like the mantle Garibaldi used to cover Enrico with when he was wounded at Palermo, or the famous red shirts, berets, trousers and, of course, weapons. Traces of glory were also relics, such as diplomas, medals or the tricolour flag hung from the balcony of the family townhouse in Pavia when Garibaldi visited in April 1862. Lastly, relics also included personal objects and souvenirs, such as cufflinks, pen cases, inkwells, paper weights, card holders, wallets, passports, notebooks, gloves, scarves, loose leaf notes, a bouquet of flowers gathered on Caprera and more.

One of the most moving objects, both visually and emotionally, that has come down to us is the reliquary box Adelaide made herself, which bears witness to her fetishism. On a piece of satin are hung bone fragments extracted from Enrico and Benedetto's wounds, with explanatory notes in Adelaide's own hand (Fig. 3).

During the last three years of her life, from 1869 to 1871, weakened by illness, including nervous disease, and by now disinterested in politics, Adelaide's sole purpose in life was to prepare her domestic museum in Groppello, with the adjoining mausoleum, to be opened to the public. She wished to reserve for herself the place which, together with her children, she had earned within the circle of the "martyrs of Italian freedom", thus virtually updating the list of martyrs published by Atto Vannucci, which enjoyed great popularity during the era of the *Risorgimento* and which was certainly present in the Cairoli family library.[24] Proof of this intention is offered by the captions of many objects and documents written in her own hand, together with the active collaboration of Gualberta Alaide Beccari in preparing an album dedicated to her by the women of Italy, implicitly intended to be placed on display.[25] Right to the end, Adelaide continued to squirrel away papers, icons and objects/relics, helped by her niece Fedelina Cavallini Duranti, who had long played the role of acolyte to Adelaide's high priestess. But Mother Cairoli did not

23. Susanna Zatti, "Arte figurativa risorgimentale: committenza pubblica e privata a Pavia", in *Risorgimento pavese. Saggi, documenti, immagini*, Pavia, Formicona, 1982, pp. 52-53.

24. *I martiri della libertà italiana dal 1794 al 1848. Memorie raccolte da Atto Vannucci*, Livorno, Poligrafia italiana, 1849. The volume was first printed in 1848 in Florence. After the exended edition of 1849, it had several successive ones.

25. Tafuro, *Madre e patriota. Adelaide Bono Cairoli*, pp. 144-148.

live to see her design completed.[26] In her will she assured that the family and some few intimate friends received the objects most precious to her, the jewels with the images and the bodily "pieces" of her sons. For this reason, buttons, rings, brooches and bracelets that were jealously guarded by the benefactors and their heirs are no longer been visible, if not through photographs and the painting that was the starting point for the present study. The only exception is the ring containing the bone splinter extracted from Enrico's forehead, which Benedetto Cairoli gave to the General, receiving a predictably emphatic thanks.[27] For a time, this object, which later became the protagonist of a tale invented by Clelia Garibaldi,[28] became part of the *memorabilia* of Caprera, Garibaldi's last home and place of death, and so was certainly observed by the hundreds of pilgrims and visitors which, at various times, came to that place.

4. *Benedetto: the survivor overwhelmed by relics*

Upon his mother's death, Benedetto Cairoli was overwhelmed by a profound sense of anguish that plunged him to the brink of depression. Perhaps for the first time, he became fully aware of the thorough and religious work of collection and conservation Adelaide had performed and felt the moral urge and political duty to "gather, order and transmit to the coming era [...] the papers, as a monument of devotion to the nation".[29] However, aside from the papers, a plethora of objects had been scattered in an unruly way around the house. The last of the Cairolis thus began to write a list, without any particular classificatory criteria.[30] When he came to number 78 of the list, busy with his many political and parliamentary engagements, he must have realised that he could never hope to bring order worthy of a museum to such a great mass of materials, and he laid down his pen.

In Groppello, where Adelaide had finally come to rest alongside her sons, the number of visitors dwindled over the following two years. This was partly because the main reason for the pilgrims to flock there in previous years had been to see the museum replete with its most precious piece, Mother Cairoli herself. Everything remained untidy and unmoved, just as she had left it. The only novelty was the Cairoli Album, imposing in its size, precious for its artistic binding and rich in symbolic value. Gualberta Alaide Beccari had finally sent it, but too late, as Adelaide had already passed away. It was displayed on a table in the salon.

26. She died in Groppello, on 27 March 1871 at the age of 65.

27. "Caprera, June 13, '71. Dear Benedetto, I have received our good mother's most precious gift: a ring and a piece of the skull of our hero Enrico. For life, G. Garibaldi. The ring and the skull will lie alongside my ashes", in Elena Romano, "Lettere e biglietti autografi di Giuseppe Garibaldi a cittadini pavesi", *Bollettino della Società pavese di Storia patria*, 3 (1907), p. 319; *La Libertà*, 19 July 1871.

28. Clelia Garibaldi's story, *Mio padre* (Florence, Vallecchi, 1948, p. 55) is said not to be a believable account by Mengozzi, *Garibaldi taumaturgo*, 49.

29. Benedetto Cairoli's letter to Fedelina Cavallini Durandi, 30 October 1871, Museo Centrale del Risorgimento, Rome, Fondo Cairoli, b.600, fasc.1, n. 15.

30. Archivio storico civico, Pavia, Fondo Cairoli, cart. VI, n. 17: four handwritten pages.

The editor of the newspaper *La Donna* was one of the few people outside of the family to explore those spaces after Adelaide's death, and told her readers of the pilgrimage to Groppello. She described the numerous "relics of martyrdom" inside the house and mausoleum and concluded that "everything, everything [...] in the Cairoli househould [...] is sublime and transcendent".[31]

The first turning point in the use of Adelaide's collection came about in 1873, when Elena Sizzo Noris became a part of the family through her marriage to Benedetto. The husband immediately assigned her the task of preserving and handing down the sanctified memory of his brothers and mother, in the form of the material that had stratified within the house. Understanding her duty, but less emotionally involved in it, Elena set to work. She made a summary reorganisation but above all gave her mother-in-law's project a tangible outcome by dedicating a wing of the villa exclusively for display. Although the boundaries between the archive/exhibition area and the couple's living space remained permeable, this rationalisation of the spaces allowed the "Groppello complex" to be better appreciated in its dimension as a museum. The broad, frescoed room known as the "Arms Room" was furnished with specially made shelves and opened to the public, though not continuously, with the intention of attracting homage to the site. And that is just what happened. Combat veterans, political personalities and friends came to Groppello, individually or in small groups. On several occasions, the visit to the domestic museum and the mausoleum was undertaken with great solemnity, in the form of a true pilgrimage (Fig. 4).

On 24 October 1875, in front of the gates to the Groppello villa, a monument eternalising Adelaide's figure in marble was inaugurated. Hundreds of people came, and in the front rows there were representatives of the retired soldiers' associations, the local authorities and members of Parliament close to Benedetto, including Felice Cavallotti. The doors of the house, and the newly completed domestic museum, were opened. Emanuele Baccio Maineri described the interiors of the house:

> Cairoli House is a temple [...]. In its entirety it speaks of Italy, of freedom, of humanity [...]. But what strikes one, upon entering, is the second hall [...]. There, in tall and broad glass display cases one glimpses tunics, trousers and helmets peppered with bullet holes, remnants left behind by those martyrs whose effigies are visible in marble busts, in paintings and in photographs of different sizes. And albums of every make, among which the one given to Adelaide by the ladies of Venice particularly attracts attention, [and also] a white banner with the following motto at its centre: *Monte Pairoli. 23 Octobre 1867*.[32]

Nine years later, upon the occasion of the inauguration of Ercole Rosa's monument dedicated to Enrico and Giovanni on May 27 on the Pincio Hill in

31. Cited in Tafuro, *Madre e patriota. Adelaide Bono Cairoli*, p. 168.

32. *Il Monumento a Adelaide Cairoli in Groppello Lomellino. 24 ottobre 1875. Memorie raccolte e ordinate da Emanuele Baccio Maineri*, Milan, stab. Angelo Zanaboni, 1875, pp. 8-9. The author had edited a publication in memory of Giovanni Cairoli: *Spedizione dei Monti Parioli (23 ottobre 1867) raccontata da Giovanni Cairoli con proemio e note di Emanuele Baccio Maineri*, Milan, Levi, 1878.

Rome,[33] the same journalist returned to Groppello and wrote about the emotions of the visit.[34] In the domestic museum the usual atmosphere of relic fetishism reigned, if anything intensified by a recent episode. Indeed, the call of blood to be spilled as a sacrifice for the nation was redoubled, but this time due not to battle, but to an act of courage and abnegation on the part of the last living Cairoli. Indeed, in the "Arms Room" a place was found for the torn and bloodied suit that Benedetto had worn on 17 November 1878 when, in his role as Prime Minister of Italy, he had accompanied King Umberto I on a visit to Naples. He had shielded his sovereign from the knife lunges of the would-be regicide, Giovanni Passannante, and had received wounds to the leg.[35] Furthermore, two objects – Benedetto's ceremonial dress uniform and the honourary collar of the Order of the Annunziata, the Italian crown's highest honour, received in 1887 – bear witness to the partial change in the values and meaning of the objects in the Groppello museum. The traces of the original patriotic exaltation and self-denial for the Nation, and then of the disappointed Garibaldian cause, which had distinguished the first phase of the exhibition, gave way to a message of political and patriotic reconciliation, though always within that diplomatic and progressive current incarnated in Benedetto himself. In fact, the domestic museum had become a monument raised first and foremost to that "surviving son", as his mother had called him, who summed up in his person the sacrifice made by the entire family for the cause of the *Risorgimento*, but who also distinguished himself by his actions in post-Unification Italy. Certain photographs[36] show that the large boards in the "Arms Room" were once hung with objects that regarded above all Benedetto. Without doubt, the political role he had assumed as the "standard bearer of the left" and his three terms of office as Prime Minister[37] had made Benedetto a "celebrity" in his own right.

The domestic museum of Groppello was now perceived not only as a Cairoli family Pantheon, but also as a national monument, and it remained open to the public even when the *Risorgimento* Museum of Pavia was inaugurated in 1887.[38] Benedetto figured as the honourary president of the founding commission of the latter, but did not deem it necessary to make any donation to it. This apparent

33. The plaster model was donated by the artist to the *Risorgimento* Museum of Pavia, where it is currently on display.

34. Emanuele Baccio Maineri, *Inaugurazione del monumento ai fratelli Cairoli*, Pavia, Bencini, 1884, p. 36.

35. Marina Tesoro, "L'attentato Passannante. Lettere al Ministro degli interni Giuseppe Zanardelli", in *Zanardelli. Una famiglia ghisleriana*, Como-Pavia, Ibis, 2005, pp. 27-52.

36. The originals of six photographs, undated, of the domestic museum and mausoleum at Groppello, as well as some postcards, are in the photographic archive of the *Risorgimento* Museum of Pavia, Ris C 37-43. See also Gigliola De Martini, "Mito e celebrazione del Risorgimento: documenti nelle collezioni del Museo", *Museo in Rivista*, 3 (2003), pp. 120-121 and 125-127.

37. Michele Cattane, "Benedetto Cairoli: la traduzione politica di un mito garibaldino. 1860-1889", *Società e Storia*, 15 (2016), pp. 283-314.

38. Donata Vicini, "Il Museo pavese del Risorgimento", in *Risorgimento pavese. Saggi, documenti, immagini*, pp. 10-11; Massimo Baioni, *La "Religione della Patria". Musei e istituti del culto risorgimentale (1884-1918)*, Quinto di Treviso, Pagus edizioni, 1994.

incongruence demonstrates how he intended to preserve the original dual function of the domestic museum and mausoleum, with an eye to continued acts of homily to the tombs of his family members. In any case, "the fame of Groppello, by all accounts, [was] far superior to that of the civic institution of Pavia".[39] In 1888, the name of the village was even changed from Groppello Lomellina to Groppello Cairoli, confirmation of the fact that the identity of the place had become fused with the identity of the family itself.

Benedetto Cairoli died on 8 August 1889, far from home like his brothers, but in a very different context, in Capodimonte Palace in Naples, where he was the guest of the king. His solemn funeral in Groppello, attended by a great many people, was widely featured in the newspapers, and *L'Illustrazione Italiana*, a national magazine, offered a detailed account with a description of the house, the "Arms Room" and the mausoleum.[40] Elena's final decision in bringing closure to her work of arranging the exhibition of the reliquary for posterity was to have Benedetto's body petrified and a small window set in his sarcophagus to make his face visible.

The following year, on the first anniversary of Benedetto's death, a pilgrimage to Groppello was organised by several associations of veterans and ex-servicemen of the *Risorgimento* wars.[41] A lengthy feature was devoted to it in *La Tribuna illustrata*.[42] The most interesting aspect of this printed historical source is iconographic: besides the "eye-witness illustrations", two photographs were published – one of Adelaide's desk in the library, crammed with small objects and silver-framed portraits, and another showing a "memorial display case" in the "Arms Room". For the first time a broad spectrum of Italians, as broad as the readership of this popular magazine, could see "inside" the Cairoli villa, with all its contents. Meanwhile, on 20 March 1890, the Italian Parliament had approved a law that recognised the mausoleum as a national monument.[43]

5. *From the mansion to the museum*

For some years pilgrims and visitors continued to come to the "house of heroes". On two occasions there were gatherings of particular solemnity: on 14

39. Gigliola De Martini, "'È un museo di memorie sacre alla famiglia Cairoli e alla Patria'. La collezione Cairoli dal sacrario famigliare al Museo del Risorgimento di Pavia", in *Musei nell'Ottocento alle origini delle collezioni pubbliche lombarde*, ed. by Maria Fratelli and Francesca Valli, Turin-London-Venice-New York, Umberto Alemanni, 2010, p. 272.

40. *L'llustrazione italiana*, 18 August 1889. Another detailed description of the domestic museum and mausoleum is to be found in *La Provincia pavese*, 11 August 1889.

41. *Nel primo anniversario della morte di Benedetto Cairoli. Commemorazione fatta nome del Comizio dei veterani lomberdi 1848-49 dal presidente del consiglio direttivo Colonn. Giacinto Bruzzesi*, Milan, Tipografia degli operai, 1890.

42. *La Tribuna illustrata*, 10 August 1890.

43. N. 6696, G.U. n. 77 1890. Indeed, the official decree would only arrive 118 years later: legge n. 200, 22 December 2008: http./monumentinazionali, it/regioni/lombardia/sepolcreto_fratelli_cairoli_pavia.htm.

June 1900, when a national monument to the mother and her sons was inaugurated in Pavia, the work of the sculptor Enrico Cassi, and on 7 May 1911, when the town by the Ticino River received the gold medal "for patriotic merit", during the 50th anniversary celebrations of the Unification of Italy.[44] The domestic museum and the garden with its mausoleum were once again invaded by crowds of people.

Even though such acts of devotion continued for some time,[45] the sentimental and civic appeal of Groppello gradually faded. It was then that Elena Cairoli, the last priestess of the family religion, having no direct heir, began considering the idea that the *Risorgimento* Museum of Pavia might be the place of choice in which to transmit, if no longer the cult, at least the memory of, and profound respect for, the Cairoli family. "Whereas normally – as has been observed – it is the step from home to public institution to determine the shift in the symbolic value of objects from being sacred to the memory of individuals to being sacred to the memory of the collective, in the case of the Cairoli family [...] this shift occurred in the house of origin".[46] Nevertheless, after the death of Benedetto, the time seemed to have come to find another direction and to consign the collection to the memory of society and to history, lending it new meaning as a precious heritage of documentary, written, iconographic and material sources.

During the "Cairoli Celebrations" held in Pavia in May and June 1900, Elena made her intentions known. She entrusted the unpublished papers and images to the compilers of a "single issue" prepared for the occasion and also allowed furnishings to be photographed, including those in Adelaide's bedchamber, as well as prints, paintings, jewels – such as the brooch containing Benedetto's bone fragments – and various objects from the "Arms Room" and other spaces in the villa.[47] The Cairoli widow had no doubts about her moral obligation to transmit the historical heritage of the family to the city's museum. Nevertheless, for a long time she held back from formalising the donation because she did not consider the exhibition spaces to be adequate. Thus, for many years, during WWI and after, the Cairoli collection remained in stasis in its original collocation. It was beginning to show signs of neglect and no longer represented a particular attraction for the general public.

Elena Cairoli died in July 1920. Hers was the last funeral celebrated, with many honours, in Groppello. Her will stipulated that the mansion was to become a hospice for the mutilated and invalids of war. The entire content of the "Arms Room", the archive and certain paintings kept in other rooms were donated to the

44. Gigliola De Martini, "Eternare nel marmo le gesta di quei valorosi...", in *Le memoria in piazza. Monumenti risorgimentali nelle città lombarde tra identità locale e nazionale*, ed. by Marina Tesoro, Milan, Effigie, 2012, pp. 179-181; Tesoro, *Pavia città garibaldina*, pp. 79-80.

45. Mario Franci, *La casa degli eroi a Groppello. I Cairoli. Poemetti*, Rome-Milan, Soc. editrice Dante Alighieri, 1904, p. 16, note 45 records the lay procession to Benedetto's tomb on the 25th anniversary of his death, on 8 August 1904.

46. De Martini, "È un museo di memorie sacre alla famiglia Cairoli e alla Patria", p. 274.

47. *La Famiglia Cairoli. Ricordo per l'inaugurazione del monumento*, single issue, Pavia, Tipografia Fratelli Fusi, 1900.

museum.[48] The original inventory of the "Cairoli Donation" has unfortunately been lost,[49] but Cairoli inventories were to be reconstructed later, when the museum was moved, and the collection was moved with it. The first transfer from Groppello to Pavia was undertaken in two operations, from summer 1920 to winter 1921. Over the following years, many objects that pertained to the Cairoli family in one way or another were donated or lent to the museum by admirers, acquaintances or friends.

In the summer of 1939, an appraisal of the Groppello villa was conducted, which had recently come into the spotlight once again. Indeed, on 4 July 1938, in the presence of Fascist "black shirts" and with many a pennant and banner flying, a "reconsecration" ceremony had been held at the mausoleum:[50] a propagandic operation on the part of Mussolini's government. This attempt to revitalise the cult (and the myth) of the Cairoli family in general, and of the sacrificial mother in particular,[51] was well suited to the radicalisation of moment, with its warlike tones and re-proposition of the theme of death in battle as beautiful and regenerative. On that occasion, certain papers and prints, paintings and objects were found, and immediately transferred to Pavia. The Cairoli donation, thus completed, has ever since represented the added value of the otherwise rich heritage of the *Risorgimento* Museum of Pavia. Nevertheless, the Cairoli-related materials have long been undervalued, above all for reasons of space. It was not until the years after World War II that the situation improved. In 1967, perhaps to compensate the civic pride of the people of Groppello, to whom nothing remained apart from the mausoleum and the monument to Adelaide, the City of Pavia decreed that a part of the "Cairoli Donation", the so-called deposit, allocated in the *Risorgimento* Museum, should be returned to the village. After many years, a portion of the villa was newly transformed into a museum, though it never again achieved the evocative power it had once exercised.[52] Eventually, after much litigation between the City of Pavia and Groppello, in 1996 the concession was revoked and the nucleus relative to the Cairoli family was once more united in the *Risorgimento* Museum of Pavia and placed on display again in 1998 in the definitive and, at long last, adequate context of the Visconti Castle.

An entire hall is devoted to the Cairoli family, interrupting the otherwise chronological order of the exhibition.[53] From the communicative point of view, it

48. The handwritten will of Elena Sizzo Cairoli, dated 25 July 1919 and the letters of her benefactors relating to the inheritance are in the city Archive of Pavia (1931-1940), cat. IX, 4A.

49. Giovanni Zaffignani, "Il fondo risorgimentale presso l'Archivio storico civico", in *Risorgimento pavese. Saggi, documenti, immagini*, p. 70.

50. *Il Popolo di Pavia*, 6 July 1938. Other sources in the city are in Archive of Pavia, Fondo Cairoli, cart. LX, b.5. An interesting photographic document by the Guglielmo Chiolini Studio of Pavia, showing the state of the garden and the mausoleum both before and after these renovations, is to be found in the Fondo Frediani, Istituto pavese per la storia della Resistenza e dell'età contemporanea, serie 28.

51. Erminia Ghiglione Guidetti, *Visione romana. Ad Adelaide Cairoli la "mammina" dei volontari d'Italia*, Pavia, Superstampa, 1939.

52. [M. Milani], *Casa Cairoli. Guida al museo Cairoliano*, Groppello Cairoli, s.n., 1971.

53. Gigliola De Martini, *Il Museo del Risorgimento di Pavia*, Milan, Guide Skira, 2007, pp. 57-61.

was a particularly effective choice to reconstruct the interior of a house of the high bourgeoisie, such as the Cairolis, so exceptional from some points of view and so typical of their era from others. Within this display other mementoes have been placed with efficacy. From the historical point of view, it is also philologically correct to have reconstructed the familial dimension, in combination with the political and military aspects, given the case of the Cairolis, who continually breached the confines between the public and private spheres. Alongside furnishings that are either original or from the era, paintings and photographs, some new display cases house a significant sample of objects, including Adelaide's famous reliquary. These items have thus been restituted to the general public in their original meaning as material traces of history.

1. Pacifico Buzio, Portrait of Adelaide Ciroli, oil painting on canavas, (1896?). Pavia, Museo del Risorgimento (n. inv. P 1487). Mourning dress and jewels.

2. Funeral notice of Ernesto Cairoli, tempera on cardbard, 1859. Pavia, Museo del Risorgimento (n. inv. P 618).
3. Box for relics preserving fragments of bones, silk and paperboard, with handwritten notes by Adelaide Cairoli. Pavia, Museo del Risorgimento (n. inv. Ris 138).

4. Showcase in the Arms Room of Villa Cairoli in Gropello (PV). Undated photo. Pavia, Museo del Risorgimento, Pavia (n. inv. Ris C 40). On the right side, Benedetto Cairoli's crunchs are visible. They were long used due to the wound he received in Palermo on 27 May 1860.

Index of Names

Contributors

ARIANNA ARISI ROTA (PhD) is Full Professor of Contemporary History in the Department of Political and Social Sciences at Pavia University, where she teaches courses on 19th-century history and the history of diplomacy. Her research falls along two main axes: the history of diplomatic machinery and the history of politicisation in 19th-century Europe, with special attention to generational mobilisation and to memory-building. She is the author of *I piccoli cospiratori. Politica ed emozioni nei primi mazziniani* (il Mulino, 2010); *1869: il Risorgimento alla deriva. Affari e politica nel caso Lobbia* (il Mulino, 2015); and *Risorgimento. Un viaggio politico e sentimentale* (il Mulino, 2019), among other works.

ROBERTO BALZANI (Forlì, 1961) is Professor of Contemporary History in the Department of History, Cultures and Civilizations at the University of Bologna. After graduating in 1985 (Department of Political Science, University of Florence), he was a scholarship recipient at the EUI (1986-1989) and then, beginning in 1992, a researcher in Contemporary History at the Department of Political Science in Florence. Since moving to Bologna, he has worked at the Department of Humanities since 1995, then at the Department of Cultural Heritage Preservation (including as Dean from 2008-2009), and since then he has continued his activities in the Department of History, Cultures and Civilizations (2014-present). He is a board member of *Il Risorgimento* and *Rassegna Storica del Risorgimento*. He also runs the Museums of Bologna University (2015-present) and the Archives of Bologna University. He served as President of the Institute for Cultural and Natural Heritage of the Emilia-Romagna Region (2017-2020) and is also a member of the ANVUR Commission on VQR Third Mission, 2015-2019 (2020-present). His most recent book is *Memoria e nostalgia nel Risorgimento. Percorsi di lettura* (il Mulino, 2020).

SILVIA CAVICCHIOLI teaches Contemporary History at the University of Turin. Her recent publications include: *Public Uses of Human Remains and Relics in History* (ed., Routledge, 2020); *Anita. Storia e mito di Anita Garibaldi* (Einaudi, 2017). In recent years, her research interests have focused on memory studies, in particular on: the history and celebration of the Italian *Risorgimento*; gender history; the 19th-century ruling classes; the history of the Kingdom of Sardinia and post-Unification Italy; museum collections and art related to national identities; and public uses of human remains and relics.

SANDRO MORACHIOLI (Genoa, 1981) is a Research Fellow in Contemporary Art History at "Federico II" University in Naples. His research focuses on the connections between artistic languages, media and cultural systems in the 19th and 20th centuries. In addition to a number of essays and articles on art history, he is the author of a monograph on the birth of modern visual satire in Italy titled *L'Italia alla Rovescia. Ricerche sulla caricatura giornalistica tra il 1848 e l'Unità* (Edizioni della Normale, 2013).

Simon Morgan is Head of History at Leeds Beckett University. He has published extensively on the culture of the public sphere in the 19th century, with particular reference to urban elites, radical politics and cultures of celebrity. He is co-editor of the four-volume *Letters of Richard Cobden* (Oxford University Press, 2007-2015) and author of the monograph *A Victorian Woman's Place: Public Culture in the Nineteenth Century* (I.B. Tauris, 2007), which developed from his PhD research. His chapter in the present volume grew from the research for his most recent monograph, *Celebrities, Heroes and Champions: Popular Politicians in the Age of Reform, 1810-1867* (Manchester University Press, 2021).

Álvaro París is a Juan de la Cierva Postdoctoral Fellow at the University of Zaragoza. He received his PhD from the Universidad Autónoma de Madrid (2016) and has been a postdoctoral fellow at the Universities of Toulouse-Jean Jaurès and Clermont-Auvergne. His research focuses on popular politics, counterrevolutionary movements and royalist militias in Southern Europe and Spanish America (1789-1848). He has edited three special issues for various journals (*Claves. Revista de Historia*, *Investigaciones Históricas* and *Jerónimo Zurita*) and published numerous articles and book chapters.

Alessio Petrizzo is a postdoctoral researcher at the University of Bari and teaches Contemporary History at the University of Padua. He holds a PhD from the University of Florence and has since worked at the Universities of Padua, Lausanne (within the Swiss Government Excellence Scholarship Programme) and at the IAS Collegium de Lyon. His research centres on politicisation processes in 19th-century Europe using an approach that draws on media history, historical anthropology, visual studies and material culture, and the history of the body. His recent works include the exhibition and catalog for *Icone politiche. Celebrità e nuovi media al tempo del Risorgimento* (Mantua 2018, with Gian Luca Fruci and Costanza Bertolotti) and *Visualità e socializzazione politica nel lungo Ottocento italiano*, ed. by Alessio Petrizzo, *MEFRIM. Mélanges de l'Ecole française de Rome - Italie et Méditerranée*, 1 (2018).

Rolf Reichardt is Professor h.c. of Modern History at the Justus-Liebig-University in Giessen, Germany. He is an author and co-author of books and articles on the political culture and social imagery of the French Revolution. He is also the general editor of the *Lexikon der Revolutions-Ikonographie in der europäischen Druckgraphik 1789-1889*, 3 vols, over 2000 ill. (Rhema-Verlag, 2017).

Jordi Roca Vernet is Serra Hunter Lecturer at the University of Barcelona. He is the author of two monographs: *La Barcelona revolucionària i liberal: exaltats, milicians i conspiradors* (Fundació Noguera, 2011) and *Tradició constitucional i història nacional (1808-1823): llegat i projecció política d'una nissaga catalana, els Papiol* (Pagès, 2011). His work centres on transnational liberal revolutions in the 19th-century western Mediterranean, the political discourse of liberalism and the history of urban politics in European cities from a cultural, social and geographical perspective.

Marina Tesoro is Full Professor in Contemporary History. She taught in the Department of Political and Social Sciences at the University of Pavia (1980-2019) and coordinated PhD courses in History at the University of Pavia (2000-2016). Her main research fields include: Italian parties and political systems from the Liberal to the Republican age; antifascism and political exile; political representation, especially women's suffrage in Italy and Europe; the language of nation-building in the 19th-20th centuries; monarchy and republic in Italy. Her recent publications include: *Monarchia e repubblica. Istituzioni, culture e rappresentazioni politiche in Italia. (1848-1948)* (Bruno Mondadori, 2011, with Maurizio Ridolfi); *La memoria in piazza. Monumenti risorgimentali nelle città lombarde tra identità locale e nazionale*, (ed., Effigie, 2012); "Les republicains dans l'Italie libérale: de l'abstentionnisme à l'action parlamentaire 1861-1922" (with Maurizio Ridolfi), *Parlement(s), Revue d'histoire politique*, 2018/3 (N° HS 13), pp. 57-79; "La Facoltà di Scienze politiche", in *Storia dell'Università di Pavia*, vol. III/1 (2021), pp. 259-286.

Finito di stampare
nel mese di ottobre 2021
da The Factory
Roma